Also by Teresa Carpenter

MISSING BEAUTY
A Story of Murder and Obsession

MOB GIRL
A Woman's Life in the Underworld

WITHOUT A DOUBT
(with Marcia Clark)

THE
MISS STONE
AFFAIR

∽∭∾

*America's First
Modern Hostage Crisis*

TERESA CARPENTER

SIMON & SCHUSTER

NEW YORK LONDON TORONTO SYDNEY SINGAPORE

SIMON & SCHUSTER
Rockefeller Center
1230 Avenue of the Americas
New York, NY 10020

Simon & Schuster and colophon are registered trademarks
of Simon & Schuster, Inc.

For information regarding special discounts for bulk purchases,
please contact Simon & Schuster Special Sales at
1-800-456-6798 or business@simonandschuster.com

Manufactured in the United States of America

1   3   5   7   9   10   8   6   4   2

Library of Congress Cataloging-in-Publication Data

Carpenter, Teresa.
The Miss Stone affair : America's first modern hostage crisis /
Teresa Carpenter.
p.   cm.
Includes bibliographical references (p.) and index.
1. Stone, Ellen Maria, 1846–1927. 2. Macedonia—History—1878–1912.
3. Missionaries—United States—Biography. 4. Missionaries—Macedonia—
Biography. 5. Abduction—Macedonia. I. Title.
DR2218.S76C37 2003
949.5'6072—dc21   2003042540

ISBN 0-7432-0055-1

To my mother

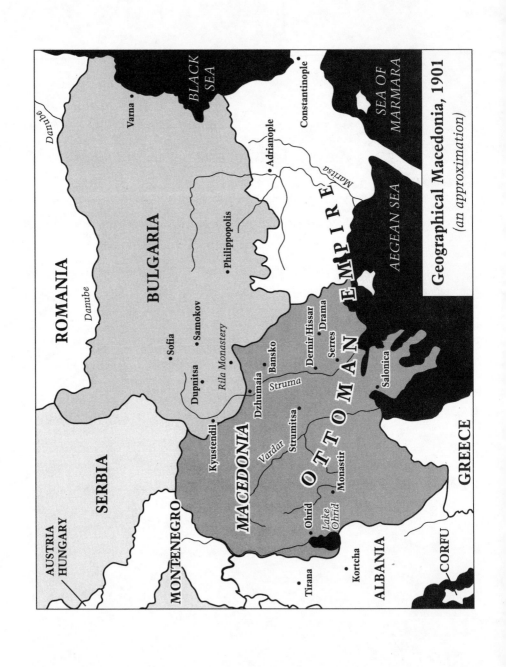

Geographical Macedonia, 1901
(an approximation)

CONTENTS

PREFACE

In September 1901, an American missionary named Ellen Stone was kidnapped in Macedonia, then a southerly province of the Balkans. Her capture by a band of unidentified revolutionaries caused a sensation throughout Europe and America. This excitement was due in part to the times—it was the Victorian era when the honor of an unmarried woman was still a proper cause for mobilizing armies. It was also due to the place. The Balkans at the turn of the century were in the throes of a long, percussive revolution.

The Christian states in the west of the peninsula—Greece, Serbia, Montenegro—had already waged successful wars of independence against the Ottoman Turks who had ruled the Balkans for over five hundred years. This insurgency had spread east to Bulgaria. In the capitals of Europe, diplomats of the Great Powers met to carve up the carcass of the staggering Ottoman Empire and to discuss how to fill the void left by its impending collapse. The Eastern Question, as it was known, was the subject of endless debate.

The United States had not been invited to participate in that debate. As of the late nineteenth century it was not yet a world power. Isolated by two oceans, it did not stand to be affected directly by an Ottoman implosion. Most Americans, moreover, could not have located Macedonia on a map of Europe—making it all the more improbable, therefore, that Miss Stone, a middle-aged spinster from Massachusetts, should have strayed into the line of fire.

The American Board of Commissioners for Foreign Missions, the missionary society to which Miss Stone belonged, was headquartered in Boston. Its mission was Evangelical and characterized by a crusading zeal. The first of their number arrived in Constantinople in 1819. From there they hoped to launch a latter-day crusade against the Muslim Turks. Although their hymns were militant, the invasion was largely metaphorical. The enemy they'd envisioned was the Turk of Christian memory—the Seljuk Turk who had ruled the Holy Land during the Middle Ages and who had crossed swords there with Christian Crusaders. But the Seljuks had since been supplanted by the Ottomans. And the Ottoman sultan dealt with this fresh Christian intrusion by ignoring it.

The Ottomans had arrived from the plains of Anatolia at the end of the Middle Ages. In the fourteenth century, descendants of a warlord named Osman led a deadly efficient army over the Dardanelles and into Europe. One by one they conquered the faltering Christian kingdoms of the Balkans, defeating the Serbs at the Battle of Kosovo in 1389 and engendering religious and racial hatreds that would last for centuries.

At the height of its power, the Ottoman Empire had spread as far east as the Caspian Sea, as far south as the tip of Arabia, as far west as Algeria, and as far north as Belgrade. Not until the late sixteenth century were its forces turned back, when Eugene of Savoy thwarted Sultan Mustafa II's siege of Vienna at the Battle of Zenta on September 11, 1697. After that, Ottoman power began to wane. By the nineteenth century, the prestige of the Empire was so reduced that the Western press referred to it by the less respectful name of Turkey or with plain contempt as the "Sick Man of Europe." When Sultan Abdul Hamid II strapped on the sword of Osman in 1876, he had inherited an exchequer deeply in debt to European bankers.

The Sultan was, by nature, a recluse. His own subjects never saw him except on Fridays when he climbed into an enclosed coach and rode a few yards to pray at a mosque just outside the palace gate. If they strained, they could catch a glimpse of a sunken, hawk-nosed man with haunted eyes and artificially blackened hair. (Custom did not permit a sultan to show signs of mortality.) In place of the sable robes of his forebears, Abdul Hamid wore a Stambouline, an ugly black frock coat worn by Ottoman gentlemen to proclaim their Europeanization.

Abdul Hamid's paranoia became so acute that he ordered built on the grounds of Yildiz Palace an authentic replica of a European outdoor café where he sat and sipped coffee while his bodyguards lounged at adjoining tables. He carried an ivory revolver. Startled once by a gardener, he shot the man dead.

Early in his reign, Abdul Hamid tolerated the Protestant missionaries. He perceived that their arrival antagonized the Eastern Orthodox as well as the Roman Catholics, and anything that set Christians to fighting among themselves worked to his advantage. But as the revolts among his Christian subjects grew, the Sultan's rule became increasingly harsh, culminating in massacres by Muslim irregulars called *bashi-bazouks*. He suspected, correctly, that the American Evangelicals were encouraging rebellion in Armenia and elsewhere. Spies followed the Protestants, recording their comings and goings in confidential reports to the palace.

Since the United States didn't enjoy full diplomatic relations with the Ottomans, the two countries had never exchanged ambassadors. The Americans wouldn't take the initiative, waiting for Turkey to make the first move. Turkey didn't see the need. American interests were represented, instead, by a lesser dignitary, the U.S. Minister. He presided over a legation that occupied a small rented palace in the diplomatic quarter of Constantinople. There was also an American consul whose job it was to safeguard the interests of U.S. citizens within the empire. One of these consuls, Eugene Schuyler, rose above the mundane confines of his office to write a white paper protesting the slaughter of Bulgarians in 1876. On balance, however, the Americans had little influence and could be manipulated or safely ignored.

In the spring of 1898, all of that changed. The American Asiatic Squadron surprised and sank the Spanish Fleet at Manila Bay. That Spain was already tottering—and the Yankee fleet was a slow, ungainly assortment of steam and canvas–driven vessels—did not alter the fact that America was now a power to be reckoned with. The Sultan was said to be very impressed, particularly as the battle had been won without the loss of a single American life. Negotiations for an exchange of ambassadors with Turkey were underway when they were overshadowed by the sudden kidnapping of Ellen Stone.

Kidnappings in European Turkey were hardly new. The highjacking of Europeans was already a cottage industry among roaming bands of *comitadji*. Their victims were usually aristocrats, industrialists, and foreign consuls. Their ransoms were usually paid by the victim's family or associates while his government coerced the Ottomans into reimbursing it. As the Empire was nearly bankrupt, these so-called "indemnities" were difficult to collect. Americans had so far been spared as victims, probably because prior to 1898 the United States was still regarded abroad as a crude confederation of provinces rather than an actual country, and its citizens had appeared too insignificant to command a ransom. With the capture of Ellen Stone, Americans had to reckon with one of the unforeseen consequences of world power.

Faced with the problem of rescuing Miss Stone, the American Department of State was at a loss for precedent—the nearest thing in its experience being the cases of sailors captured by Barbary corsairs. The kidnapping posed a dilemma. Did the United States of America negotiate with kidnappers or did it not? Would it pay a ransom, or no? If the nation's honor was at stake, would President Theodore Roosevelt take the perilous step of sending warships through the Dardanelles?

During the six months of Miss Stone's captivity, American and English tabloids fueled public outrage. Before its ultimate resolution, the kidnapping had drawn the governments of America, Turkey, Russia, Britain, and Bulgaria into a web of diplomatic intrigue.

The Miss Stone Affair, as it came to be known, would go down in history as America's first modern hostage crisis. Turn-of-the-century negotiators would find themselves having to deal with a shadow adversary who could fade into mountains beyond the range of conventional weapons. The art of hostage negotiation, Americans would learn, required finesse, *politesse*, patience, and unapologetic deception. The Stone affair, driven as it was by ancient ethnic hatreds and banner headlines, seems as timely today as it was on that brisk autumn afternoon in 1901 when Miss Stone was forced off her horse at gunpoint.

To trace the roots of modern terror we must look back to the beginning of the twentieth century. Back to a time when news traveled by cable and diplomats traveled by horse-drawn carriage. Back to an era when the American Foreign Service boasted more amateurs than professionals. Back to the strange case of Miss Ellen Stone.

CHAPTER ONE

Miss Ellen Stone

Ꙩꙮꙩ

The photograph which stands on my desk is not the strong face of the (mature) woman, now familiar to the public, but the picture of a winsome girl whom we called Nellie. She is the sort of individual whose personality makes a strong impression, and her crafty captors are aware that in seizing her they have taken one of the choicest representatives of American womanhood.

Frances J. Dyer,
The Congregationalist and Christian World,
October 19, 1901

ELLEN MARIA STONE was no fragile Victorian flower. A photograph taken of her in her late teens reveals a substantial, somewhat plain young woman whose ordinary features are graced by large almond eyes, a high forehead, and a firm, determined mouth. If she ever had a suitor, she never wrote about him.

Her family manufactured and sold leather goods in Boston and to the north in Haverhill, Massachusetts. Their modest fortune did not put them on an equal social footing with the Adamses or the Lodges. The drawing room banter of Brahmin society might have struck them as frivolous. The Benjamin Franklin Stones were plain people—Puritan bluebloods, sprung from the oldest Protestant roots in America.

On her mother Lucy's side, "Nell" (as she was known to friends and family) could trace her lineage back to Miles Standish, military leader of the Plymouth Colony. Her paternal grandfather was a veteran of the Revolutionary War. His son served in the same regiment, later recruiting a company of his own to fight in the War of 1812.

When the Confederates took Fort Sumter in the spring of 1861, Ellen's two oldest brothers—she had four—enlisted for the Union—George in the Army of the Potomac and Edwin Cornelius in the Navy. Edwin was aboard the frigate *Minnesota* when it escaped from the Confederate ram *Merrimac*. Ellen's father, old Benjamin, joined the Union cause near the war's end, and upon his return home produced for his family a copy of the New Testament, cover torn and twisted by a bullet meant for his chest.

Reared to the tattoo of a battle drum, Ellen Stone was as patriotic as she was devout. A schoolmate later recalled high school commencement exercises at the town hall where Nell recited a poem by Elizabeth Browning:

> *Dead! Both my boys!*
> *One of them shot in the sea in the East*
> *One of them shot in the West by the sea.*

The point of Browning's pacifist verse was apparently lost on the speaker as surely as it was on her listeners, who were carried away by the force of her declamation. It was the height of the Civil War, after all, and Ellen had two brothers at the front.

Had she been a boy, Miss Ellen Stone would certainly have

been a soldier. But her life's course was set at birth: her mother dedicated her to God. For a time, Miss Stone taught high school. Later, she took a job as children's editor of a religious monthly, *The Congregationalist and Christian World,* where she would work for nearly a decade.

By the mid-1870s, the country was swept up in a delirium of revivalism. The faithful and the simply curious streamed into tent meetings where the Holy Spirit often overtook them and they fell to the floor writhing in religious ecstasy. The man, woman, or child thus blessed was said to have experienced an "awakening." Those who were inspired to spread the Gospel had received "the call."

The leader of this movement was the Reverend Dwight L. Moody, a compelling figure who set himself up as defender of the faith against Darwinism. In the winter of 1878, the Reverend Moody held a week-long revival at Boston's South End Tabernacle. Ellen attended with a friend. It was during a chorus of "Christ for the World I Sing," the companion later recalled, that Miss Stone's face began to glow. Not long after, she received the call to become a missionary.

The call was not a grim summons to a life of toil and self-denial. For a young Christian woman, it offered an opportunity to travel, live and work in exotic lands, and meet unusual people—in short, to have a life less ordinary than was usually the case. For a female with no marital prospects, it presented the opportunity for a career.

The American Board of Commissioners for Foreign Missions (ABCFM), the governing body of an Evangelical society headquartered on Beacon Street, usually preferred married couples. One of the values the board wanted to export was the example of the Western family. (The "heathen" families in other lands were too often polygamous and extended.) In fact, the board would sometimes arrange marriages for men going abroad.

As a single woman, Ellen Stone fell into a slightly different category. Unfettered by the cares of domesticity, she could become a dedicated and tireless worker, and as long as she was sent into an environment dominated by married couples, she would prove an asset. She would earn a small salary, have her modest living expenses paid, and enjoy the title of assistant missionary.

Ellen Stone was posted to the Principality of Bulgaria.

In China and India, missionaries of the American Board had enjoyed considerable success. The Near East, however, was different. Early on, the Evangelicals encountered difficulties. The first to arrive in Constantinople around 1819 apparently imagined themselves heirs to the Crusaders, but they had no tangible blueprint for conquest, nor did they enjoy the backing of the U.S. government, which was scarcely a diplomatic presence in the region. A death sentence, moreover, awaited any Ottoman citizen who converted to Christianity. The Protestants failed completely in their assault upon Islam.

The Evangelicals cast their eyes west to other promising fields of opportunity and their gaze came to rest upon the Bulgarians, who were growing increasingly restless under Ottoman rule. That the Bulgarians had been Christians for over 1,000 years did not seem to bother the missionaries. To the contrary, Eastern Orthodoxy, to their way of thinking, was the Oriental cousin of Roman Catholicism. And the Catholics, with their adoration of icons and relics, were for all practical purposes heathen.

From the Evangelicals' worldview, the Orthodox should not be merely ready but eager to embrace Protestantism. After suffocating for centuries in a stupor of incense and stultifying ritual, they asked themselves, must not the Slavs be yearning for a more modern form of worship? Protestantism offered a creed that denounced the adoration of saints and the vulgar wealth and power of patriarchy. It held out the means for a man to talk directly to God.

The Protestants misjudged their own appeal, however. The Bulgarians, as it turned out, loved the sensual beauty of their Orthodox service. The poor especially found in the liturgy a mystery and mysticism lacking in their everyday lives. Protestantism, with its insistence upon plain dress, plain church, and plain services, seemed sterile by comparison. In day-to-day life, moreover, the Bulgarians were stubbornly secular. The Protestant creed appeared to them a dreary list of prohibitions: no drinking, no smoking, no gambling. The Evangelicals were finally forced to conclude that the Bulgarians had an inadequately developed sense of sin.

The most serious obstacle to Protestant progress, however, was political. To Bulgarians, being Orthodox was synonymous with nationalism. To be a Bulgarian Orthodox therefore was to be a patriot. To leave the faith was treason.

Letters from missionaries to the American Board in Boston reflect their disappointment. "We do not see the multitudes flocking to Christ as we have hoped we might before so many years should pass away," wrote one in May 1885, "but we dare not become discouraged."

In marked contrast to these failures there was the Girls' Boarding School in Samokov. The girls' school and its companion institution, the Boys' Collegiate and Theological Institute, were the showpieces of Protestant evangelism. Wealthy Bulgarian Christians, who had no interest in converting to Protestantism, nonetheless had a strong desire to see that their children acquired a Western education. Shortly after the school's founding, the parents of several Orthodox girls objected to the missionaries' attempts to proselytize, and they withdrew their daughters from class. Although the school had to close briefly, it later reopened along a slightly more secular model, and it thrived thereafter.

The education of females would become the most enduring legacy of the American Board in the Balkans. Having remained so long under the Turkish yoke, Bulgarian society had an orientalized view of women. Even in Orthodox services, females were often obliged to sit behind screens. They bore children, tended huts, observed feast days, and, with a few literate exceptions, remained mute.

The American missionaries brought to the Bulgarians of European Turkey what they believed was an enlightened view of the sexes. Women enjoyed not an equal but a complementary role. The hand that rocked the cradle was the extension of a soul and even, certain progressive men would concede, an intellect. Because female intelligence informed the nursery, it should be fortified and refined for the task. Women should be educated if only that they might be better mothers.

In September 1878, Miss Ellen Stone and her luggage arrived at the door of the missionary compound in Samokov. She had been assigned to assist the directress, a formidable, iron-willed matron named Esther Maltbie. In that secondary capacity, she was charged with a sacred mission, the "emancipation of Oriental womanhood."

IN THE TOWN OF Samokov, which lay about forty miles south of Sofia, living conditions were primitive. Plumbing took the form of mountain streams diverted into pipes made of pinewood. These, according to missionary accounts of the times, gurgled constantly. The cobbled main street slanted from the sides toward the middle, so that when an important person was due to visit, the townspeople could divert a river through it to flush out the filth. Every Saturday, housewives scrubbed the interior and exterior of their homes with brick dust, which made the entire town glow an unearthly shade of pink.

Far from shrinking from the strangeness, Miss Stone embraced it. Although she was not required to learn her students' native language—classes at the Girls' School were conducted in English—she mastered the Cyrillic alphabet and learned to read, speak, and write fluent Bulgarian. As a teacher, she seems to have been imperious yet affectionate. She called her students her "childies." They called her *kaka*, meaning sister, or "Auntie Stone." Those who complimented her became her pets as she was unfortunately susceptible to flattery.

Miss Stone spent about twelve years in Samokov and would probably have remained there for life but for a series of clashes with Miss Maltbie. In 1883, she was transferred west to Philippopolis. Here, Miss Stone found herself under the thumb of yet another difficult personality, the Reverend George Marsh. When Serbia declared war on Bulgaria in 1885 and Miss Stone volunteered without permission to minister to wounded soldiers in Sofia, Marsh reprimanded her for leaving her post.

Miss Ellen Stone, however, did not allow herself to be stifled by the ill-tempered Marsh. By now she was a power in her own right.

While male missionaries were obliged to petition for funds from the notoriously conservative ABCFM, female assistants had the option of applying to the Women's Board, a well-funded auxiliary that seemed to be answerable to no one. Miss Stone drew on the Women's Board's reserves to recruit and help support a platoon of native "Bible Women," itinerant female workers who spent their time traveling a circuit of remote villages, passing out Christian pamphlets and holding classes in infant care and hygiene. They could sometimes persuade village wives to open their doors and listen. Often, these poor women were under the impression that the missionaries had come with food for their children. Once the personal contact was made, an ordained minister would follow up the visit.

Miss Stone had nineteen Bible Women under her command. Some of her male colleagues were resentful. "The ladies can appeal to the wheel within the wheel," complained the Reverend John Baird of Samokov. "That is gallantry, but is it

Christian justice to men?" Another referred to Miss Stone's "little Bishopric." What irked them most was that Ellen Stone was now a law unto herself.

Miss Stone had been at Philippopolis about fifteen years when she received the call to Macedonia.

MACEDONIA, ANCESTRAL SEAT of Alexander the Great, was roughly the size of North Carolina. From the Rila mountains to Salonica on the Aegean Sea; from Lake Ohrid to the River Mesta, it was a region of splendid beauty and the scene of continuing carnage.

The year that Miss Stone arrived in Bulgaria, the Russians declared war on the Turks, sweeping through the eastern Balkans and liberating along the way their blood relatives, the Bulgarians. In their capital of Sofia, the Bulgarians celebrated the arrival of their Russian liberators. Their joy was short-lived, however. The Great Powers, chiefly Great Britain, were afraid that Russia would finally get its warm water port on the Aegean, and a month later, at the Treaty of Berlin, they forced Tsar Alexander II to give back much of what his armies had taken. As a result, the northern half of Bulgaria was declared a principality—autonomous, yet nominally under Ottoman rule. The southern half, from the rugged Balkan Mountains down to the sea, was tossed back to the Sultan. This lower sector, Macedonia, was left under Turkish rule.

Macedonians fled by the thousands over the border into the principality. Those unable to make it out were harassed or slaughtered by local Muslim militiamen, the *bashi-bazouks*. Although it was official American Board policy to stay clear of politics, many of its missionaries sympathized deeply with the Bulgarians. To the Evangelicals, the Ottomans became "the Unspeakable Turk."

Having been shortchanged by diplomacy, Macedonia now

loomed large in the missionary mind as a land of opportunity. The American Board hoped that the large Bulgarian population south of the line of demarcation might be more humble and approachable than their kinsmen to the north. A new railway from Belgrade to the sea made it practical for the Evangelicals to consider establishing a new station in Salonica. In 1894, the ABCFM dispatched to this new outpost one of its most able workers, Dr. Henry House.

Henry House was a patient, intelligent man. His father had been an abolitionist, and during the Civil War, the House home in Ohio was a stop on the Underground Railroad to Canada.

When Henry and Adeline House sailed for the Balkans in 1872, they were newlyweds. During their twenty years at the Samokov station, Addy gave birth to seven children. A marvel of endurance and industry, she not only suffered the demands of her boisterous brood, she kept her home open day and night to prospective converts. The Houses were the living ideal of the Christian family.

Upon their arrival in Salonica in the autumn of 1894, the Houses found a large home in a Bulgarian neighborhood. Its most appealing feature was a garden for the children. The living compartments were arranged on either side of a palatial foyer that was Mrs. House's despair. The simple sticks of furniture that they'd brought with them from Samokov would not fill the open, yawning space. Their few Turkish rugs looked forlorn, like "little islands on a sea of pine boards."

The Houses held regular services here, but the only persons in attendance were a young missionary couple, the Edward Haskells, who had been posted to Salonica about the same time. They rarely had other visitors. The Greek Orthodox of the city scorned them, the Bulgarian Orthodox regarded them as dangerous, and the Jews, like the Turks, proved impossible to convert.

The missionaries' isolation increased. Then, only a year

after their arrival in Salonica, the Christians of Armenia revolted against the Ottomans. Instead of sending government troops to curb backlash from the *bashi-bazouks*, Abdul Hamid II sent Kurdish irregulars, known as "the Sultan's Own," to suppress the revolt. The slaughter was extensive and dreadful.

Afterward, there was blame spread all around: the *bashi-bazouks*, the Sultan's Own, the Sultan himself. Among those who had blood on their hands were Americans of the Near Eastern mission. They had marched into Armenia earlier that century singing "Onward Christian Soldiers." Now they were in the embarrassing position of explaining to the vanquished Armenians that the phrase "marching as to war" was not to be taken literally.

Until the Armenian uprising, Abdul Hamid had tended to be tolerant of the American missionaries. He could see that Christians were split into many factions and that he could profit by pitting one against another. Now, however, the Protestants became the objects of his paranoia. The activities of Americans were observed and recorded by many of the 20,000 spies accredited to the palace. Their reports ended up in the Sultan's infamous private *djournals*.

In Salonica, resentment toward the Americans ran especially high. Anti-Christian placards were posted in mosques. At the same time, young Bulgarian Macedonians met in attics to plot revolution. The British sent a fleet of forty warships to keep the peace.

One afternoon, a pair of English sailors called on Dr. House. They were members of the Salvation Army and wanted to know if the mission had space to lend them for services.

"Here was a use for our big room," Adeline House exulted in her memoirs. "Never again were we to complain of its size. . . . There was much coming and going to our house then, for each day the number [of English seamen] would increase. They would come about four o'clock, play with the children, then sit and talk of their homes. After that they shared our simple supper of bread and jam with tea."

The yardstick of the Salonica mission's success became the number of individual teas served to British seamen, virtually the Evangelicals' only constituency. Shut out by the citizens of Salonica, Dr. House turned his attention toward the Macedonian interior. But for that, he would need the help of a woman to help persuade villagers to open their doors. The American Board sent him the acknowledged dean of Bible Women, Miss Ellen Stone.

Miss Stone, now stout and famously stubborn, was advancing into middle age when she arrived at her new post in 1893. There she found herself surrounded by old friends, the Houses and their seven children, as well as by new ones, the Haskells who now had three of their own. Very likely, she felt like the odd woman out in a station where fecundity was rampant. And yet, her letters home were filled with affection for Salonica. She marveled at the privilege of walking in the footsteps of the apostle Paul who had preached here in ancient times. The view from the mission house left her breathless.

In the harbor and the sweeping crescent bay beyond, warships of the Great Powers dropped anchor. On the Sultan's birthday, fountains of fireworks burst from their decks, lighting up the headlands. Their searchlights played over the outlines of minarets and onion domes sprawling up the hill to an ancient citadel. The great walls of Salonica had stood for twenty centuries, encircling first a Greek city, then a Roman city, which for a time became a free city, and then a Byzantine city. The Venetians bought it from the Greeks, who lost it to the Ottoman Turks. At the dawn of the twentieth century, Salonica was a Levantine metropolis second only to Constantinople.

Axes and shovels chipped away at the old fortifications, which were now too confining to progress. The ancient stones were being used to modernize the quay. European money built railroads linking Ottoman Europe to Belgrade and Paris. *Cafés chantants* presented Viennese operettas by the glow of gaslight. (Electricity was not permitted since, it was said, the Sultan had confused "dynamo" with "dynamite" and considered it subversive.)

In Salonica, each ethnic class kept to its own quarter. The Greek craftsmen from the Lower City withdrew at day's end to the apartments behind their storefronts. In the Upper City, wealthy Jewish merchants luxuriated in their fantastically ornate mansions. High above it all, like eagles in their aeries, the Turks, from the privacy of hearth and *harem*, surveyed their domain.

Only rarely did these peoples mingle. That was usually on summer evenings when children from every quarter gathered on the quay to watch the flaming sun set behind Mt. Olympus across the bay.

Most newcomers fell under the charm of Salonica, and Miss Stone was no exception. "The blue waves sparkle . . . beautifully in the sunlight," she wrote in a dispatch to *The Congregationalist*. "The transparent air enwraps the scene in wondrous brilliancy."

Among her new responsibilities was to correspond with the British marines who had visited the mission. She was pleased to report success in steering these men clear of Oriental fleshpots.

It was in the field, however, that Miss Stone showed her grit. She toured between 50 and 150 days a year, riding many hours over rough terrain on horseback, putting up with the discomforts of smoky inns, or *khans*, and sleeping on filthy, flea-infested pallets, often sharing a room with strangers. Her capacity for hardship was legendary. And she was fearless.

Travelers over Macedonian highways, usually rutted oxen paths, were often attacked by bands of robbers. These brigands, as the Victorians called them, were often nothing more than professional thieves, distant relations of the legendary *haramii* who robbed from the rich and gave to the poor. Often a band would be in the hire of a certain village, whose town fathers would pay for protection and reap their share of the spoils. Every nationality had its own *comitadji,* or militia, whose careers were tinged with romance and sometimes political purpose. The Greeks terrorized the Bulgarians. The Bulgarians terrorized the Greeks. Both terrorized the Turks. The Albanians, the only nationality to convert in large numbers to Islam, were particularly brutal and terrorized everyone.

The Turks had built guardhouses at four-mile intervals, but they couldn't guarantee safety. Foreigners were advised to ask the regional governor for an escort of *zaptiehs,* or military gendarmes. Because the escorts also gave the Turks opportunity for spying, the missionaries routinely declined the courtesy. After twenty years in service, Ellen Stone had accepted an escort only twice.

In the spring of 1901, Miss Stone was recovering from a cold and a touch of malaria she'd contracted from the mosquito-infested swamplands of the Vardar River. Still, she managed to tour more days than the men: 140 to Dr. House's 109. For most of the following summer, the mission was nearly deserted. The Haskells were on furlough in America, the House family visited Paris, and the Bairds, a third family to join the station, had been transferred north to Samokov, so Miss Stone held down the fort with only her handsome Salonica tabby for company. The months of June and July she spent in rapturous anticipation of August, when she would preside over the annual meeting of her Bible Women, planned to be held that year in the highlands of northwestern Macedonia.

The village of Bansko had been chosen as the meeting place, though not because of its strategic location. It was, in fact, very difficult to reach. Situated on a high plain, it was surrounded on all sides by mountains: Rila to the northwest, the Rhodope range to the east, and the Pirin massif to the south. The main road into the village led from the border town of

Dzhumaia, and it was scarcely a path. The only way in was on horseback or on foot. Bansko, however, was cooler than surrounding regions, certainly more pleasant than Salonica, which sweltered in August. It was also very beautiful.

Even as they were being rebuffed elsewhere, the Protestant missionaries had enjoyed unusual success in Bansko. The *Banskali* were free-thinkers. Several of the prominent local families were feuding with the Orthodox church over dogmatic issues such as Lent and celibacy. These families broke away and began to practice what they called a "home-grown Protestantism." In the early 1870s, they had actually written the Americans asking them to send missionaries to Bansko. Two had responded to the call and founded the Bansko Evangelical Church, the first of its kind in European Turkey.

To this day, it remains unclear whether these "home growns" ever broke entirely with the Bulgarian Orthodox church. The Orthodoxy was still associated with patriotism, and the *Banskali* were intense patriots. Families like the Peter Ushevs, who were among the town's first converts, kept a foot in the Orthodox world, paying an annual tithe to maintain the family seat at the town cathedral.

When money and gifts flowed in from America, Protestant membership rolls swelled. If the largesse slowed to a trickle, the faithful fell away. The Evangelicals bemoaned these fair weather conversions, but opportunism was a way of life among the *Banskali*.

The congregation of the Bansko Evangelical Church had recently built a large stone parsonage. It was, however, without a pastor. In the spring of 1901, Pastor Atanas Hristov had been accused by the Turks of sedition and had fled over the border to Bulgaria. This incident increased the political tension between the *Banskali* and the Turks, who suspected the townspeople of harboring *comitadji*.

MISS STONE, it would later be said, should have had the sense to hold her Bible meeting in a safer spot, such as Salonica or Samokov, but her resolve was firm. She was protected by her Bible and a small American flag, which she always kept pinned somewhere on her person. In early August, she set out by horse-back for the highlands, taking for company two young Bulgarian female teachers, a muleteer, and a young native boy.

During part of her stay in Bansko, Miss Stone was a guest of the Stephanovs, a prominent merchant family whose compound occupied a town block. They were referred to generally as the Pop, or "Pope," Stephanovi, since they counted at least two Orthodox bishops among their forebears. Such a family was naturally a prized addition to the Protestant fold. The Stephanovi had been converted by their eldest daughter, Katerina.

Katerina was a woman in her early thirties. While studying nursing in America, she had met and married an Albanian Protestant named Grigor Tsilka. He was a graduate of the Union Theological Seminary in New York City.

Katerina had come home to Bansko that summer of 1901 to visit after an absence of nine years. She brought her only child, a three-month-old infant named Victor. Shortly after arriving at his grandparents' home, however, the baby developed cholera and died. Katerina herself became dangerously ill. She had tried to make the fifty-mile journey to Samokov but was detained so long in quarantine that she missed the missionaries' general meeting. By the time the Bible Women began arriving in Bansko, Mrs. Tsilka had regained her strength and was bearing her loss stoically.

During their retreat in the highlands, the Bible Women, about ten of them, read Scripture. Mrs. Tsilka offered classes in nursing.

Miss Stone led them all on a tour of surrounding villages "to inspire the hearts of Christian friends." Miss Stone and her acolytes also took long walks through the cobbled lanes of Bansko. At the end of three weeks, the Bible Women said their emotional farewells.

MISS STONE'S PLAN was to begin traveling on September 3 with a caravan of horseback riders to Dzhumaia, where she would spend the night at a local inn. She intended to continue west the following day to Strumitsa, the closest railway station, and catch a southbound train to Salonica. Miss Stone was wary enough of the dangers of the highway to pick a Tuesday, the day before the *Banskali* took their goods to market in Dzhumaia, when the road would be well traveled.

Her party, larger than the one that had accompanied her in, included her assistant, the widow Kerefinka Usheva. Madame Usheva was the daughter-in-law of old Deacon Peter Ushev in whose home the first Protestant preaching service had been held thirty-five years earlier. There were, in addition, three young teachers who were to ride with Miss Stone as far as Dzhumaia, then on to their respective villages.

Grigor and Katerina Tsilka were to travel with Miss Stone as far as the border, then continue east on horseback to Albania. That morning, the couple said good-bye to family and friends, a tearful scene as they were leaving behind a small grave. The Tsilkas left Bansko on horseback at about 10:00 A.M., two hours ahead of Miss Stone. Some distance down the road, they stopped to wait for her.

Miss Stone was late getting out of town. A member of the Bansko congregation had died the night before, and she paid a sympathy call upon his family. The Protestants, who came to see the Bible Women off that sunny September day, hung garlands of carnations and pinks around their necks and gave them gifts of honey, pastry, cheese, and roast fowl. The young teachers took sausage cured in a pig's stomach, a specialty of the Raslog district, for the winter.

A little past noon, Miss Stone, Madame Usheva, and the young teachers left Bansko in the company of three muleteers. Miss Stone noticed that the head *kiradjee,* or muleteer, was leading them out through the big gate in the upper part of town. This was unusual, but Miss Stone wasn't sufficiently alarmed to insist that the boy take the customary road in the lower town. In a couple of hours, Miss Stone's party caught up with the Tsilkas. The company had now grown to ten: six women and four men. Grigor, the only one armed, carried a revolver hidden in his coat.

At about four o'clock, the party passed a Turkish guardhouse. A little farther on, the riders dismounted in a grassy clearing shaded by beech trees, where they unpacked a picnic of meatballs and Bulgarian pastry. Madame Usheva was seized by stomach cramps, possibly the result of some honey she'd eaten in the morning, though Miss Stone and Mrs. Tsilka had sampled the same batch with no ill effects.

While they were eating, Madame Usheva's nineteen-year-old son, Peter, and a friend caught up to the party. They were going as far as Dzhumaia and then to Samokov, where they were students at the Protestant Boys' Institute. They were in the company of a man later described as a servant.

When lunch was cleared away, everyone remounted. Peter led his mother's horse by the bridle to the head of the column, and the party, now thirteen strong, set off down a steep mountain trail in single file. They were nearing a place called the Divide, the valley where the southern hills of the Rila and the Pirin meet. Ahead loomed a landmark called the Hanging Rock, a large granite boulder that jutted over the path in such a way as to force riders to steer their mounts aside into a rushing stream.

Madame Usheva's horse was the first into the water. As she rounded the rock, she looked startled. Her horse tried to scramble to one side, but an armed man was bearing down on her with his rifle butt raised as if to strike her. Usheva turned a horror-stricken face to Miss Stone and swayed as though she might faint.

In a matter of moments, it was over. The travelers' luggage and its intimate contents lay strewn along the riverbank. There was no one left at Hanging Rock—not a sound but the rushing of water. Miss Stone and her company had disappeared into the mountains.

CHAPTER TWO

Alert

᠔ᴍᴍᴏ

I cannot help thinking that . . . the whole plot is a bit of
Moslem cunning (half devil and half child) . . . the scheme
might drive our missionaries out of Turkey.

Second Assistant Secretary of State Alvah Adee
to Secretary of State John Hay,
October 5, 1901

D R. AND MRS. HOUSE had been asleep for several hours
on the night of Wednesday, September 4, when they
were awakened by a rapping on the door. It was a Turkish messenger with a telegram from a Protestant pastor in the Raslog
district. It read, "Stone and Madame Tsilka on their way from
Bansko to Djumaa [sic] at the place of the rocks were carried off
to the mountains."

Henry and Adeline House sat in the strong moonlight reading the words, too stunned to comprehend. It had been Mrs.
House's worst fear that her husband might be robbed or killed
by highwaymen. But a woman? Not even the Albanians were
so brazen as to take a gentlewoman and a persona grata such as
Miss Stone. The House children were sleeping peacefully, but
their safety—everyone's safety—was now threatened.

House dressed quickly and, taking along a Christian friend for moral support, readied a carriage. Ahead lay a ride of about an hour across town to the home of Pericles Hadji Lazzaro, the American vice consul in Salonica.

It was not the custom of the State Department to fill vice consulships with Americans, because they demanded salaries. The office was honorary and often sought by local characters looking to exploit the connection to line their pockets. Lazzaro had better credentials than most other vice consuls. He was a Greek who traveled on a Russian passport, but he was well connected in Washington, D.C., his mother having been the daughter of a U.S. senator from Virginia.

When Dr. House roused the vice consul at one o'clock in the morning Lazzaro was eager to be of service. He had had a recent tiff with the American Legation in Constantinople and as the result was feeling ignored and neglected. Now he was glad to have his services solicited so urgently.

Kidnappings were common in European Turkey, he told House. British, French, Italian, and German citizens had been seized in other parts of Macedonia. The Turks' natural inclination was to pursue the culprits, but when they did, the hostages were invariably killed. The most grisly Balkan kidnapping in European memory was that of Lord and Lady Muncaster, two British aristocrats, who had taken an excursion to the plains of Marathon in 1870. They were set upon by Greek brigands, who stole Lady Muncaster's jewels. Her husband and several attachés were taken prisoner. The British government had agreed to pay their ransom when Greek soldiers jumped the gun and pursued the kidnappers. Lord Muncaster and his aides were murdered and their bodies mutilated.

Lazzaro promised House he would meet with the Ottoman Vali, the provincial governor of Salonica, and urge him to hold back his troops.

The vice consul didn't wait for the Vali to appear at the

offices of the provincial governor that morning but went straight to his home. Tewfik *bey,* a former governor of Jerusalem, was characterized by a severe practicality. Owing perhaps to the earliness of the hour, his demeanor was chilly and his manner blunt. Miss Stone herself was to blame for not availing herself of a military escort, he groused. Lazzaro was schooled enough in the ways of the Levant not to argue the point. He did manage to extract from the Vali a promise to hold back his troops except for surveillance.

At dawn, Salonica stirred. From the docks rose the babble of tongues, the clanging of the coppersmith's hammer, the braying of donkeys, and singsong rhymes of Persian pastry vendors. Oblivious to the clamor around them, House and Lazzaro spent the morning at the Turkish telegraph office sending urgent cables: House to his missionary colleagues in Turkey and Lazzaro to his superior, Charles Dickinson, the U.S. consul general in Constantinople.

The vice consul was inclined to believe that the brigands had taken the Bulgarian woman, Madame Tsilka, as a messenger to send back their ransom demands. If so, she would be released shortly. Lazzaro knew from long acquaintance with the region that the Ottomans could be pressured through diplomatic channels to pay these ransoms. But the Sultan's treasury was so poor that it was customary, in the interests of expediency, for the captive's own government to advance the money. The correct way to handle the matter, in the opinion of the vice consul, was quietly. He himself should go to Bansko, with House as interpreter, and try to make contact with Miss Stone's captors. In his telegraph to Charles Dickinson, Lazzaro urged the consul general to be ready to pay the ransom promptly. But valuable hours passed, and there was no reply.

What happened to Lazzaro's telegram once it reached Constantinople is a mystery. It was addressed to the consul general, whose proper task it was to tend to commercial matters and to lend assistance to Americans in distress on Turkish soil. The telegram landed, however, on the desk of the U.S. Minister, John Leishman. Leishman's proper province was foreign affairs, so the kidnapping of Miss Stone was already on its way to becoming an international incident.

Leishman telegraphed the news to Washington, D.C. What response it would have received had it arrived on an ordinary business day, we'll never know, because only hours after the minister's cable reached Washington, the State Department was swept up in an event so convulsive that it blotted out nearly every other concern. At four o'clock on the afternoon of September 6, 1901, President William McKinley was shot by an anarchist.

The President had been mingling with the crowds at the Pan-American Exhibition in Buffalo when he was approached by the assailant, a lone gunman named Leon Franz Czolgosz, who pulled a revolver and fired twice. The first bullet, which pierced McKinley's chest, had not done much damage. The second, to his stomach, was more serious. His condition was grave but not hopeless. The President's cabinet and advisers moved en masse from Washington to upstate New York to be near his bedside. Among them was the vice president, Theodore Roosevelt.

Owing to his military exploits during the Spanish-American War—and a genius for self-promotion—Roosevelt was one of the best-known figures in public life. Even before he was named McKinley's running mate, he had made a name for himself as a naturalist, big game hunter, prolific author, city government reformer, war hero, and relentless champion of U.S. naval power. The joy that Roosevelt took in warfare disturbed even some of his own party. Upon learning of Roosevelt's nomination, McKinley's campaign manager, Mark Hanna, groaned, "There's only one life between that madman and the Presidency."

By the time Roosevelt arrived in Buffalo, he found McKinley improving. Barring a turn for the worse, Roosevelt would be required to tend only to routine matters of governing, so he left for a retreat in the Adirondacks with his family. If the President failed, he could be reached there by cable and quickly sworn into office. In the interim, all of the executive orders signed by McKinley remained in force. Given the possibility that these might have to be reissued and signed by his successor, government was in a state of limbo.

As Americans hung on reports issuing from the President's bedside, House and Lazzaro, far away in Salonica, kept their own anxious vigil for Miss Stone. They were still waiting for word from the consul general when they received a message from the Vali. Mr. Dickinson, who had been so curiously unresponsive to their telegrams, had wired the Turkish governor directly asking him to order out troops—the very sort of reckless move that Lazzaro had hoped to avoid. The British consul to Salonica, Sir Alfred Biliotti, had served in the past as a friend and adviser to the Americans, and as a native of the region, he knew perfectly well the risks that pursuit of the kidnappers posed to the captives. He offered to visit the Vali and attempt to persuade him to stand down, but it was too late: the Turks were already scouring the province in pursuit of the culprits. In the absence of any official response from his superiors in Constantinople, Mr. Lazzaro's hands were tied.

OVER THE NEXT few days, Dr. House managed to learn a good deal more about Miss Stone's disappearance. On the morning after the kidnapping, remnants of Miss Stone's party—Grigor Tsilka, Madame Usheva, and the three young teachers—had come straggling into Bansko. They were interviewed first by the Turks and then by their missionary colleagues. Shortly after reaching Hanging Rock, they said, they'd been surrounded by a gang of armed men and forced to dismount. After climbing the side of a mountain at gunpoint, they said, they were robbed of money and watches. Their attackers led Miss Stone away from the others; a little later, they took Mrs. Tsilka as well. The rest of the group was kept under guard through the night. At dawn, the sentry had disappeared. They looked around the quiet, dew-soaked clearing and realized that they were free to leave.

Who were these men, and what did they want? No one knew. Grigor Tsilka had identified some of the band as "Turkish soldiers." Not long after, the *Sofia Evening Post* published an article identifying the brigands as "Turkish deserters." This seemed plausible on its face, since the Ottoman military was forever in arrears on payment to regulars.

Other witnesses, however, cast doubt on the Turkish deserter theory. Young Peter Ushev, who slipped away to Samokov instead of Bansko, told the Reverend John Baird that the bandits, about forty in all, were dressed like Turks but spoke "bad Turkish" and "good Bulgarian." As they were rooting through the baggage, they fell upon the bacon and ham, eating it ravenously. Good Muslims would not have touched the pork. Their rifles, moreover, were modern Mannlichers carried by the Bulgarian army rather than the Mausers used by the Ottomans.

Henry House suspected that the kidnapping was the work of Macedonian revolutionaries, possibly backed by Bulgarians. These insurgents were known as the *Comitate*. If this were true, then the Stone kidnapping was not an incidence of common banditry but of political brigandage.

Dr. House wrote to James L. Barton, the American Board's corresponding secretary in Boston, "I have a suspicion—it is only a suspicion—that the band is a Bulgarian one, and that this is a political demonstration to show that Turkey is unsafe. Even in that case a ransom will probably be asked."

IN BOSTON, Miss Stone's family was frantic. Her ninety-year-old mother had taken to her bed. The two younger of Ellen's four brothers, Charles and Perley, begged the American Board and the State Department for news.

The Stone family's personal fortune was not large. For a time, they had owned the shoe manufacturing plant in Haverhill, but Charles and Perley had since retired to the retail end of the leather goods business. The Stone relations were hastily pooling their own funds so that when the ransom demand came, it could be met. They expected that the American Board would make up a shortfall. At first, it seemed that they could rely on this assistance. When the board's financial committee met on September 23, it authorized William W. Peet, its treasurer in Constantinople, to "provide the ransom if Turkey or the United States is not ready immediately to do so."

Over the following days, however, its resolve began to waver. The Rooms, as the American Board headquarters were known, were receiving confidential complaints from missionaries in the field. Paying a ransom would set a dangerous precedent: *Comitadji*, political and otherwise, would come to view nabbing missionaries as a steady source of cash. Sobered, the board backpedaled, sending a more carefully worded set of instructions to its treasurer at Constantinople. In the event that Miss Stone's kidnappers should demand "an absolutely unreasonable" amount, he was expected to wire headquarters for special authority to dispense the money. What would happen next wasn't spelled out.

Three weeks passed, families and friends of the captive women waiting in agonized suspense. The U.S. Legation and Consular Court in Constantinople remained alert for a sign from the kidnappers. Late Tuesday night, September 24, it came.

THE EDWARD HASKELL family, recently returned from furlough in America, had retired to bed in their temporary quarters at Samokov. Miss Mary Haskell, the missionary's daughter, was awakened by a tap on her window. Looking out, she saw a tall man who motioned that he wanted to give her something. He pushed a letter through the slats of the blinds. She heard the sound of many feet running from the house.

The letter was written in Bulgarian and addressed to W. W. Peet, treasurer of the American Board's Near East Mission in Constantinople. The handwriting was unquestionably Miss Stone's. It was dated "Macedonia, Sept. 20."

> *My Honored Friend,*
>
> *My first letter, which I sent eleven days ago, I now learn has not been forwarded to you by the person in Raslog (Macedonia) into whose hands we entrusted it. Therefore I write you again to inform you that on the 3rd of Sept. I was captured by a great number of armed men (some 40) as I traveled from Bansko to Dzhumaia. . . . The price which they demand for us is 25,000 LT, which sum must be paid without the knowledge of the Turkish and Bulgarian Governments—in a term of 18 days from today. . . .*
>
> *Therefore I beg you to hasten the sending . . . of the ransom demanded and that as much as possible you will insist before the Turkish Government that it stop the pursuit of us by the soldiers and "Bashibazouks"—otherwise we shall be killed by the people in whose hands we are.*

The missionaries' elation gave way to shock. The brigands were asking for 25,000 Turkish liras—nearly $110,000 (the modern equivalent of $1 million). How could so large a sum be raised by the deadline, only two weeks away? Clearly, the captives would be executed if the money was not paid. There was also the disturbing news of Mrs. Tsilka.

"In my first letter," wrote Miss Stone, "I had mentioned that the condition in which Mrs. Tsilka is, decided the limit as she is to give birth to a child in three months."

Katerina had apparently told no one but her husband and mother, and Grigor, out of a sense of Victorian propriety perhaps, had withheld that fact from their friends.

It was apparent from reading Miss Stone's letter that her captors had sent a ransom note a week after the kidnapping, but the message had been lost or misdirected. The missionaries couldn't take the chance of this one's wandering astray. Mr. Haskell would carry it personally by train to Constantinople.

News of the kidnapper's demands hit Boston like an arctic chill. The American Board reneged. After conducting a review of its own history, it announced that it was not allowed to negotiate with brigands and that it had always warned its missionaries not to take unnecessary risks. The responsibility for Miss Stone's rescue, the missionary society insisted, lay with the U.S. government. Judson Smith, a corresponding secretary of the ABCFM, wired the secretary of state requesting an audience with the new president, Theodore Roosevelt.

WILLIAM MCKINLEY had died on September 14 of an infection in his stomach wound. After waiting a decent interval for his prostrate widow to vacate the White House, Edith Roosevelt and the couple's six children swept in. She dismissed the state housekeeper and assumed those responsibilities herself. Her husband took over the duties of his own office with equal decisiveness, yet his usual bellicose conduct had been replaced by a restraint, which disarmed his critics.

The assassination had sent tremors through the stock market, and Roosevelt's first priority was to restore public confidence. He promised to continue the policy of President McKinley, which extended to keeping his entire cabinet, including the venerable secretary of state, John Hay.

Roosevelt himself was knowledgeable about foreign affairs owing to his tenure as assistant secretary of the navy. He'd connived to bring about the war with Spain, which, fortunately for him, ended in victory. The conquered territories spread halfway across the globe from the Caribbean to Asia. Roosevelt did not foresee, however, that a policy of imperialism, while it might elevate the nation to the ranks of a world power, required expensive maintenance. He'd inherited an ongoing rebellion in the Philippines. The rebels there were apparently no happier being repressed by the United States than by Spain. Although the uprising was all but put down by the time Roosevelt assumed office, American soldiers were still at risk in an Asian jungle. It became one of the new president's top priorities to quell the disturbance and "help these people [the Filipinos] upward along the stony and difficult path that leads to self-government."

The Panama Canal Treaty, being negotiated in London, consumed the energies of Secretary Hay, and the elder statesman was frankly weary. Four decades earlier, he'd begun his career in Washington as private secretary to Abraham Lincoln, and he was ready to retire. The death of McKinley, doubtless recalling the murder of Lincoln, had hit the Secretary hard, and he was spending a good deal of his time at his home in New Hampshire. He left lesser business, including the Stone matter, in the hands of the second assistant secretary of state, Alvah Augustus Adee.

Adee had been in Washington almost as long as Hay. He was an odd little man, just over five feet tall. Nearly deaf due to a childhood bout with scarlet fever, he was obliged to carry an ear trumpet. His mind was exceptionally keen and his wit sharp; he was a notorious punster. Temperamentally suited to the intrigues and periodic absurdities of international relations, Adee was, in the words of one State Department historian, invariably "serene and cheerful."

The Stone matter, however, left him, if not flustered, at least stumped. This was the first time in memory that an American had been kidnapped on foreign soil. The U.S. government had no clear-cut policy on the payment of ransom. The closest historical precedents, neatly stored, no doubt, in Adee's encyclopedic memory, all involved capture and enslavement of American mariners on the high seas.

Since the 1600s, pirates from the Barbary states of northern Africa had threatened American merchant vessels. As colonials, American ships had sailed under the flag of Great Britain, but after the American Revolution, they were stripped of that protection. In 1784, the brig *Betsey* was captured by Moroccan pirates, its crew taken as slaves. Americans were so enraged that the Congress voted $80,000 to buy the captives' release. The Moroccans agreed to settle for only $30,000 in gifts. They returned the prisoners and after that let American ships pass in peace.

Other corsairs kept up their raiding. The Algerians succeeded in capturing 119 American citizens whom they impressed into slavery. Congress would gladly have appropriated funds to redeem them, but the new republic was already staggering under debt to European banks. The United States couldn't send a fleet to rescue the captives; it didn't have one. Secretary of State John Jay dealt with the problem by feigning indifference in hopes that sympathetic French priests might buy the prisoners back on reasonable terms. The slaves were held for over ten years until 1796 when the United States sent its final negotiator, a poet named Joel Barlow, who managed to finesse their freedom. By then, however, a third of the original hostages had died, and the United States was compelled to pay a ransom of almost one million dollars.

America's grievances against the Barbary Muslims peaked at the beginning of the nineteenth century, after treaty negotiations between the United States and Tripoli stalled. The Tripolitans cut down a flagstaff at the U.S. consulate. The Americans sent warships to block their harbor. Unfortunately, one of these, the frigate *Philadelphia*, ran aground on a reef. The Tripolitans boarded the distressed ship and captured over three hundred U.S. sailors, demanding $1.69 million in ransom. The standoff ended when an American seaman, Stephen Decatur, stole aboard the *Philadelphia* and torched it. Americans also landed a small detachment of marines—fewer than a dozen, but enough to persuade the *bashaw* to negotiate. The entanglement with the Tripolitans was America's first foreign war since the Revolution. The affair would also be remembered as the new nation's first "victory," even though release of the *Philadelphia*'s crew required a payment of $60,000.

Although Americans had traditionally prided themselves on paying "not a penny for tribute," the record showed quite the opposite. If Miss Stone's countrymen hoped to recover her alive, they almost certainly would have to produce a ransom.

Adee now felt that the American Board's reluctance to front the money was "a deliberate death sentence." He asked the President's opinion on the matter. On October 2, Roosevelt sent him a confidential memorandum:

> *My dear Mr. Adee:*
> *... Of course everything that can be done must be done to try to rescue Miss Stone. Equally of course the government has no power whatever to guarantee the payment of the money for the ransom. As far as I can see, all that can be done is to say we shall urge upon Congress as strongly as possible to appropriate money to repay the missionaries in the event of its proving impossible to get from the Turkish or other Government the repayment. ... Every missionary, every traveler in these wild lands, should know, and is inexcusable for not knowing, that the American Government has no power to pay the ransom of anyone who happens to be captured by brigands or savages. All that we can do is what we are doing. ...*

On a testier note, the President added:

P.S. Not for publication, but as an expression of my own belief, I would say that women have no earthly business to go out as missionaries into these wild countries. They do very little good and it is impossible not to feel differently about them than about men. If a man goes out as a missionary he has no kind of business to venture to wild lands with the expectation that somehow the government will protect him as well as if he stayed at home. If he is fit for his work he accepts the risk as an incident to the work and has no more right to complain of what may befall him than a soldier has in getting shot. But it is impossible to adopt this standard about women, and therefore my own view is most strong that they should not venture into places where they are apt to meet with such adventures as befell Miss Stone.

The President may have been referring to two Protestant missionary women who were beheaded in China during the Boxer Rising of 1900.

Theodore Roosevelt regarded women sentimentally. Formal and prudish, he shuddered at the "hideous and inhumane" crime of rape, and it was quietly supposed that Miss Stone and Mrs. Tsilka were being subjected to daily outrages at the hands of their captors.

The American press was slow to pick up on the Stone incident, overshadowed at first by the assassination of President McKinley. The case was followed more avidly by the French, whose interest in ravaged virtue had been piqued by the kidnapping six years earlier of a certain Mlle. Gerard de Trincville. The hostage, a beautiful French heiress, had been forced to marry one of her brigand captors after a corrupt Turkish negotiator made off with the ransom money. Seven months later, she was rescued in a shootout by her father, who killed her bandit husband. Mlle. de Trincville subsequently became a nun.

By late September, American tabloids were awakening to Miss Stone's story. Joseph Pulitzer's New York *World* was publishing insinuations that Miss Stone, like Mlle. de Trincville, might be condemned to a "forced marriage." Of Mrs. Tsilka, a *World* correspondent wrote, "The young and beautiful Bulgarian woman may have met a terrible fate already," suggesting that she had been sold into a *harem*. To make matters worse, Mrs. Tsilka was with child. Although she was not an American citizen, so technically the State Department had no responsibility for her, to allow her to be executed was to sacrifice an innocent child. Now, with the *World* on the case, it was only a matter of time before Hearst's *New York Journal* would enter the fray. Appearing to abandon a pair of missionary women to possible sexual exploitation and death was politically unwise for the President.

Adee wired Roosevelt's sentiments to Minister Leishman in Constantinople. The people of the United States, he wrote, were "thrilled with horror at the kidnapping of Miss Stone." He must step up pressure on the Sublime Porte.

AT CONSTANTINOPLE, foreign ships anchored in the choppy, blue waters of the Bosporus flew their flags at half-mast to honor the fallen American president. Along the coast of Therapia, where foreign diplomats kept their summer palaces, an Ottoman man-of-war had lowered its own flag. It was the first time, Minister Leishman reported to Washington, that he could recall this happening. Leishman was due for a leave of absence, which he postponed, at Hay's request. Though many hours of each day had been occupied by the planning and protocol of memorial services for the fallen president, he had been working quietly on Miss Stone's behalf.

On September 5, he had sent a communiqué to the Turkish minister of foreign affairs asking him to take "immediate steps" to ransom the missionary and capture the "miscreants who have dared to lay violent hands upon an inoffensive American Citizen." The foreign minister, Tewfik Pasha, assured him that that the Vali of Salonica was doing everything in his power to help the American lady.

Minister Leishman himself, however, was due to take "the cure" at a hot springs in Europe and apparently felt he could no longer delay. With Dickinson packing for Bulgaria, Minister Leishman left the legation in the capable but inexperienced hands of his chargé d'affaires, Spencer Eddy.

Time was running out for Miss Stone and Mrs. Tsilka. According to the terms laid out in the ransom letter, the hostages were to be executed on October 8. With only three days remaining, Judson Smith and Daniel Capen of the American Board arrived in Washington, D.C., for their meeting with President Theodore Roosevelt.

The President had set aside two hours to deal with the missionaries, but his message to them was succinct: using public money to pay ransom was illegal unless it was authorized by an act of Congress. Adee, who was present at that meeting, reported to John Hay that he had found the minds of the missionaries "virgin soil on all matters of fact, law and history." They believed that the ransom demand was a bluff and were "appalled at the intricacies of the international questions involved."

The missionaries were also taken aback to hear that Miss Stone's family had taken it upon themselves to raise funds by public subscription and that a publication called *The Christian Herald*, in New York City, had started a fund drive. A campaign such as this required publicity, and publicity involved the press. Now, more journalists would be hectoring the State Department for confidential information, and that could only hinder negotiations. Smith and Capen left the President's office chastened, and Adee was certain that they would now see their way clear to put up the ransom. But as the deadline neared, the board remained firm in its refusal to pay.

"The Missionaries are a curious lot," Adee observed to Hay. "Their consensus seems to be that it would be more economical and convenient in the long run to let Miss Stone be killed—a practical proposition, which I admit while reserving opinion on the score of charity."

Adee considered the situation "intensely grave." In a telegram to Hay on October 5, he raised for the first time the possibility of sending a warship or warships through the Dardanelles. There had technically been no European Squadron since the spring of 1898, when it was disbanded and redeployed to the Philippines. Now, with insurrection there subsiding, two vessels, the *Chicago* and the *Nashville,* had joined the *Albany* in the Mediterranean only two weeks earlier. The new European Squadron was now at anchor in Genoa, Italy.

Roosevelt's predecessors, Presidents James Garfield and William McKinley, had each kept a respectful distance from the straits lying on either side of Constantinople. Since the Ottoman capital occupied such a strategic location between Europe and Asia, travel through the Dardanelles and Bosporus was strictly governed by international law. Specifically, they were off-limits to ships of war in time of peace. Although the United States had not signed and was not technically bound to any treaty, sailing into the straits with hostile intent was certain to alarm the Europeans as well as the Turks. (In 1900, the *U.S.S. Kentucky* was diverted from regular maneuvers to Constantinople, where it dropped anchor just as the American chargé d'affaires was trying to extract an indemnity from the Porte. The ship's presence seemed to have no immediate effect on the negotiations.)

Sending ships to Constantinople might rattle the Sultan, and that would no doubt have been satisfying to the President who, as assistant secretary of the navy, had once declared that

Spain and Turkey were the powers he would most like "to smash." It appeared increasingly unlikely, however, that the Turks had any part in Miss Stone's kidnapping. Did America aim simply to strong-arm the Ottomans into putting up the cash? Could a warship squeeze blood out of a stone? Was it possible to pressure the Turks to pressure the Bulgarian government to strong-arm this mysterious *Comitate*? Bulgaria, unfortunately, was for practical purposes landlocked, its only ports being on the Black Sea. American vessels could reach them by sailing through the Bosporus, but what then? Would they bombard the seaside resort of Varna? The Bulgarian capital of Sofia lay many miles inland, beyond the reach of the *Chicago*'s eight-inch guns.

For the time being, Adee felt, the State Department should avoid escalating to gunboats until it had exhausted diplomatic remedies. The next step, he advised the President, was an appeal to Bulgaria. The consul general to Constantinople, Charles Dickinson, was already on his way to Sofia.

CHAPTER THREE

The Captives

ᏙᎲᏗᏙ

What those two women will suffer can be imagined. May
God guard them.

The Reverend John W. Baird,
September 7, 1901

A LATE MORNING SUN glinted through the beech trees
as Miss Stone and her party left Bansko. The carriage
road leading out from the big gate soon narrowed to a bridle
path, and the party fell into single file. Outside town, Grigor
and Katerina Tsilka sat on horseback waiting for them.

Apart from the muleteers urging the ponies on, no one
spoke. The Protestants were mourning the death of a parish-
ioner. The Tsilkas, who had arrived in Bansko full of joy, eager
to show off their baby to his grandparents, now started their
return to Albania without him.

After almost three hours, the travelers stopped near the
Bulgarian border at a guardhouse. Turkish soldiers inspected
them cautiously, then checked their traveling papers and
waved them on. The mood of the party lightened considerably.

Beyond the checkpoint lay a narrow valley running between
the Rila and Pirin mountains, and the party stopped to admire

the beauty. A turbulent stream cut through the pines. Near the water's edge, there was a clearing, and someone suggested a picnic. The travelers dismounted and pulled down hampers of winter provisions, which they spread on the grass.

Miss Stone's companions later described a scene of perfect contentment that early September afternoon: Miss Stone, sitting ramrod straight, surrounded by her young acolytes. Spirits soared higher still when the elderly Mrs. Usheva's son, Peter, and his two classmates from the missionary school in Samokov joined the picnic. After they'd eaten, the boys began to sing. Even the young muleteers, whose demeanor bordered on sullen, seemed more talkative.

After lunch, the travelers continued, still close by the stream, into a narrow gorge. Here, they paused by the enormous boulder that hung over the path. Mrs. Usheva was the first to make the turn. In an instant, some twenty to thirty armed men sprang from behind trees and rushed her.

Some of the attackers appeared to be Turkish military. Three or four others wore the national Albanian costume, a white skirt of wool and short jackets with black braid. A few others wore European trousers. Some had blackened their faces or covered them with handkerchiefs. They carried a variety of weapons—daggers, Russian Krimki, but mainly Mannlichers, the general issue weapon of the Bulgarian army.

"Surrender you unbelievers," they shouted. Their Turkish was poor.

An order was given to dismount. Peter Ushev, who had been walking to the rear, now hurried to his mother and eased her gently off her horse. The women were driven into the rushing stream, the water soaking their skirts and petticoats. Amid the chaos, Miss Stone had the chance to observe that Mrs. Tsilka had been allowed to remain on her horse. Only after rounding the rock did she leave her mount. The attackers drove their captives stumbling up a mountainside.

During the scramble, Miss Stone had seen that Mrs. Usheva was having trouble keeping up and she asked the men, in Bulgarian, not to push so hard. They didn't reply but seemed to understand. If they weren't Turks and they weren't common bandits, what, she asked herself, did they want?

From a short distance away came the crackle of gunfire. Several of their kidnappers rushed in that direction, and when they returned, they were pushing ahead of them a tall man. His hands were tied behind his back, and blood was running down his face.

The kidnappers would later insist that he was a spy who had trailed the party, and seeing the attack in progress, he had turned and run. As his pursuers gained on him, he'd turned and fired, wounding one. Others among the kidnappers would describe him as a "Pomak," a Christian convert to Islam, later insisting to their captives that the man was the overseer at the estate of a local Ottoman *bey*, or lord. According to this story, he'd raped at least two Bulgarian girls and deserved to die. (American inquiries later established that the man was a hapless merchant who had stumbled upon the scene.)

Several of the kidnappers, Peter Ushev later recalled, seemed young and inexperienced. Those boys turned pale at the sight of the Pomak advancing toward his death. Four of the older men took charge. After exchanging a few words, they pushed the prisoner face down on the ground, lifted their daggers, and plunged them into his back.

Grigor Tsilka and the male students stood stunned and motionless. Mrs. Usheva fainted. The young teachers wailed. Katerina started forward, then withdrew and covered her eyes with her hands. Miss Stone remained calm, even after one of the kidnappers motioned for her to follow him.

Miss Stone, her ample form shrunken a bit by terror but still massive and erect, disappeared into the woods. The students and young teachers whispered among themselves that they were all to be killed, or worse. This conviction deepened when the man who led Miss Stone away returned moments later and beckoned to Mrs. Tsilka. She followed him into the woods, where she found Miss Stone sitting behind a tree, not a hair disturbed.

At dusk, the two women were ordered to climb higher, to a point where they found two horses waiting. There, they were lifted and thrust almost violently into the saddles. As she was carried away, one of the last images to remain in Miss Stone's memory was that of Grigor Tsilka, still on horseback, "holding the halter of his bare-backed horse with one hand, while he leaned his face on the other in deep dejection." Grigor, she knew, was carrying a concealed revolver.

THEY TRAVELED by moonlight, Miss Stone recorded in a memoir published after the event: "As the quiet of the night calmed our fevered nerves, we observed the brigands marching noiselessly around us. Their moccasined [sic] feet made little sound. If they had occasion for conference no word was spoken aloud, nor could even their whisperings be heard. As if by magic, men were deployed upon one side or the other as scouts, the path often changing direction without apparent command. There was a weird fascination about the scene."

The kidnappers avoided highways, holding to mountain trails and goat paths. A gigantic man went before them breaking off branches that might sweep the women off their horses. Miss Stone's mount stumbled and fell. Lying on the rocky ground, she was filled with "a sweet content" at the idea that this might end her ordeal. There was no conversation, only occasional murmurings. She caught the phrase, "Think how many liras!"

At dawn, they camped in a small ravine. The kidnappers spread out a wool rug and ordered the women to sit. Since the picnic, the women had eaten nothing but pears, which their captors had given them in the place of water. Now the very large man with thick blond curls brought a kettle of milk and a couple of wooden spoons. He also produced crumbs of the pastry that Katerina's mother had packed for the trip.

Wilted flower petals still clung to the bodice of Miss Stone's dress. One of the kidnappers noticed this and brought her a fresh bouquet of wild cyclamen—a strange gesture, she thought, as she recalled how they had murdered the Muslim.

THE KIDNAPPERS ordered the women to lie on the ground. Then four or five of them cut branches, which they laid on top of the prisoners as camouflage. Tsilka would later write:

> From where we were lying, we could see only the sky and the trees. There was no wind and the silence was so complete that our nerves were strained to the utmost. Miss Stone began to move her hands in such a queer way and to roll her eyes from side to side that I thought she was going insane. Suddenly, she jumped up in a standing position and cried: "I can't [endure] this any more and I am not going to stand it." Then she began to cry. "We must know why we are here," she said, "does not one hear me? Who is the chief? I want to see the chief."
>
> The (giant) was at once by us. "Are you the chief?" asked Miss Stone. "No, but I will ask him to (come), if you wish" said he.
>
> Very soon a man seemed to emerge from a pile of branches and came near us. He looked nervous and confused and hesitated in his speech. "Please," I said, "Tell us, are you Christian bandits or Turks?"
>
> "Oh, he said. "We are a mixture of faiths and nationalities. Among us are Bulgarians and Albanians, Serbs and Macedonians. We have even a Jew with us. But we are no

bandits. You shall know very soon why you were captured." He told us to be patient and stay where we were without getting conspicuous, because it wouldn't help anybody, least of all us.

By twilight, the caravan was on the move. After several hours, the women were hoisted off their horses and given heavy goat's hair cloaks with large hoods, which were pulled over their faces. Then they were led through a door into a small room with a single barred window, where they waited.

Finally, three men filed into the room: the Chief, the giant, and a third man, stouter and gruffer than his companions. Cartridge belts were slung over their chests and around their waists. Daggers and revolvers hung at their sides. They stacked their guns in a corner.

The men squatted in the Turkish fashion but spoke in Bulgarian. The Chief, Miss Stone wrote, explained that he and his men were "highwaymen" and that she and Katerina had been taken prisoner for ransom. "If it is not paid," he said, "there will be a bullet for you and a bullet for her"—indicating Mrs. Tsilka.

Katerina Tsilka would have a different recollection of this encounter. The brigand chief, she wrote, explained that he and his comrades were "freedom fighters" looking to overthrow the Turks. Both women, however, recalled the amount of the ransom: 25,000 liras, $110,000.

At hearing this figure, Miss Stone protested, "But my people are not millionaires, and the missionaries are poor." The men seemed unconvinced. If the ransom wasn't paid within eighteen days, the women would be shot. Miss Stone and Mrs. Tsilka began to weep. The men departed, leaving behind the odor of cigarette smoke and the stench from their filthy clothing.

For three, perhaps four, more days, Stone and Mrs. Tsilka were kept on a forced march. They slept when they could during the day and traveled by night. The attitude of their captors was perplexing—one minute threatening, the next almost polite. Miss Stone, unused to being touched by men, stiffened when they lifted her onto her horse. She smelled alcohol on their breath. Stone was a temperance worker, and she knew what could happen to men under the influence of drink. Although she continued to dress her hair in a bun, she wore a kerchief over it. During the trip out of Bansko, Mrs. Tsilka, an attractive younger woman, had let her hair fall long. Now, she pulled her own kerchief forward so that it nearly covered her face.

Once, as Katerina's horse climbed a steep hill, the saddle girth broke, and she fell backward down a stony slope. The kidnappers came to her rescue, but, Miss Stone recalled, "She shook like an aspen leaf from the nervous shock, and she burst into almost hysterical weeping." When the party finally came to rest in a vineyard, the women were taken to a dirty, bare room in an inn. Two men insisted on staying in the room that night to keep watch.

Although Stone insisted that it was not proper to have men in their chamber, they refused to leave. The captives spent a miserable night tossing on a blanket infested by bedbugs. By morning, Mrs. Tsilka was sick and feverish. There was a small window barred with iron rods, and she rested her face against the cool bars, fighting down panic. Finally, she could contain it no longer. "Kill me, kill me," she screamed, "but get out of here!"

The men retreated.

Miss Stone stroked her sick companion's temples until she was calm.

CHAPTER FOUR

Diplomacy

⟨⟩⟨⟩⟨⟩

*This has been a peculiarly hard week for me, and my mind
is black and blue all over with the coming of the blessed
Saturday afternoon. I have been worse off than (Saint)
Stephen,—I have been Stoned all the time with a continu-
ous but unfatal result."*

Second Assistant Secretary of State Alvah Adee
to Secretary of State John Hay,
October 5, 1901

B Y THE TIME THE AMERICAN consul general, Charles
Dickinson, reached Sofia, the Bulgarian capital was full of
foreign journalists. Six thousand miles and an ocean to the
west, the American public had awakened from its trance of
mourning. Leon Czolgosz, the President's assassin, had been
found to be acting alone, quieting fears that anarchists were
about to seize the levers of government. The press was now
fully alive to the possibilities of Miss Stone.

Pulitzer's *World* wanted an exclusive—pending a happy
outcome. Should Miss Stone agree to couch her memoirs in the
form of a long telegram containing 10,000 words or so of "inter-

esting matter," the paper was prepared to pay a large, though as yet unspecified, sum. Hearst's *New York Journal* had dispatched its own man to Sofia. He too was reputed to be carrying a fat purse—largesse that would doubtless find its way into the palms of telegraph operators and bellboys in exchange for information.

Correspondents congregated next door to the hotel at the Grand Café de Bulgarie, to drink *raki* and trade gossip. One, from Paris's *Le Figaro*, claimed to have visited the American missionary in a remote mountain canyon, where she was being treated in "queenly fashion." Two of her captors had been assigned to her as servants. They had, in fact, made a long trip to Constantinople to buy her Kodak film. A less sanguine account of Miss Stone's captivity found its way into the *New York Journal.* "Bulgarian Clergymen" had visited a brigands' camp where they found the captive "semi-mesmerized and in danger of losing her mind."

The consul general refused requests for interviews, grumbling about the danger that this feverish interest posed to his mission. In fact, Charles Dickinson was perfectly confident in his ability to handle gentlemen from the press.

Dickinson had, as publisher of the *Binghamton Republican* in upstate New York, helped to turn an ineffectual handful of small news organizations into what would become the Associated Press. He was also a published poet. One of his verses, "The Children," was widely anthologized, although its fame seems to have rested in part upon an early misconception, due to a compositor's error, that its author was Charles Dickens. Dickinson had spent much of his life trying to get the credit due him. This had happened only after Dickens's son wrote a letter saying the poem was assuredly not his father's.

In the spring of 1875, Dickinson had suffered a nervous collapse after losing his only child, a son, to diphtheria and for several years had confined himself to landscaping his Binghamton,

New York, estate. He regained his health, thanks to the outdoor work, which directed his thoughts into "health-giving channels." He then set off on a world tour, which left him with a lasting appreciation for the charms of the Old World. It also convinced him that the American diplomatic service was run inefficiently. What it needed was a businessman's touch—naturally, his own. Through his connections with the New York Republican corrupt political machine of bosses Thomas C. Platt and Roscoe Conkling, he landed the U.S. consulship in Constantinople.

WHEN DICKINSON ARRIVED in January 1898 at the Palazzo Corpi, the small Italianate mansion that housed the American Legation on La Grande Rue de Pera, he received an icy reception. The U.S. Minister and his staff had a long-standing suspicion of arriving consuls, fearful that the latter might be tempted to overstep their prerogatives and meddle in foreign policy matters. Dickinson asssured his new colleagues that he had "no desire for a ministry and the social functions that would go with it." His sole ambition, he declared, was to promote American business.

Until Dickinson arrived in Constantinople, American goods had barely trickled into Turkey. Europeans who controlled shipping in the region shut out all other exporters. The new consul general scored his first triumph by convincing a tramp steamer line to deliver American goods straight into the Golden Horn. When British and German shippers hired the son of the grand vizier to use his father's influence to impound American flour on the docks, an enraged Dickinson asked the secretary of state for permission to threaten "retaliatory measures." In doing so, he ran afoul of Alvah Adee, who was afraid of offending the Turks. The flour incident left relations between Dickinson and Adee permanently strained.

Dickinson was, in fact, more ambitious than he let on. Two years after arriving in Constantinople, he announced his intentions of opening Bulgaria to American business. He wanted an appointment as U.S. Minister to Sofia.

TURN-OF-THE-CENTURY Sofia was not one of the glittering capitals of Europe. It was tiny, muddy, and in transition. The Oriental character of the town—indeed, anything that reminded Bulgarians of the recent Turkish occupation—had been ripped out and replaced piecemeal with Western-style buildings. There was a charming royal palace in the French style. The area around it was paved with cobblestones or brick. Unlike Salonica, still captive to the Sultan's prejudice against "dynamos," Sofia had electricity, which ran an impressive system of streetcars and illuminated public buildings and many private homes. The residential areas, which lay beyond a two-block radius of the palace, however, were a jumble. Every citizen was responsible for the paving in front of his own home. Some did. Sofia reminded one British visitor of an American cow town.

That Sofia had an oddly American air was no accident. Nearly all of its political leaders had been educated at Robert College, a missionary school in Constantinople. After the Treaty of Berlin in 1878, Bulgarians had adopted an American-style democracy, including a popularly elected legislature. Its constitution, the most liberal in Europe except for Switzerland's, guaranteed freedom of religion and press, and right of assembly, and it forbade the rule of monarchs. Strangely, it made provisions for a prince. Alexander of Battenberg was only twenty when he was recruited to the throne. Greatly loved by his own people, he was not favored by Tsar Alexander III, who forced his abdication. A blue-ribbon delegation then made an exhaustive canvass of Europe to find a replacement who would be acceptable to the Russians. They settled on a grandson of Louis Napoleon, the last emperor of France. He was Ferdinand of Saxe-Coburg and Gotha.

Republic or not, the Bulgarians felt they needed a royal on the throne, if only to remind themselves of their lost imperial glory. During the Middle Ages, their own Tsar Ivan Asen II had ruled much of the Balkans. His court, according to one British author, was "far more refined, elegant . . . and cultivated intellectually than the English king's." More than that, however, the Bulgarians needed a symbolic warrior who could rattle a saber at the Serbs to the west and the Turks to the east. The twenty-six-year-old Ferdinand, however, was no one's idea of a warlord. He was, in the confidential assessment of the committee that acquired him, a "spoilt child . . . more fit to lie on a sofa than to sit in the saddle."

At the prodding of his ambitious mother, Princess Clementine, Ferdinand accepted the crown and played his ceremonial role gamely. He had a scientific bent that made him receptive to progress. Still, he was said to despise Sofia, preferring to spend his time at his summer palace in Varna, collecting and classifying insects. During these long absences, a personal representative of Alexander III saw to the Prince's interests in the capital. Russia, as always, was the power behind the Bulgarian throne.

Bulgaria, then, was an odd hybrid: a nominal Ottoman principality, an American-style democracy, and a Russian client state. Doing business in Sofia therefore required all the finesse and *politesse* that a career diplomat could muster.

Whatever his virtues as a businessman, Dickinson lacked *politesse*. Neither did he speak French, the universal language of diplomacy. He succeeded, however, in convincing the State Department to appoint him—if not minister, then at least to the lower and more nebulous position of "U.S. diplomatic agent" to Sofia. President McKinley signed the letter of credence, which Dickinson hoped to present personally to Ferdinand in the summer of 1901.

The Prince, while accepting Dickinson in theory, refused to receive him. Ferdinand and his ministers were troubled that Mr. Dickinson proposed to remain consul to Constantinople. Turkey was, after all, Bulgaria's old enemy, and having one man hold both posts was an "incompatible accumulation of functions."

In early August, Dickinson vented his frustrations in a letter to the State Department. There were "influences at work"— Russian, he suspected—to keep Americans out of Bulgaria. Because his presentation at court had been "indefinitely postponed," he proposed to take up his post without formal recognition. "They want our farm machinery," he declared bluntly, assuming that the juggernaut of American commercial imperialism would roll right over this toy prince. The State Department held Dickinson in check—until *l'affaire de* Miss Stone.

Charles Dickinson had met Ellen Stone socially. Few details of that encounter survive, except that it occurred during the year prior to her kidnapping and that she had found him a "sagacious man and earnest Christian." In later correspondence, he refers to her with respect, even affection. Why he displayed such apparent lack of concern for her by ignoring Vice-Consul Lazzaro's pleas for help has never been explained. Dickinson was most likely playing his cards close to the vest, not sharing information with anyone, waiting to be dispatched on a mission of mercy that could, as a fortunate by-product, put the seal on his appointment to Sofia.

When Dickinson arrived at the Bulgarian capital on Friday, October 4, he carried only the vague title of "diplomatic agent" and had no formal authority to negotiate a ransom. The instructions he had received from the State Department were cautious. He was to observe a "strict reticence," avoiding committing himself or his government to any course of action. He was, moreover, to refrain from discussing questions of "ulti-mate responsibility," although it was the current belief in Washington and Constantinople that the women had been car-ried over the border by Macedonian revolutionaries.

To the best of the State Department's information, the operational center of the Macedonian revolutionary organiza-tion was Sofia. Until recently, it had operated quite openly under the leadership of Lieutenant Boris Sarafov, a reputed familiar of Prince Ferdinand who had a reputation for ruthless-ness. He didn't hesitate to collect contributions to the cause at "revolver's mouth." Sarafov was also a man of considerable charm. He had traveled widely in Europe raising funds for a war against the Turks. This included seducing the plain daughters or bored wives of wealthy men and persuading them to make donations to the revolutionary cause. During the Spanish-American War, he'd proposed to rent Macedonian mercenaries to the United States, but his offer was declined. Sarafov had apparently overstepped his prerogatives by plot-ting the assassination of a Romanian newspaper editor who had published unflattering remarks about the *Comitate*. The journalist's murder brought Bulgaria and Romania to the brink of war. Sarafov was stripped of his chairmanship. Tried and acquitted in the spring of 1901, he'd dropped out of sight. The Turks were now circulating his photograph on their side of the border.

The missionaries did not seem to favor the Sarafov theory, holding instead that the kidnapping was the work of the local committee in Samokov. Two years earlier, the Reverend James F. Clarke, a teacher at the Boys' Institute, had received an anonymous letter from the *Comitate* demanding a contribution to the "holy cause" under the pain of death. When he turned the letter over to Bulgarian authorities, his barn was burned.

The missionaries seemed to feel that the mischief, and sub-sequent kidnapping of Miss Stone, was the work of one Asen

Vacilov, chairman of the local revolutionary committee. Young
Vacilov was "smart and reckless and a café orator," according
to one American newspaper, which added, "He has never
earned an honest dollar and has lived off contributions to the
local revolutionary fund." Vacilov had studied at the Protestant
boys' school but had since taken to taunting and persecuting
the staff. Miss Mary Haskell had tentatively identified him as
the man who thrust the ransom letter into her window the
night of September 24. Since then, he'd been taken into custody
by local Bulgarian police. No one—not the missionaries nor
even the consul general—was allowed to interview him.

The Evangelicals were perfectly aware of an impending
showdown between Bulgarians and Turks in Macedonia, and in
principle, they were neutral. They were in the business of saving souls, they declared, not playing politics. Certain of the
Americans, however, actively despised the *Comitate*. The Reverend John Baird for one condemned it as "socialist" and "anarchist." And the line between politics and humanitarian aid was
often blurred. During the winter of 1879, Clarke, over the
objections of his superiors, spent two months distributing relief
to Macedonian refugees. His efforts had apparently given the
impression of partisan sympathy, and the *Comitate*, their
request for funds rebuffed, now apparently felt betrayed.

Miss Stone had never made a secret of her dislike for the
Turks, but neither had she—as far as anyone could recall—
expressed any sympathy for the revolutionists. A story, unveri-
fied but persistent, now circulated that as recently as July, she
had been asked for a "contribution" but had refused. Perhaps
the *Comitate* hoped to make an example of her to force the
missionaries into a more generous attitude of giving.

Dickinson deputized the Reverend Baird and sent him to
Bansko to find out what he could about the kidnapping. The
consul general then paid a call on the British chargé d'affaires,
James McGregor. Since the "Liberation" in 1879, the British

had handled American matters in Sofia. For the past few weeks, McGregor had been quietly gathering intelligence about Miss Stone. He had interviewed Stoyan Danev, the Bulgarian foreign minister, whom he suspected of having planted the "Turkish deserter" story in the *Sofia Evening Post*. Danev had admitted to McGregor that the principal suspect, Boris Sarafov, was indeed involved with the Macedonian "secret committee." General Sarafov had applied for a passport and intended to leave soon for England. McGregor asked that he be detained; Danev declined to do this without a specific accusation. It was McGregor's private opinion that Sarafov had nothing to do with the kidnapping. Since he had fallen out with Ferdinand, the loss of prestige had probably "ruined him" with the Macedonians.

Dickinson himself wanted to meet with the foreign minister, but Danev, who had received advance warning, avoided him. Undeterred, Dickinson found the minister's address and went straight to his home. He was turned away but was so persistent that Danev sent a note to his hotel that he would agree to meet him at his office the following morning, a Sunday.

Despite his instructions to tiptoe around the question of responsibility, Dickinson came directly to the point. The kidnapping, he charged, was the work of a secret committee led by Boris Sarafov. He demanded that all known members of this subversive organization living near the frontier be arrested and jailed. Danev was ready with a reply.

After learning about the kidnapping from the British, he told Dickinson, the princely government had taken vigorous measures to guard the frontier and arrest the perpetrators before they could cross into Bulgaria. Military posts had been reinforced under the command of new chiefs, and fresh troops were sent to the frontier.

Danev was telling the truth—though perhaps not the entire truth. Internal government memos of the period indicate that the Stone kidnapping had taken Bulgaria by surprise. The foreign minister and the Ministry of the Interior had moved quickly to evacuate all woodcutters, shepherds, or anyone else who might assist the kidnappers from border areas. These had been replaced by soldiers who had been ordered to conduct a manhunt to rule out the possibility that the kidnappers crossed into the principality. These measures would exclude the possibility of subversives' lurking on the border. Mr. Dickinson could put his mind to rest about that.

ON TUESDAY, October 8, the ransom deadline, there was silence. No word from the kidnappers. No letter from Miss Stone. Dickinson, McGregor, and Bulgarian politicians scanned the columns of the *Sofia Evening Post* for news. The *Post*, whose editor was a reputed familiar of Boris Sarafov, seemed to be getting information directly from Miss Stone's captors. It had, for instance, published the amount of the ransom even before the letter containing that demand reached Dr. Haskell. But the *Post* that day carried no news about the missing women.

In Washington, Roosevelt had decided to "strengthen Mr. Dickinson's hand." At the President's request, Adee drafted a communiqué to Dickinson, which the consul general could then pass to Danev with the knowledge that it would find its way to Prince Ferdinand.

"In view of emerging evidence of complicity of Bulgarians," it read, "the President directs you to say to the Bulgarian Government with all earnestness that if harm come to Miss Stone the American people will be satisfied with nothing less than *unhesitating ascertainment of responsibility and due redress.*" The last phrase, Adee observed sensibly to the President, was "sufficiently elastic" to be interpreted as anything from a verbal dressing down to the appearance of U.S. warships in the Black Sea.

For the next few days, according to his diary, Dickinson

worked late into the night collecting evidence and sifting through clues. The Ottoman commissar in Sofia, with whom he seemed to enjoy good relations, passed along reports that Miss Stone had been taken to the Rila Monastery near the Turkish border. Rila had long been a sanctuary for revolutionaries. The redrawing of frontiers had left it inside Bulgarian territory and out of reach of Ottoman troops. Dickinson shared this intelligence with the Bulgarian minister of the interior, who had dispatched a patrol to check it out. The women were nowhere to be found.

The Bulgarians, meanwhile, had received a copy of the President's cable, and they were incensed. Where did the United States find the audacity to blame Bulgaria? The kidnapping had occurred indisputably in Turkish territory. Even if Bulgarians were involved, they were acting as individuals, not on behalf of their government. If the tables were turned, no one would think of trying to hold America responsible for the misdeeds of its own citizens abroad—for instance, the assassination of King Umberto of Italy the previous year by an American anarchist named Gaetano Bresci. Nor would anyone suggest that the United States arrest all anarchists living within its borders on mere suspicion. That would be as unconstitutional in Bulgaria as it would be in the United States. Sensitive to any hint of slander against their new republic, ministers of the princely government took the cable as proof that the Americans, British, and Turks were conspiring to discredit them.

Danev fired back a challenge: "If the Government of the United States should [persist to affirm] that such a secret committee exists in our country and that it considers it to be the moral author of this odious act . . . I . . . beg of you, instantly, Monsieur le Consul General, to be so kind as to furnish me with all the evidence and information that you possess."

Dickinson considered this outburst encouraging. "The resolute character of the President is well-known," he wrote to the State Department. "I think the Bulgarian Government fully realizes at last the gravity of the situation."

DICKINSON, MEANWHILE, had received a letter from an Englishman who taught at the American school in Samokov. The Reverend Robert Thomson had gotten word from a trustworthy messenger that Miss Stone and Mrs. Tsilka had been spotted by villagers as recently as the previous Saturday on Gul-tepe, a low mountain whose thickly wooded summit straddled the border between Turkey and Bulgaria. The women looked well, he reported, although Mrs. Tsilka was far advanced in her pregnancy. The band, apparently feeling pressure from patrols on both sides of the border, was threatening to resist to the death if surrounded by Turks.

Dickinson pondered this information and concluded it had the ring of truth. If one accepted the premise, as he did, that the princely government was sympathetic to the Macedonian cause, then the rebels must know they would be safe from prosecution in Bulgarian hands.

Dickinson was anxious for results to report to his superiors at the State Department. The news of a purported sighting of the prisoners increased his sense of urgency, and he began making plans for a military rescue. It was a daring move, but one he probably felt would appeal to the reckless temperament of President Roosevelt. He envisioned sending a detachment of Bulgarian troops onto the Turkish side of the ridge and having them push the band north over the border, where they would be arrested by Bulgarian authorities. He posed this scenario to Danev's lieutenant, a Monsieur Vernazza, who found Dickinson and his plan both strange and ludicrously naive. He doubted very much, he said, whether the Turks would allow Bulgarian troops onto their territory.

Dickinson, however, had a contingency plan; one that involved military action by the Turks alone. Ottoman troops would push the band over the hill into the waiting hands of Bulgarians. It is possible that Dickinson had even gotten some kind of verbal agreement of cooperation from the Ottoman military. At any rate, the consul general gave the impression that he had military forces at his disposal when he wrote to the State Department on October 11 asking, "Shall I move troops?"

Word of possible military activity along the frontier reached Constantinople where the young American chargé d'affaires, Spencer Eddy, was nervous. During the week or so that Dickinson had been in Sofia, he had not bothered to keep in touch. The excuse Dickinson offered was that the legation had never given him its code, so he had been forced to send encrypted messages through the American ambassador to Russia, who then relayed them from St. Petersburg to Washington. (Dickinson may have deliberately avoided getting the code as a ploy to cut the relatively inexperienced Eddy out of the loop, thus ensuring direct access to the State Department.)

Spencer Eddy was alarmed at the idea of Ottoman roughriders galloping up the slopes of Gul-tepe. He cabled Washington that such hostile movement might bring about the captives' instant death. He suspected that Dickinson had surreptitiously telegraphed the Vali of Salonica asking him to send out the troops that would drive the kidnappers over the border. For nearly thirty-six hours, Eddy attempted to reach the Vali before he satisfied himself that Turkish troops were not on the move.

Secretary John Hay tried to restore harmony between his fractious envoys. To Dickinson, he cabled instructions to stand down. The department, he wrote, "deems it too hazardous to ask that troops move on either side of the frontier against the brigands. This should not be done without the understanding and concurrence of chargé d'affaires to Turkey." To young Eddy, he wrote assurances that the department fully approved of his actions so far and had advised Dickinson to suspend his rescue efforts. As for a ransom, he added that he had information from an informer that the *Comitate* hoped to get 25,000 liras but would settle for 2,000.

It was the first time the State Department had officially mentioned the possibility of paying a ransom. Getting the kidnappers to settle for eight cents on the dollar, however, would require delicate and persuasive negotiation.

THAT WOULD BE extremely difficult now that Miss Stone was a cause célèbre. Her family's appeal had moved the nation. Sunday school children from coast to coast were emptying their piggy banks into collection plates. Western Union and the Postal Telegraph Company had donated their services to *The Christian Herald,* which sent telegraphs to devout families throughout the country soliciting contributions. In New York City, an "army of messengers" brought pleas to wealthy merchants; $2,000 was raised within six hours. In Washington, D.C., the envoy of the Empress of China gave $100 to demonstrate her majesty's gratitude for American help to her people during the recent famine and floods.

When the Stone brothers began their subscription drive on October 5, only three days had remained before the ransom deadline. They were certain, however, that God would work a miracle of loaves and fishes. By Tuesday morning, October 8, American Christians had managed to raise $35,000, a small fortune. Still, it was only a third of the amount demanded. There simply wasn't enough time. The Associated Press wire carried a hopeful bit of news that Mr. Dickinson had succeeded in contacting the kidnappers and extending the deadline. But this story, like so many others, was nothing but smoke.

The State Department now cautioned the bankers, Miss Stone's family, and the American Board to keep silent as to the amount raised. But the drive had taken on a life of its own. Even after the deadline passed, the fund continued to grow: $64,000 . . . $66,000 . . . $77,000. The amounts were posted and carried along by the wire services, thanks in large part to Dickinson's journalistic innovations, to every European capital, including Sofia. The *Evening Post* carried the running totals, making them readily available to Miss Stone's kidnappers. What incentive, after all, did they have to release captives whose value appreciated daily?

William Peet, the American Board's treasurer in Constantinople, sent a cable to America asking that the collections cease. There were recriminations all around. The government blamed the American Board for slipping the amounts to the press; the American Board blamed the government for coming up with this ill-considered scheme to begin with. Of course, the government had opposed the subscription scheme from the start, but it would have been tactless to lay the blame where it actually belonged: on the victim's family. Charles and Perley Stone had organized the fund campaign with the best of intentions. They had not foreseen how their appeal to Christian sympathy might have far-reaching political consequences.

The subscription drive gave an already irresistible human interest story the moral dimension of a crusade. A maiden lady at the mercy of assassins. How would she be killed? Shot in the head? Hanged? Decapitated? And her virtue? Wasn't the violation of this woman an affront to American manhood? The kidnappers, whoever they were, had thrown down the gauntlet. At stake was national pride, as Consul-General Dickinson explained in a letter to Minister Danev:

> *The Bulgarian Government can hardly understand the*
> *intense feeling which exists in the United States over this*
> *most deplorable affair. . . . This, as I believe, is the first*
> *instance in our national history in which an American*

citizen has been seized and carried off by brigands. And
when to this is added the fact that the American thus
seized and carried off and subjected, it is believed, to
untold hardships and indignities, is a woman of refined
and beautiful character, engaged in the work of an Ameri-
can Society of commanding influence, it is easy to under-
stand how powerfully those facts appeal to the chivalric
and outraged feeling of the American people and with
what irresistible force that feeling is impressed upon the
highest officials of the Government.

For Americans, the Stone kidnapping was a bewildering
blow. One of the consequences of world power was obviously
increased vulnerability, something the English, French, Germans, and Italians had felt for years. Until the victory over the
Spaniards, no American had apparently been considered valuable enough to kidnap. Now an American abroad was, as one
columnist put it, "a pigeon to be plucked."

How did one strike back?

In Boston, one Congregationalist pastor longed openly for
"a first-class battleship with decks cleared for action." In New
York, the *Evening World* picked up the refrain, and other editorial columns followed suit, wondering when Teddy Roosevelt,
hero of San Juan Hill, would call out the fleet.

The new European Squadron of the American fleet was still
at Genoa at the time the first ransom deadline came and went.
A week later the *U.S.S. Chicago* put out onto the Mediterranean to practice firing its big guns. At the time, it was three
days' cruising distance from the Dardanelles.

The situation along the Bulgarian border, meanwhile, grew
increasingly dangerous. Danev had told Dickinson the truth
when he reported that troops had been sent to the frontier. The
Bulgarians had strengthened border troops with two additional
companies of infantry and additional cavalry. These were

intended, only in part however, to hunt for Miss Stone's kidnappers. The Bulgarians had watched the increased activity of Turkish patrols south of the border with alarm. They were afraid that the Ottomans might try to use the Stone kidnapping as an opportunity to mount an invasion.

THE WESTERNIZATION of the Ottoman Empire in the early 1800s had left the Sultan with a fully modern European-style military, uniformed and equipped by his new friends, the Germans. His infantry was supplied with Mausers and supported by Krupp field guns. He was desperate to keep what remained of his disintegrating domain and would have liked to strengthen his toehold in Europe by retaking Bulgaria.

It was not clear, however, how much longer his depleted treasury would support the military. At border crossings, Turks in their handsome blue uniforms with red braid often had buttons missing. How daunting it must have been for them to look across the bridge into the eyes of Bulgarian guards in their crisp new Russian uniforms, carrying Mannlichers of recent issue.

Although Prince Ferdinand had no taste for the military life, he took an intellectual interest in military organization and modern armaments. "No nation but France," according to one British intelligence report, "has sacrificed more in military preparedness than the Bulgarians. They have had more shooting practice than the Turks and could be mobilized in eight days to full war status." Indeed, after beating back a Serb invasion in 1885, the young Bulgarian Republic had set about modernizing its own army—with the help of Russia, it was assumed in the West—still hoping to use it offensively to push the Turks out of Europe. Among the top echelon of Bulgarian officers were a large number of former Macedonian refugees who hoped to use this new military machine to cross the border and recapture Macedonia. This possibility was very much on the mind of the

Ottomans. A private communiqué from the Turkish foreign minister to the grand vizier described the call-up of Bulgarian reinforcements as an "excuse for a military buildup."

There were 150 miles of border, Bulgarians on one side, Turks on the other, and five hundred years of grievances between them. Any spark could have set the mountainous frontier aflame. If the Bulgarians and Turks went to war, would they not draw in their patrons, Russia and Germany? And England, historical protector of Turkey against Russia. Could it stand by? And France, which was currently bullying the Sultan over petty fiscal matters with a show of naval force. And America? The United States had no stake, save Christian sympathy, in the historical quarrels between the Bulgarians and the Turks, but the issue on the table was the life of one of its citizens. This improbable Ellen of Troy stood to send the *Chicago* and its escorts streaming toward the Dardanelles.

TR WAS QUIET. So were his advisers. Due to the lack of a coherent intelligence-gathering operation, they probably never comprehended the full danger of an impending clash on the Bulgarian border. And yet they had recognized the Stone situation as potentially explosive. It was also clear that continuing to pursue a diplomatic solution threatened to pull the country into a web of Old World alliances. A better choice was to find a well-connected, back-door negotiator.

This required going hat in hand to the Russians.

Teddy Roosevelt did not particularly like the Russians. Their high birthrate struck him as menacing, particularly as his own countrymen weren't reproducing rapidly enough to suit him. He boasted privately that he and Edith at least were winning "the warfare of the cradle." Later, in 1905, when he would be called to mediate a peace between the Russians and the Japanese, he felt America had more in common with the latter.

Under ordinary circumstances, the Russians wouldn't have put themselves out locating a missing American missionary. The Russian Orthodox church disdained Protestants as much as or more than did their Bulgarian Orthodox counterparts. Miss Stone was the odd exception. Her twenty years in Bulgaria had left her with a wide range of social connections. Among these was Mrs. Ivan B. Kasurov, Bulgaria's most influential businesswoman.

Kasurova had been a pupil of Miss Stone's at the Girls' Boarding School in Samokov. She had married a Sofia bookstore owner who died without heirs. This was 1876, when Bulgaria was still under Turkish rule. Oriental custom made it almost impossible for women to inherit a business, let alone run it. The plucky Kasurova, however, braved censure by picking up where her husband left off, and she made a success of the store. As years went by, men who had first scorned her now greeted her courteously in the street. Many young women followed her example. Madame Kasurova was lauded by one contemporary commentator as a "typical example of what an American education and American ideas introduced by the missionaries can do for a Bulgarian woman, and illustrates the advancement women have made in the East under missionary influence."

At the time of Miss Stone's disappearance. Kasurova's business, the Court Book Store, stood across the square from the royal palace. As official stationer to the princely government, she had influential friends at court. One of these was Mary Bakhmetieva, wife of the Russian envoy.

Charles Stone was perhaps aware of friendship between Kasurova and his sister when he sent a letter to the secretary of state early in October begging him to seek Russian intervention. His pleas fell on the sympathetic ears of undersecretary Adee, who, as it turned out, was himself an old friend of Madame Bakhmetieva. He had known her as the former Miss Mary Beale, an American from California. Her father, General

Edward "Ned" Beale, had been President Ulysses S. Grant's roommate at West Point and had remained one of his closest friends.

After Mary's marriage to the Russian, Adee had socialized with the couple for nearly twenty years in Washington, D.C., before Bakhmetiev's posting to Sofia.

With John Hay's approval, Adee telegraphed Mary, hoping to reach her influential husband. The couple happened to be away from the capital, so Adee then cabled the American ambassador to Russia, Charlemagne Tower, requesting him to ask the imperial government to reach out to Bakhmetiev. When the Russian envoy returned to Sofia, he found instructions from his superiors in St. Petersburg to do what he could to help the Americans.

An odd and secretive man, Bakhmetiev was a favorite of the Grandduchess Olga, sister of Tsar Nicholas II, and it was through her influence that he had gotten the appointment to Bulgaria. The Russian Ministry of Foreign Affairs regarded him as an uncouth palace protégé, but he had found favor with Ferdinand, who respected Bakhmetiev for his ability to close a deal over a cup of coffee. The Russian was, moreover, a staunch supporter of monarchy.

As he read over his instructions from St. Petersburg, Bakhmetiev grasped the subtext. The American woman had been kidnapped by Macedonian revolutionaries or their Bulgarian sympathizers, who doubtless hoped to use the ransom to buy guns. The confidential instructions Bakhmetiev had received from his own government before taking the post were to discourage Bulgaria's territorial ambitions in Macedonia. Russia didn't want trouble there, especially as war with the Japanese loomed as a possibility in the Far East. Bakhmetiev's mission was to find the American woman and stabilize the frontier.

It was the third week in October when Dickinson was invited to Bakhmetiev's home. In the best of worlds, the two men might have come to an understanding over a cup of coffee.

Unfortunately, they detested each other on sight. After brief salutations, Dickinson later reported to the State Department, Bakhmetiev launched into a diatribe against American Protestants who, he said, "had no business proselytizing a country that had been Christian for nearly two thousand years."

Had Dickinson possessed the restraint of a career diplomat, he might have held his tongue. But he couldn't let the insults pass. "I should have been a very poor American representative," he explained in a memo to the State Department, "if I could have listened to such attacks without expressing my emphatic dissent."

Monsieur Bakhmetiev insisted to Dickinson that it was pointless for him to continue pressuring the Bulgarian government. It had no control over the Macedonian *Comitate*. Indeed, the committee was stronger than the government. Officials who dared stand up to it risked assassination. The only way to rescue Miss Stone was to set up immediate negotiations with the revolutionaries for a ransom. How much was Mr. Dickinson prepared to pay?

Dickinson claimed not to know the exact amount in the Stone family subscription fund. (This may or may not have been the case. He did not, in fact, know at this point if it was his to spend.) The State Department had, in the beginning at least, tried to distance itself from the fund-raising campaign, taking the official position that the U.S. government did not "obstruct private charity." At the heart of the matter, however, the very idea of ransom appalled him. A great power like the United States should not capitulate to blackmail. Now this Russian was declaring "only ransom, not force" would free the captives. Dickinson concluded that Bakhmetiev was acting on behalf of the kidnappers.

He stalled. He'd not received orders from his superiors. He must check to see if it was possible to pay a ransom, however small.

Bakhmetiev was disgusted that the American had not come to the table prepared to negotiate. Personally, he doubted that Miss Stone was still alive, but felt it was necessary to find out. Without waiting for Dickinson to cable for further instructions, he set about locating the kidnappers himself.

Bakhmetiev sent his wife to Madame Kasurova, asking her if she would send a letter to Miss Stone. She agreed and wrote tenderly:

> *My dear Kaka [older sister],*
>
> *You must think by this time that your friends have forgotten you, but remember that you will find when once you are with us again that your true friends have tried to do all that they can for you, and more than that, God has put it into the hearts of others who have never known you, to work, perhaps, the hardest of all, for you to be saved. . . .*
> *God be with you!* Please write on the same letter with your own hand *[emphasis added] what you have to say, and if possible, of your condition, and send it back by the same man who brought it to you.*
>
> *Hoping to see you soon, I am with love,*
> *Your Little Sister.*

Madame Kasurova passed the letter to a colleague, Konstantin T. Boyadzhiev, who was also a Sofia bookseller as well as a friend of Miss Stone and Mrs. Tsilka. Boyadzhiev then enlisted the help of Lazar Tomov, a student at Sofia University, as his messenger. (Tomov would be identified in the American press as a "reformed brigand.") The young man was dispatched, carrying a letter from Kasurova to the village of Dupnitsa on the Bulgarian-Turkish border. There it would be put into the hands of a reputed revolutionary named Nikola Malashevski, who had been hired, at Bakhmetiev's expense, to take the letter to the kidnappers.

CHAPTER FIVE

Thread and Soap

꧁꧂

Miss Stone & Madam Tsilka cut to pieces by brigands . . .
& buried on the spot.

Cablegram to the New York *Evening World*,
Vienna correspondent,
November 9, 1901

T HE MYSTERIOUS BAND remained on the move. It traveled at night only. During the day, the women were shut
away in closets or other enclosed spaces, forbidden to move or
make a sound. They were taken at one point to a wine cellar,
then—when the air became too foul—to a room above it, where
the ventilation was better. Peering through wide cracks in the
walls, they could see that they were in a hut on a hillside.

Stone had no idea how many, if any, of the details of her
kidnapping had reached the outside world. Her traveling companions, left behind at gunpoint, might be dead. She and Tsilka
had been in captivity not quite a week when the Chief, the
giant, and their rude companion made another visit. The men
squatted near an old charcoal heap and reaching into a knapsack
pulled out paper, pen, and ink. Giving Miss Stone a wooden
plank, they ordered her to compose a ransom note. She should

choose some trusted Protestant friend in Bansko to deliver the demand to Salonica, where it should be sent to the treasurer of the American Board in Constantinople.

Miss Stone chose an elderly colporteur named Konstantin Petkanchin. She wrote to him and also to treasurer William Peet with a request for 25,000 liras inside eighteen days or she and Mrs. Tsilka would die.

The kidnappers stood over Stone's shoulder as she wrote in Bulgarian, making sure she didn't try to insert some message in the script. When she finished the two letters, the men left, taking with them all of the unused paper as well as the pen and ink.

Another week passed. Then ten days. The kidnappers grew impatient. On the eleventh day, the delegation of three paid the women another visit. This time, the Chief and the giant were silent, leaving the talking to their companion, whom Miss Stone and Mrs. Tsilka had privately dubbed the "Bad Man."

"Your man in Bansko has done nothing," he growled. (In fact, Petkanchin had been so terrified when the letters were deposited on his doorstep that he hid them, discarded them, or turned them over to Turkish authorities, who must have ignored them.)

The man told Miss Stone that she would be given one more chance to save herself. He and his companions had decided to let her write another letter. This one would be taken on foot to Samokov on the Bulgarian side of the border. There, a messenger of her choice should deliver it personally to Mr. Peet in Constantinople.

A ten-day extension wouldn't be enough, she insisted. There must be twenty. After much haggling on this point, the Chief cut off debate by declaring a compromise of eighteen days.

"I arose from our corner," Stone wrote, "and seated myself upon a projecting beam. . . . I begged them to relieve us of their presence while I should complete the two letters. They said that was impossible. 'Who knows what else you would write for your own purposes if we did not watch you?' I protested that . . . they would see every word; but they sneeringly disregarded my plea, and continued their watch."

The letter that Miss Stone addressed to Dr. Edward Haskell, her colleague in Samokov, evoked the threat of imminent peril. By the time Stone finished the two letters along with a copy of each, she had a severe headache. Her captors, however, had another demand. She must write an authorization allowing the bearer of it to receive the entire amount of the ransom.

With less than thirty days to live, Miss Stone had, nonetheless, some breathing space to assess her situation. That she was the main target of the kidnapping had been clear from the beginning. These men imagined her to be a rich American, which was untrue. Although a blueblood, she was not rich. Their belief that she represented a missionary society with large assets was closer to the truth. Although the American Board was not itself wealthy, its impeccable credit could have secured a loan from Boston bankers to cover the whole ransom within the course of an afternoon.

But why had these men taken Katerina Tsilka? From certain hints dropped by the kidnappers, Miss Stone learned that Tsilka, whom they referred to as "Gospozha," or "the Missus," had been brought along as a chaperone. The men had originally intended to take old Mrs. Usheva, but had seen that she was too frail to bear up under the strain of captivity. How, Miss Stone wondered to herself, had the kidnappers known that Mrs. Tsilka was the only other married woman in the party? She puzzled over this with Tsilka, and together they decided that it was God's plan.

Gospozha was, at the time of her capture, five months pregnant, a fact obscured by loose riding clothes and apparently undetected by her kidnappers. Her condition now posed a serious threat. The forced marches exposed her to dangers, like the fall from her horse. She might miscarry. If the baby were born, the kidnappers might smother it rather than run the risk of its making noise. They might also be tempted to kill her rather than drag around an expectant woman.

"Mrs. Tsilka," Stone wrote,

> had told me of her sacred secret, of her coming mother-hood, which she had hardly breathed as yet to mother or husband. Although it seemed almost like the desecration . . . with her consent I had acquainted the brigands with the fact of her delicate situation, on one of the first days of captivity. Then I based upon it a strong plea that they should free us, while there was yet time, and not lay themselves liable to the curse which highwaymen hold in special horror—the curse which they believed to be entailed if they cause any injury to a woman with child, or to her little one either before or after its birth. The men looked grave as they listened to me. Perhaps they thought it was a ruse of ours to escape. At any rate they answered, "It is too late. The dance which we have begun we must dance through to the end."

It is not clear whether the idea to appeal to folk superstition originated with Miss Stone or Mrs. Tsilka, but it was a shrewd move and apparently effective. By the time the giant, whom the women now knew as "Stoyan" (not his real name, of course), was dispatched to Samokov carrying the letters for Dr. Haskell, the kidnappers seemed to be going out of their way to accommodate the demands of Katerina's pregnancy. One, a plump, good-natured man whom the women called Stouty, was assigned to cook for them. He displayed great skill, Tsilka recalled, and a "fanatical cleanliness."

"WE WAITED in a state of growing despair," Tsilka wrote, "our moments of hope alternated with long periods of hopeless weeping. 'Is my husband living?' I often asked, but they never gave me a straight answer, so I took it for granted that he had been killed. Miss Stone seldom thought about her own needs; she was more concerned about me. I was expecting a baby four or five months later and my state was worrying not only her but also the whole band. They would go out of their way to search appropriate food for me, especially eggs."

The Chief had, in fact, sent out one of his men to collect eggs from local villagers. The brigand, named Antony, came back with a story of how he had tried at several houses without success. Finally, he pulled a revolver and ordered the family and their chickens into a room. There they sat for hours until the hens started laying. The scene was so ridiculous that Antony started laughing. Even the family he held hostage began to laugh. He returned to camp with a handkerchief full of hard-won booty.

"The men laughed," Tsilka recalled, "and it was a relief to us to see them gay. Their mood was often indicative of the imminences [*sic*] of danger. The nearer the danger of being attacked, the sterner and gloomier their faces became."

By the end of three weeks, the relationship between captor and captive had become complicated. Both women would claim that they had no clue as to the real identity of their kidnappers. They had given nicknames to the ones they saw daily: the Good Man or the Chief, the Bad Man or simply the B. Man. There was Stoyan. There was Stouty, also called Chaoosh the Terrible, because he wasn't very brave. There was someone called the Doctor, a pharmacist who had studied a little medicine, and a pair of young boys, Meeter and George. Miss Stone named the latter because he had an honest face. (Meeter was most likely the fifteen-year-old Dimitur Konstantin Pitsin Stephanov, one of the two young muleteers and a cousin of Katerina on her father's side; George his adolescent companion, Georgi Matsurov.)

The women remained under constant guard, even when they slept, although the guards were ordered to keep their backs turned and eyes averted. The women never had enough privacy to undress.

"Finally, in desperation," Miss Stone later recalled,

> we bethought ourselves of a plan. . . . We took the one piece of stout cord, which had been provided for the tying of our blanket during our nightly journeys, and stretched it across one corner of that black place. Over it we hung our homespun blanket, making a secluded corner in which we could hide ourselves to a degree, with our misery. At length we began to interest ourselves in watching the feet of the brigands as they passed in and out, and taught ourselves to distinguish the different guards by the way they wound the straps which held their foot-gear.

Only rarely were they permitted to bathe. (Turkish intelligence reports claim the women were seen twice emersed in thermal pools in the vicinity of a hot springs.) For six months they shared a single bar of soap. And then there was the question of feminine hygiene. One day, one of the guards inquired shyly as to whether the women had brought a change of undergarments. "No," Miss Stone reportedly replied, "we've nothing but what we wore when you captured us."

In 1901, the discussion of intimate apparel was scandalous to either sex. It was certainly a humiliating subject for the captives and an awkward one for the captors, whose sense of Victorian propriety was sufficiently cultivated to have seen the need for a chaperone.

The women were told to make a list of their most urgently required items. The Good Man disappeared for several days, then returned with supplies—men's undergarments and socks. He also brought material, thimbles, thread, and shears for new blouses. Mrs. Tsilka's had been torn to tatters.

"Here, then," Stone recalled, "was work for us to do. With

what avidity we set about it. We cut our white cotton cloth with our new shears, giving ourselves each four handkerchiefs, and then we hemstitched them, to make our work last as long as possible. What a blessing that work was to us!"

It was not only their own needs that now filled the women with a sense of purpose. The baby was coming and would need proper swaddling clothes. The wool was too coarse for an infant's skin, but Tsilka suggested that it would grow softer with washing. From that material, she cut three small dresses, two caps, and several shirts.

"The hours and days sped away more swiftly," Miss Stone recalled. She noticed how Katerina's "loving fingers often folded and rearranged the little garments which, in our rude surroundings, actually seemed soft and dainty. We varied our work with investigations in the saddlebags to see if happily there remained any apples or pears with which the brigands occasionally supplied us. We were fortunate, indeed, to have so many of them, and some varieties were very nice."

At other times, they occupied themselves by reading to one another from the Bible. Stone had managed to hang onto one of her two Waterman pens. When she was satisfied that no one was looking, she would underline passages of Scripture. The ink finally ran out, and they passed the time throwing crumbs from a window and watching birds gather to peck at them. During the day, Mrs. Tsilka recalled, the kidnappers lounged idly. But "with the coming of darkness they came out; some were stationed on guard duty while the rest ran about, played and danced. We were also taken out to walk in the woods."

Once, Miss Stone wandered too far and tumbled over the edge of a bank, resulting in a bad scrape from the edge of her hairline to below the cheekbone. The Good Man produced some antiseptic cotton. Although there was enough gravel left in the wound to produce lasting scars, she recalled, it was healed several months later almost without a trace.

For the most part, the women were kept indoors and out of sight. Once when Mrs. Tsilka opened a shutter too wide, a passing shepherd caught sight of her white kerchief. The brigands were so angry that the women were shut away again, without light.

BY LATE OCTOBER, cold winter rains swept the Balkans. In Salonica, the open verandas had been shuttered against the Vardar winds. Gloom hung over the Protestant Mission House. Henry and Addy House soldiered on with the help of reinforcements, the Reverend Holway and his wife. But they went about their labors in a state of constant dread.

In Boston, the Stone brothers took turns sitting at the bedside of their ninety-year-old mother. The old woman was too feeble to move, yet her mind was clear and her faith unshakeable. "If God still has work for Ellen," she pronounced, "he will spare her." Charles urged the State Department to prod the Russians.

In Samokov, Dr. Haskell waited for another visit from the brigands. Miss Stone's note, slipped through the blinds of his daughter's bedroom window one month earlier, had specified that the ransom must be paid in Samokov. Haskell had delayed returning with his family to their regular post at Salonica in hopes that the messenger would reappear. Night after night passed without a sign. Sick at heart, Haskell wrote Boston that the kidnappers had been frightened off by newspapermen.

On Thursday, October 25, a second messenger appeared. Neither Haskell nor Baird, who was also present that evening, recognized the man. He was not young Asen Vacilov whom Mary Haskell thought she had seen running from her bedroom window. He appeared to be about twenty-four and was of medium height. The Reverend Baird later recalled that he had high cheekbones and coal black hair and eyebrows—possibly dyed. His dress and manner were those of an educated man, and he spoke a cultivated Bulgarian. Haskell guessed he was a teacher.

The young man gave the missionaries a second letter, this one dated October 8, the first ransom deadline. It was in Ellen Stone's hand. Why, she asked, had no one responded to her pleas? The brigands had now given a ten-day extension, but that new deadline had come and gone. The dark-haired youth told the missionaries that he and his comrades intended to use the ransom money for a "holy cause," and if they knew what it was, they would not begrudge them the money.

Like Dickinson, Haskell did not know how much had been raised, but he could say for a certainty that it was not the whole sum. He would telegraph the treasurer of the American Board in Constantinople, he said, to see what there was. The messenger seemed to take heart at this. He, too, would return to his comrades to find out the lowest figure they would accept. It would take him five days, at the end of which he'd come again.

"Things seem to be working at last," Haskell cabled Dickinson. But he warned the consul general not to come to Samokov for fear of attracting attention. Should he arrive trailing reporters in his wake, the kidnappers might conclude that their confidence had been betrayed.

If anyone knew the difficulty of keeping secrets in Bulgaria, it was Dickinson. He had already complained to Monsieur Danev's assistant that telegrams were routinely opened and their contents given away or sold. Mail sent by government post arrived with the wax seals broken or missing. Miss Stone, however, had been Dickinson's ticket to Sofia, and he was not about to be pushed to the sidelines. After the meeting with Bakhmetiev, he had received a cable from Spencer Eddy in Constantinople placing $66,000 at his disposal. The Stone family's bankers had converted the dollars into gold and turned it over to the American government. Dickinson interpreted this to mean that he, not Haskell, was now the duly authorized negotiator.

The consul general proposed that he should come to Samokov "under the guise of collecting evidence." Before Haskell could say no, Dickinson was on his way.

As Haskell had predicted, news of the consul general's presence was published in the press. The police in Samokov staked out Haskell's house with a plain-clothes detective. Five days passed. The young man with dark hair did not return.

On November 4, the consul general returned to Sofia empty-handed. He found a stack of cables—some from the State Department, others from Eddy in Constantinople—demanding details. How many negotiators were in the field? How many lines of negotiation? Secretary Hay, moreover, was unhappy with Dickinson for antagonizing the Russians.

As he was trying to placate the State Department, Dickinson received encouraging news. Kasurova's letter had hit its mark. The dark-haired young man, on his way back from Dr. Haskell, had stopped in Dupnitsa, where he found Nikola Malashevski holding the letter for him. The kidnappers were willing to negotiate with Dickinson—not through an intermediary but face-to-face.

THE ENSUING MEETINGS—three of them—were conducted in absolute secrecy. The details that remain are scant. Dickinson was hesitant to file detailed reports, even with the cables encrypted.

Two members of the brigand band arrived in Sofia the last day of October, where they stayed with the student *cum* reformed brigand Lazar Tomov. On November 5, one of the two negotiators slipped past a gaggle of foreign journalists in the lobby of the Grand Hôtel de Bulgarie to meet with the U.S. consul general. Dickinson described his visitor as "bright, alert, with light eyes and hair, from twenty-five to thirty years of age and with a rather pleasant face." He was favorably impressed.

The young man handed the consul general Madame Kasurova's letter. On the back was the reply from Miss Stone:

My Dear Little Sister,
    As though the sun in all its splendor has shone out despite the rain falling on us from thick clouds, so great is my joy at having received your letter this morning. What a blessing your dear words bring to me and also to Mme. Tsilka, your countrywoman.

There was second letter addressed to Dickinson. Stone wrote:

Dear Friend, this I received of one of my friends in Sophia the first word which my companion and I have received from anywhere since we have been taken and today is the 56th day.

She went on to report that Mrs. Tsilka had reached her last weeks, if not days, before giving birth to a child and they were often compelled to travel by night:

    If you could see us surrounded with armed and cruel-faced men who keep us sometimes sheltered from the weather with only some branches in some ravine or like to-day sitting in a cave as the rain falls you would understand that if there is any hope of being free then that must be done as soon as possible.

The negotiator, who spoke through an interpreter, suggested that his side was willing to come down from its original demand, but only slightly. Dickinson, however, had specific instructions from Spencer Eddy to bargain with the kidnappers, beginning "as low as possible." He offered 10,000 liras. At this, the young man's pleasant expression turned, in Dickinson's words, "forbidding and low," and he stormed out of the hotel.

Three days later, negotiations resumed with the second of the two brigands. This man was short, dark, and cruder than the first. He also took a tougher line: the full 25,000 liras was the price. He also railed on about a "holy cause." Dickinson wrote to the State Department, "They are apparently revolutionists."

This negotiator also threw up his hands and left in disgust. The American had not come to the table ready to deal.

Five days passed before Dickinson saw the brigands again. He explained the delay to the State Department as a ruse on the part of the kidnappers to convince him that their camp was located far away over the border in Turkish Macedonia. Dickinson was still convinced Miss Stone was being held in Bulgaria.

On November 13, both brigands reappeared at the Grand Hôtel de Bulgarie. This time they seemed more conciliatory. They felt very kindly toward the captives, they said, and they would never injure them. Indeed, Miss Stone and Mrs. Tsilka knew them and called them by name. The ladies were free to walk where they liked and were extended every possible courtesy. The band, however, was prepared to hold them as long as necessary. The men had read reports in American newspapers about the subscription campaign. If the whole amount had not been raised, it soon would be. For the present, they insisted, they were owed an advance for not having injured their captives.

Under those conditions, Dickinson insisted, a settlement was impossible. He planned to return within a few days to Constantinople. If they should decide in the meantime to accept his offer of 10,000 liras, they should contact Boyadzhiev.

It was a dangerous bluff, but one Dickinson intended to play to the end game. Appearing disinterested, he explained to superiors, was necessary to convince the brigands that the American people were not lying awake at night worrying about Miss Stone. Quieting the press was the only way to break the impasse.

———

BY NOVEMBER, the cold rains whipping the Rila and Rhodopes had turned to snow. "Winter has already begun in the mountains," Spencer Eddy wrote sadly. The "suffering of the prisoners must be severe."

After all, Miss Stone and Mrs. Tsilka were still in their summer dresses.

CHAPTER SIX

Summer Dresses

ᏟᎥᎥᎥᎥᎾ

We were even afraid to weep; they never liked to see us crying, but now we had to restrain suffering lest we should get on their nerves and provoke some rash reaction.

Katerina Tsilka,
unpublished memoir

S INCE LATE OCTOBER, the women had been allowed outdoors for morning walks. On one of these strolls, a guard turned to Miss Stone and asked her if she knew that the American President had been shot. The news left her devastated.

"What was our nation doing?" she asked herself. "I felt lonely and desolate, a foreigner in a strange land, indeed, when none of them evinced any sorrow whatever at the tragedy."

The women at the time were living in a sheepfold. One morning Tsilka woke to find Miss Stone straining to overhear a conversation.

"Stoyan has come," she said.

The large man appeared, smiling. He had a letter for Miss Stone. It was from Kasurova.

78

"As she read the letter," Tsilka recalled, ". . . I saw her face brighten with intense joy and happiness. I saw also Stoyan's face smiling and his eyes getting extremely kind and gentle."

Miss Stone read the letter aloud, translating as she went from English to Bulgarian. When she came to the passage, "My mother and my three boys are well, praying for and constantly talking of you," the Bad Man sneered, "Yes, they pray and they pray, but where's the money?"

On the back of Kasurova's letter, Stone wrote her reply as well as her signature, dated October 29. For the first time, she was allowed to write an undictated letter, in English, to the American consul general, who, she learned, had come to Sofia to negotiate. The news that Dickinson had become involved in her case bolstered her spirits. She considered him a personal friend whose influence could get results.

Stoyan served as messenger and negotiator. When he left the camp on October 29, or shortly after, for his first meeting with Dickinson, he carried letters from Stone to Kasurova, Dickinson, and her mother and brothers and one more from Katerina to Grigor. Of his departure, Mrs. Tsilka recalled, "His pants were too short and his jacket shabby and torn, but the disguise was [so] successful that he could easily be taken for an overgrown country schoolboy. Beneath his jacket he wore a broad cloth belt which concealed his cartridge belt and two loaded guns. He took our letters and was quickly out of sight."

A new spirit of hopefulness settled over the camp. To celebrate, the kidnappers roasted a sheep on a spit. In the days to come, they showed a playful side.

"One Albanian dance," Miss Stone wrote, "was especially weird and grotesque. After the cold weather obliged [them] to put on their white woolen leggings, they seemed elfish, not human, with their legs suspended spider-like, in the movements of this dance. Sometimes they would take merrier measures of Greek, Bulgarian or Turkish dances. When chilled by cold, they danced to warm their feet. The doctor, when without his cloak, because either Mrs. Tsilka or I was wearing it, often slipped under Chaoosh's, and the two had a merry dance and song, provoking merriment in all."

The kidnappers occasionally took the prisoners into their confidence. The Chief would stop by the sheepfold to talk to the women about events in the outside world. Diplomats from Britain and Russia were now involved, he said. The American people, he marveled, had raised the money very quickly. Now it all rested in the hands of the U.S. consul general, who, he was certain, would release it after receiving Miss Stone's latest plea. He reported with pride that the women were now celebrities in Europe and abroad. French kiosks were selling postal cards with an artist's rendering of them in captivity. The prisoners listened, Stone recalled, "as if in a dream."

Nearly three weeks passed, however, with no news from Stoyan. Miss Stone had felt certain that Consul-General Dickinson would take pains to wrap up the matter before Thanksgiving in order to return to Constantinople and spend the holiday with his wife. On November 27, Miss Stone's morale seemed particularly low. Mrs. Tsilka explained to George, who was on guard duty, how Americans gathered for a traditional feast. The next day, the boy announced casually that he'd killed a turkey. How would they like to have it prepared?

Miss Stone was touched when later in the day, the Chief himself brought gift packages of woolen stockings and undergarments. He left the women to celebrate in peace before breaking the bad news: Stoyan had returned the night before; the negotiations had fallen through.

What, Miss Stone asked, had gone so wrong? The Chief let loose an uncharacteristic volley of obscenities, excoriating the diplomat Dickinson who was so arrogant he thought he could dictate terms. "Maybe he intends to tire us out by protracting the negotiations," the brigand told her, "but he is making a big mistake. We have broken off the negotiations. . . . None of us will go to him again."

Nothing could placate his rage. He would hold them for five years, he vowed. He would take them even farther into the mountains—so high that not even a bird would find them.

The men made hurried preparations for what Katerina Tsilka would call their "winter exile." She wrote:

Night after night, we climbed over snow covered mountains. The steep narrow paths [skirted] on one side high mountain peaks on the other fearful precipices. One slip of the horse could be fatal. The high mountain towering over us, the almost complete or the deceptive illumination of the moon. The silence broken only by the distant runs of the streams down below, the guerillas dashing in and out of our sight like ghostly shadows, all that seemed supernatural and to our sight like ghostly shadows, all that seemed supernatural and to our physical sufferings added the terror of superstitious fear. The wind was piercing our bodies and our feet were frozen beyond the stage of pain. "Don't drop your rubber shoes!" shouted an angry voice behind me. "You want to leave a trace, do you?" But soon he saw that my feet were numb with cold and couldn't feel anything.

Finally, we reached a mountain house. When they saw that we were almost frozen to death, the guerillas gave us some local brandy which was very strong and revived us quickly. That day two men sat down and made us two pairs of sheepskin moccasins.

The following night we put on woolen stockings, all the woolen clothes we had, the moccasins, fixed two heavy shepherd's cloaks one in front and one on our backs, but still the cold penetrated and made us shiver. We climbed higher and higher; ahead we saw a high snow-covered mountain, the rest was a sea of white clouds out of which emerged like islands white mountain peaks. The snow around us was blueish [sic] white with a perfectly smooth surface. There was no wind and the silence was complete.

Now the guerillas felt out of danger of attack and became gay and playful like children. They danced and shouted and sang very much out of tune until Shisko [one of the band] began to sing a song about mountains and brigands. His rich voice and the peculiar rather melancholy melody silenced the others who gradually were overcome by a strange nostalgic sadness.

Then one of the men pointed ahead and cried: "There is our place." It was a sort of a shepherd's hut and very small. "You better wait outside until we build the fire; there is no room for three at a time," said another one laughing. While we stood in the deep snow and waited they built a fire but it happened to be too big and burned down the hut. We did not know whether to cry or to laugh. So they took us to a nearby sheepfold where some of the men had built two big fires and were warming themselves. There we saw some of the guerillas who, we had noticed, had not always been with us. Now they turned and hid their faces from us.

The chief and the boy George gathered some straw, put it in front of the fire and asked us to sit down. Here we were to spend the remaining hours of the night and the next day hoped to reach our final destination.

The next day we resumed our journey. It was not long but very hard for us and for our horses. Then we reached the hut[s] Stoyan had built for us. They were obviously the masterpiece of a well-intentioned but utterly incapable building genius and, as Miss Stone put it, looked like their author when at his worst. Stoyan had been sent with some of his companions three days earlier to prepare a place for us. He bragged at length about the wonderful huts he was going to build, large and warm and comfortable, stocked with provisions to last us many months. Instead, the huts were made with rough planks leaving wide spaces among them through which the wind and the snow entered freely. The ground was soaked with the melting snow. One hut was so small that it could hardly hold the two of us. A fire burned near the door. Stoyan's provisions for the entire party consisted of the carcass of a goat which hung outside on the stub of a branch and lasted only a day.

We were thankful that we were allowed to walk around the hut and look at the wonderful beauty of the place. The men enjoyed complete leisure. Some of them pretended to go hunting, but never brought in any game. The nights were unbearable. Although the fire was burning all the time, it had little effect on the penetrating cold. From time to time we heard the wolves howling as if accompanied by the whine of the wind.

CHAPTER SEVEN

The Commission

ᘐᙏᙏᘑ

You will readily see from this the extreme difficulty of dealing with the case. There is such a vast number of persons concerned in it, and it has become so much an international question, that its far reaching results and the universal distrust engendered renders it almost impossible to take any direct line of action and to hold to it.

Spencer Eddy to John Hay,
December 13, 1901

B Y NOW, GOSPOZHA'S BELLY was swollen and clearly visible beneath her coarse woolen riding cloak. She was eight months pregnant. She should have been at home in Kortcha, surrounded by women, preparing to give birth to her baby. Instead, she was approaching her confinement eating carrion and shivering hour after hour in a drafty shack.

Fortunately, Katerina Tsilka was blessed with vitality. She was strong-willed and, in her own way, as indomitable as Miss Stone, perhaps the more intelligent and resilient of the two.

She had never seemed to mind her role as heroine of a Protestant fairy tale. To the missionaries, she was always the idealized convert—the little Bulgarian girl who, flouting the patriarchs of Orthodoxy, found her way to an Evangelical schoolhouse and thence to salvation. Of course, the truth was more complicated.

Although Katerina had descended from an eminent bishop of the Rila, her father, Dimitur, was not a priest, as the Protestants preferred to believe, but a merchant and teamster. As a side business, he hired young Bulgarian girls to pick cotton for local monasteries. Widowed at an early age, he inherited a modest estate from his late wife. When he married again, it was to a woman who was young and beautiful but poor. Elena Mandieva also had the unusual liability of not being able to cook. According to one of her granddaughters, she was required to put on a display of domestic skills for her new in-laws. She baked a pie that failed. "Never mind the pie," her relatives were said to have remarked. "Let us look at her beauty!"

Elena was remarkably well educated. Her mother had placed her under the tutelage of a local tailor who taught a handful of children in his shop as he measured patrons for trousers. Although Elena did eventually learn to cook and spin and weave, her passion was reading. She read not only the Bible, but also newspapers, and she yearned for a world beyond Bansko. As one of her descendants would attest, "It was grandmother's desire for knowledge that revolutionized grandfather's household."

Though not as progressive as his wife, old Dimitur agreed to allow their daughter, Katerina, to be educated. At age six or seven, she was sent to the local Orthodox elementary school but was treated so badly by the boys that she wouldn't go back. She would rather, she told her parents, go to the Protestant school in the village. Her father said no; he didn't want to risk the criticism of his neighbors. But Katerina's stubbornness prevailed.

The missionaries credited Katerina with bringing her entire family into the Protestant fold, but, in fact, she never succeeded in converting her father. When she reached thirteen, he arranged a traditional Orthodox marriage for her. According to family legend, she declared that she would not marry a man she hadn't chosen and stood up the groom at the altar.

Katerina threw in her lot with the missionaries, who offered not only a modern education but a stepping-stone to the West. After graduating from the missionary boarding school in Samokov, she returned to Bansko to teach. By now, however, the village seemed too small for her. What little money she'd saved she spent on a steamer ticket to America and sailed in the summer of 1892. A former instructor had arranged an appointment for her to teach at a private boarding school in New York City.

There was no one to meet her at Grand Central Station, so she spent her last quarter on a hansom cab to the school.

"I was taken to the place," she later wrote, "rang the bell, and when the so-called principal appeared I attempted to embrace and kiss her but she drew back and blushed as if annoyed. I swallowed my disappointment."

She had been hired not as a teacher but as a servant. For three months, she was worked hard and badly fed. Finally, a kindly neighbor woman helped her to escape and packed her off to the Reverend Dwight Moody's Northfield Seminary for Young Ladies in Massachusetts. Northfield was essentially a work camp for the physical and spiritual improvement of young Christians. Katerina recalled the three years she would spend there as a time of complete happiness.

After Northfield, Katerina studied kindergarten teaching methods and then nursing at Presbyterian Hospital in New York City. She graduated in the spring of 1900.

"That same year," she wrote, "Mr. Grigor Cilka [sic] had finished his theological studies in New York City and was making his plans to return to his country. I had known him for a long time, since he too was a graduate of the Samokov school;

we had lately become good friends and as he was going to Albania and his country . . . had the same fate as mine [both Albania and Macedonia were provinces under Turkish rule] we decided to unite our fortunes and work together."

In May 1900, they married and returned to the Balkans.

The newlyweds lived briefly in Monastir, a comparatively cosmopolitan city and formerly a stop on an ancient trade route between Constantinople and Europe. Katerina's letters to her former nursing supervisor in New York were filled with optimism.

"Do not worry about us," she wrote in August 1900. "We are perfectly happy—both because of God's love to us and our devotion to each other." For two weeks, she said, she and Grigor had been on a missionary tour, and Katerina was worried that her husband would "preach himself to death."

"I have done a good deal of medical and surgical work here," she continued. "The people are so ignorant of the laws of health! A woman will come to me with a baby in her arms. 'Sick,' she says, 'has fever.' A few questions, and I ask, 'Do you bathe the baby every day?' 'Oh, no! no!' she screams, expecting my approval. My prescription is usually castor oil, regular feeding, and a bath every day, and in a week's time the creature is just as happy and bright as any baby in America."

By January of the following year, the Tsilkas had moved out of the city to Grigor's birthplace, the tiny village of Kortcha. Katerina's spirits plunged. She wrote her old friend and supervisor in New York,

Since we arrived here, it seems as though I have sunk way down into the deeps of the sea. Shut in from all communication with the civilized world, no papers, no people of enlightenment. Mail only comes once a week, and that is not to be depended upon, for the postmaster is Turk; [he] distributes it whenever he pleases. The women are ignorant

as goats for they are not allowed to go out of their
houses. . . . All of my actions seem wonderful to them. The
men treat me very respectfully, even the Turks. I have more
nursing and doctoring here than I can possibly do. Today I
visited one of the Bey's (or lord's) houses. Everything about
the place was royal, but the women—oh, so blank!

Soon after that, Katerina gave birth to her first child, a boy.
That summer, she and Grigor took the baby to visit her parents
in Bansko. Katerina had not seen her family for nine years. Perhaps she intended to make peace with her estranged father. Her
correspondence to America stops and a curtain drops over her
thoughts.

As Katerina buried her first child, she was comforted at
least by the knowledge that another was on the way. By the
time she was taken prisoner that early September morning, she
was far enough advanced in her pregnancy to feel the baby's
kick under her ribs.

There was nothing delicate about Katerina's response to
captivity. Miss Stone would marvel at how vigorously her
young companion had charged up the mountain ahead of the
other women on the day of their capture. And the brigands
regarded their unwieldy hostage with superstitious awe. The
highwayman's curse, as Miss Stone had reminded them, fell
upon any man who brought harm to an expectant mother. Even
now, as they bundled the women onto their mounts for a forced
march into the high cloud-covered peaks, they realized their
threat to hold the women indefinitely was a dangerous ploy. It
was better for all concerned if this business was concluded
before Gospozha gave birth.

CHARLES DICKINSON had reached Constantinople in time
for Thanksgiving. He did not, however, bring the good news his

countrymen were waiting to hear. Hoping to put the best face on his retreat, the consul general wrote a long memo to the State Department.

The case involved unusual complications, he explained, but he was confident that both the Bulgarian people and the members of the Macedonian *Comitate* were interested in closing the matter and putting the scandal behind them. "The whole of Europe seems now to have reached the same conclusion that the Bulgarians and Macedonians are smarting under the indictment lodged against them by practically the whole civilized world."

While the princely government was indeed embarrassed by the kidnapping, it was in no position to deliver Miss Stone. The ubiquitous *Comitate* was not, in fact, one organization but two: a Supreme Committee that operated inside the boundaries of Bulgaria with the blessing of the Prince and the legislators and a clandestine body known variously as the "Secret Committee," the "Old Committee," or most commonly the "Internal Organization" or the IO. Inside Macedonia, the IO was a law unto itself. And while the two organizations shared the same short-term aim of driving the Turks out of Europe, they disagreed on what should happen after that. The Supreme Committee wanted to annex Macedonia to form a "Greater Bulgaria." The IO—Bulgarians still within Macedonia—wanted an autonomous state.

Lieutenant Boris Sarafov had, by dint of his commanding personality, managed to unite the two factions briefly. After his disgrace in the spring of 1901, however, the alliance collapsed. His successor, a close friend of the Prince, a General Ivan Tonchev, vowed to bring the IO to heel. During the summer of 1901, Bulgarian regulars crossed the border into Macedonia to roust the rebels. The Macedonians, who had until then been supplied with funds and guns from Sofia, were cut off. It was desperation, apparently, that had led them to kidnap an American.

Prince Ferdinand and the Supreme Committee were obviously in no position to negotiate for Miss Stone's release. They were busy making their own war on her kidnappers. This predicament was complicated by the fact that many officers in the Bulgarian military were sympathetic to Sarafov or the IO, or both.

All of this had been hidden from the diplomatic corps of Europe, for obvious reasons. The spectacle of Bulgarian fighting Bulgarian was embarrassing. Not even British intelligence, which grasped that there were rifts within the committee, seemed aware that the two factions were such bitter enemies.

To divert attention from its internal problems, the Bulgarian government had set about diverting attention from itself by going on the attack against the American consul general, Charles Dickinson. Stoyan Danev wrote to the Bulgarian envoy in St. Petersburg that Mr. Dickinson had made reckless accusations against the princely government. The consul general had displayed such a "reprehensible behavior" that the Prince would no longer consider receiving him as U.S. agent to Sofia.

In October 1901, Monsieur Bakhmetiev joined willingly in the campaign to discredit Dickinson. For his mouthpiece, he chose an American journalist, William E. Curtis.

CURTIS HAD MET Mary and Georgi Bakhmetiev nearly twenty years earlier on the social circuit in Washington, D.C. On sabbatical from daily journalism and armed with letters of introduction from influential friends (he was on a first-name basis with Alvah Adee), Curtis had set out on a world tour as a special correspondent to the *Chicago Record-Herald*. He planned to write a book about his travels. Whether Sofia was on his original itinerary is not certain. Curtis had already filed stories from Stockholm, an adulatory piece on the Swedish royal family, and from St. Petersburg, an earnest account of an American congressman's interview with Count Tolstoy, when the Stone case beckoned him to the Balkans.

He arrived in Sofia during the last week in October. The Bakhmetievs held a dinner party in his honor. Dickinson, who had been in town nearly three weeks, was not invited. Monsieur Bakhmetiev filled the ear of his American guest with the details of the consul general's incompetence. On the eve of Dickinson's first meeting with the kidnappers, Curtis's by-lined article appeared in the *Record-Herald*.

The U.S. State Department, he wrote, was certain to be "assailed by a storm of criticism" when it was revealed how it had mismanaged the Ellen Stone case:

> Mr. Dickinson's policy is disapproved by the entire diplomatic corps at Sofia. . . . Consul General Dickinson refused to send a messenger to Miss Stone, and even declined to send her a letter of sympathy and encouragement by the messenger dispatched to negotiate with the bandits by M. Bakhmetief, Russian diplomatic agent at Sofia. He refuses to spend money to secure information or open communication with the kidnappers.

Dr. Dickinson, Curtis went on to say, had quarreled with Monsieur Bakhmetiev and rejected the advice of more experienced diplomats from Britain, Germany, and Austria who had advised postponing any diplomatic controversy until Miss Stone was rescued. Curtis himself proposed offering $10,000 as a reward, not a ransom, which would allow everyone to save face. He sent a telegram to the consul general urging this approach. Scornful that a bounty would inspire every peasant in the countryside to make his own potentially disastrous rescue attempt, Dickinson did not bother to reply.

Curtis's story was picked up by newspapers in Europe and America and circulated among the Evangelical meeting halls of

Boston. Charles Stone was angry at Dickinson for having antagonized the Russians. *The Congregationalist,* sympathetic to the
Stone family's point of view, republished Curtis's accusations
in its Thanksgiving week issue.

Dickinson complained to American Board treasurer William
Peet, "I feel I have been smitten in the house of my friends."

The Congregationalist controversy widened the split between
those missionaries who favored paying a ransom and those who
didn't. Hard-liners such as John Baird and George Marsh rallied
to the consul general's defense, writing angry letters to board
headquarters in Boston.

The consul general insisted to his superiors in Washington
that his mission had not been a failure. To the contrary, he was
still engaged in a quiet contest of nerves with the kidnappers.
He had hoped that with his return to Constantinople, the jour-
nalistic interest in the case would subside and the kidnappers,
rather than see their investment depreciate, would release the
hostages.

A band of Macedonian zealots had learned to work the
levers of modern terrorism. No longer did a malcontent have to
cry unheard in the wilderness. By slipping a word to an international correspondent over coffee at a Sofia café, he could be sure
his message would travel like a bullet to publishing centers all
over the globe. The speed of the telegraph married to the power
of press syndicates allowed Miss Stone's kidnappers to plant
stories that would raise American anxieties.

As the crisis entered its fourth month, a particularly disturbing story found its way into the intelligence mill. A Turkish detective reported that the hostages had been taken into a
windmill near Rila where Mrs. Tsilka and her baby were executed. Miss Stone had died of a broken heart.

Although Henry House believed that Miss Stone was still
alive, he privately feared for her mental health:

I knew that she was inured to hardship and was a wonder-
fully good mountain traveller, but there was a much more
serious danger. She is of a most active nature, a woman of
boundless activity. It often came to me how could she be
[separated] from her . . . work of varied benevolent activity
and be shut up in cellars and . . . huts without the fresh air
and interest of life kept from all knowledge of what was
going on about her! I could not but fear the worst form
this utter impossibility—to write, to plan, to act. It
seemed as though she must break down under it.

As Charles Stone read the accounts of his sister's purported
death, his sense of helplessness spilled over into telegrams to
John Hay. "Superceding agent [Dickinson] Discredited," he
cabled the Secretary of State on Dec. 2. "Coercing Bulgaria
means inevitable conflict with Russia . . . help from Friendly
russia key of [*sic*] the situation."

The secretary of state replied:

Dec. 7

Dear sir:

*I have received your letter of the 6th of December. I
can appreciate your anxiety in regard to your sister, but
assure you that nothing has been left undone by this
Department to secure her release. One of the principal
[illegible] which has stood in our way is probably the
belief on the part of the brigands that the entire sum
they demand has been or will be raised. It is difficult to
convince men so dishonest and untruthful that we are
telling the truth when we say that the sums offered them
are all we have in hand. I greatly regret that I can give
you no assurance of a speedy termination of your sister's
[captivity]. The latest news from Mr. Eddy brings the*

gratifying intelligence that she was alive and well a few
days ago. Very truly yours, John Hay.

Charles Dickinson still considered himself the State
Department's official negotiator. While pursuing a policy of
hard-to-get, he was exploring alternatives to paying a ransom.
One scheme involved cultivating a drinking companion of the
kidnappers who could possibly bribe some or all of them to
release the captives. When this idea reached the State Department, Alvah Adee dismissed it as "opéra bouffe."

Poor Dickinson. He had never enjoyed much credibility in
Washington. Perhaps it was due to his having, early on, run
afoul of Adee over the flour shipping issue. It didn't help that
his political patrons, Bosses Platt and Conkling of the New
York Republican machine, were anathema to Theodore Roosevelt. The consul general now found himself entirely out of
favor. Secretary Hay informed him in a curt, dismissive note
that he should no longer cable the department directly but do
so instead through the legation. This was actually a sensible
step to ensure an orderly, encrypted flow of information, but it
had the effect of stripping Dickinson of his authority and trans-
ferring it to young Spencer Eddy.

Military coercion of Bulgaria remained a possibility. The
U.S.S. Chicago continued to cruise between Genoa and the
French Mediterranean port of Villefranche, stopping for regular
nighttime target practice. The bad blood between Dickinson and
Bakhmetiev, however, had complicated the scenario of sending
the ship to Varna. It would be bottled up in the Black Sea.

"I think Russian influence is against us," Eddy cabled the
secretary of state on December 11. "Russia fears exposing her
actions in stirring up trouble in Macedonia." Although the
Treaty of Paris did not strictly pertain to the United States, it
would be difficult, Eddy thought, to get permission for a ship to
pass through the Dardanelles. Unless the U.S. government was

willing to proceed to "extremest coercive measures" against Bulgaria, it should expect to hand over the amount that had been raised.

Hay passed along Eddy's dispatches to the President.

"Our Charge in Constantinople," he wrote Roosevelt, "is evidently of the impression that there is still a chance of reaching the brigands by negotiation, and I think it only fair to allow his scheme to be developed before making any change in the programme."

Convinced that Dickinson had bungled his mission, Spencer Eddy prepared to send another fact finder to Sofia. Dr. George Washburn seemed the ideal choice. He was president and founder of Robert College, the school that had educated almost every government minister in Sofia. (The American radical John Reed would characterize it as having produced "more unscrupulous politicians and financial geniuses than any other institution in the world.") Dr. Washburn was revered as the Father of Bulgaria. He was also a cousin of John Hay.

Washburn left for Sofia the second week of November and returned a couple of days later, having spoken to at least four of his former students, all government ministers. These men, who he was certain were absolutely "unable to lie" to him, swore that Miss Stone was not now, and had never been, in Bulgaria. He concluded that Boris Sarafov was most likely the instigator of the crime. As for locating the kidnappers, it was going to be difficult and most likely dangerous. The task, Washburn concluded, should be assigned to "trusty men" who knew the people and the language.

Spencer Eddy had been laying the groundwork for just such a secret expedition into Macedonia. Sir Alfred Biliotti had shared private information that one of the kidnappers might be willing to betray his comrades for a reward and safe conduct out of the Balkans.

Eddy hoped to create the impression that the U.S. government had washed its hands of the affair and that payment of ransom was now entirely in the discretion of the missionaries. The chargé drafted a commission of two men. As its nominal leader, he chose William Peet, since the kidnappers would assume that he had the ability to control money. Power over the purse, however, remained with the U.S. government, so it was necessary to send along an emissary from the legation. Eddy appointed Alexander Gargiulo.

A Levantine of Italian extraction, Gargiulo was a dragoman, or interpreter, an occupation held in low repute throughout the Ottoman Empire. During earlier centuries, the sultans' interpreters, almost all Greek, enjoyed great respect at court, but their esteem eroded as the Turks extended their dominion over Europe. They couldn't speak the languages of the conquered, so the dragoman came to enjoy an unusual amount of power to direct the course of negotiations. Because they often controlled access, they were susceptible to bribes. The havoc wrought by these middlemen gave rise to the saying: "In Pera, there are three misfortunes—plague, fire, and *dragomanni.*"

The British recruited and trained interpreters from the ranks of their countrymen, but the American Foreign Service had not evolved to this point. For nearly thirty years, the American Legation in Pera had relied on Mr. Gargiulo, who had, according to one British journalist, "perfect command of every language spoken in the Peninsula." His presence on the expedition gave it the imprimatur of the U.S. government, but if the mission failed? Well, then, he was only along as an interpreter.

Peet and Gargiulo set out for Salonica on December 13. Dr. House and his wife had invited them to spend Christmas. Henry House had not been invited to take part in the expedition. Eddy had deliberately kept the commission small so that it wouldn't call attention to itself. But it soon became apparent that his little team was critically deficient in expertise. Gargiulo's "command over every language spoken in the Peninsula" did not apparently extend to Bulgarian. Dr. House spoke the language fluently and, because he traversed the terrain regularly, was more familiar with the geography of Macedonia than perhaps any other American in the Balkans. He was drafted unofficially into the already unofficial deputation of trusty men.

On December 22, Peet and Gargiulo met with Sir Alfred Biliotti, the British consul to Salonica, who introduced them to his messenger. Little is known about this informer except that Sir Alfred's own dragoman vouched for his character. Peet and Gargiulo had brought stationery with distinctive markings. They gave this to the man, instructing him to get Miss Stone's signature. If it could be authenticated on the special paper, they would have some assurance that she was alive. Then they gave the courier a couple of hundred liras for expenses and sent him off into the interior. He was to cable them as soon as he had anything to report.

VICE CONSUL LAZZARO, meanwhile, took Peet and Gargiulo to the offices of the provincial governor for an audience with the Vali.

Tewfik *bey* greeted the deputation with all the courtesy he might have accorded visiting princes. After they had all drunk excellent, thick Turkish coffee from small round cups, the Vali delivered the frightful news: he'd received a telegram from eye-witnesses, apparently tobacco smugglers, who'd seen the women and a newborn strangled and buried on a mountainside near a house. The Turks had the witnesses in custody.

Peet studied this telegram and said he would like to interview these men and be taken to the grave site. The Vali wavered. The following day, he produced another telegram confirming that the witnesses had recanted their testimony.

Relations with the Turks had chilled. Even as Spencer Eddy reported to his superiors in Washington that the Ottomans had admitted responsibility for the indemnity, Tewfik *bey* had gone on record faulting Miss Stone for not having asked for a military escort. The Ottoman military intelligence, which the Ottomans had shared so generously with Consul-General Dickinson, was also proving unreliable. The Sultan's spies who had placed the hostages at both Rila Monastery and Gul-tepe were either wrong or intentionally misleading. The first location was in Bulgaria, the second straddling the border. In either case, it would have relieved the Ottomans of liability for the ransom. There was no convincing proof that the women had been held at either place.

The commander of the Ottoman Ninth Army at Serres, Lieutenant General Ibrahim Pasha, had written to his superiors at the War Ministry a summary of his opinions on the kidnapping of the "nun Stone." He described it as the "criminal actions of an anarchist society." The insurrectionists had several goals, among them to discredit the Ottomans and drive out the Protestants. Ibrahim Pasha then came full circle claiming that the Protestants were collaborating with the anarchists.

Had this Turkish general's memo reached the Western press, the American public would have responded with outrage at the suggestion that Protestants could have been involved in Miss Stone's kidnapping. Privately, however, certain of the missionaries were nagged by doubts. John Baird and George Marsh speculated in their correspondence that many young parishioners were revolutionaries using the machinery of the Evangelical mission to promote their cause. If a young Bulgarian could say he was working for the American church, he had some protection against his home being searched. If he had a colporteur's license to carry religious books, he might also smuggle partisan pamphlets past Turkish censors.

Naturally, they did not share these thoughts with the Turks. And so unspoken suspicions hung in the air like a fog over the Vardar as the American delegation sipped coffee with the Vali.

Had it been up to him, Tewfik *bey* would probably have

kept the American delegation out of the interior, where they could either be harmed or embolden the insurgents. Both would have unpleasant international consequences. But Peet and Gargiulo had come bearing letters of introduction from the Ottoman minister of the interior, and the Vali could not deny them traveling papers.

On the day after Christmas, the expedition left Salonica for the hinterlands. They were met at the train by a military escort. From there they traveled the two miles to Serres over winding, muddy roads. In the distance, they could make out the onion domes of the town. The caravan jostled through the cramped streets until it came to a halt at the Hôtel Salonique, the modest inn that would be home to them for the next six weeks.

They found themselves under constant surveillance. Only Dr. House, who had not been identified as a member of the commission, seemed to be able to move about unobserved. He slipped away to Drama some fifty miles to the east, ostensibly to preach but in fact to collect intelligence. He paid a call upon the local *mutessarif*, who recited the facts of the case by rote: the captives had been held at Rila; they were seen at Gul-tepe.

"So circumstantial was the story given by the spies of the Gov't," House wrote, "that I have often wondered at the relative inability of [its] Secret Agents."

In Serres, Peet and Gargiulo paid a call on the Ottoman prosecuting attorney. After reading the case files, they came to the same conclusion as House: the Ottoman position had hardened into a party line. The women had been captured by Bulgarians and taken to Bulgaria. It was pointless to look in Turkish Europe.

Gargiulo then called on the civil governor of Serres who, he learned to his dismay, had arrived at his post less than a week before and was completely under the domination of the local military commander, Ibrahim Pasha.

IBRAHIM PASHA seems to have been a cultivated man. The only known representation of him is a sketch published at the time in a London daily. "His soldierly figure," according to the caption, "is well set off by a blue cloak lined with red, and he always carries a Circassian riding-whip." He could read French, a skill acquired in officers' school. The modern Ottoman army trained its candidates in the European style. He had served his Sultan bravely at Kars during the Russo-Turk War of 1878. For two and a half years, he had been stationed at Serres, charged with guarding the border with Bulgaria. It was a thankless post, propping up the northern frontier of a collapsing empire. His men were harried by *comitadji*. Morale was low, the paymaster always late, and there was the biting cold of a Balkan winter. There was probably a good reason that the Ottoman army advanced only as far as Vienna. Winter, observed one commentator of the times, always took the Turks by surprise.

Ibrahim Pasha, however, carried out his commission with a rigorous sense of duty. During the four months since the capture of Miss Stone, tension had mounted on the border. On the other side, the Bulgarians were bringing in reinforcements. If they should be planning an invasion, it would be the Fourth Army that stood between them and Constantinople.

On December 29, Peet and Gargiulo paid a visit to the general at the Serres garrison, a handsome facility of barracks, cook house, prison, bathhouse, and stables surrounding a large parade ground—all designed by Ibrahim Pasha and paid for by voluntary subscriptions to the Turkish Patriotic Fund.

The general struck an imperious pose. He would already have caught the scoundrels who had captured Miss Stone, he said, but for Monsieur Dickinson, who had sent orders to stop the chase. Since that time, the guilty parties had all escaped into Bulgaria.

"Not even a bird" could cross that frontier without his

knowing about it, he boasted. The general seemed to be saying that he would not allow any of the band to cross back into Macedonia to negotiate. Gargiulo, who prided himself on his bulldog tenacity, was easily offended. As the ex officio representative of the United States of America, he asserted, "I am expecting to find them on Turkish territory and my mission does not extend beyond the boundaries of Turkey."

Ibrahim Pasha withdrew behind a veil of *politesse.* "Well," he said. "You look around and try."

The general had contempt for these Americans. Certainly they knew that their Protestant missionaries were in on the plot to kidnap Miss Stone. Sometime in September, Ibrahim Pasha had come into possession of what he claimed was a letter from Katerina Tsilka to her husband. She had urged Grigor to stay with her relatives, who would take good care of him. Guard your health, she warned him, or it would be bad for them both. "At the end of this story," she wrote, "we will benefit a great deal."

This was a curious phrase; certainly it was ambiguous. Ibrahim Pasha, however, seized on it as proof of the Tsilkas' complicity in the kidnapping. He sent it along to Constantinople.

On the day after they had visited him, Ibrahim Pasha dropped in on Peet and Gargiulo at the Hôtel Salonique. He expressed to them his opinion that Miss Stone was in some way implicated in the kidnapping and intended to receive a share of the ransom money.

"We repulsed the idea," Gargiulo reported to Leishman, "but this expression was sufficient for us to make out the spirit under which the Commander was laboring."

Anxious days passed as the delegation waited for news from Sir Alfred Biliotti's messenger. The dragoman of the British consulate in Salonica informed Peet that he'd heard from the man and that he was progressing. Finally, the Americans received a cable from their informant: "Much snow and wolves on the mountains." He was apparently encountering some kind of difficulty. They waited for clarification. None came. Sir Alfred's man had either failed in his mission and was too embarrassed to tell about it, or he was a fraud. Either way, he had taken the money and run.

CHAPTER EIGHT

The Revolutionists

*I have great confidence in Miss Stone's strength as a woman
and feel sure she will exercise that strength over those who
hold her in captivity. They cannot but be impressed, even
awed by it.*

J. L. Barton to Dr. Henry House,
December 24, 1901

I N THEIR MOUNTAIN REDOUBT, the prisoners had spells
of crying. Sometimes they wept together, sometimes alone.
They paced the dirt floor of the hut and sat for hours with their
faces turned to the wall. Katerina suffered from depression
brought on by physical misery—she was now entering her
ninth month—and from psychological distress knowing that
her captors were likely to kill the baby rather than risk its cries
alerting the Turks.

If the men were gruff one moment, they were jocular, playful, and even kind the next. Miss Stone desperately wanted to
believe that the men who held a knife to her throat were good
people. She would reminisce later about Chaoosh the Terrible,

who boasted that he could roast a sheep better than the others. "Toward evening one day," she wrote,

> a huge fire was kindled before the door of their hut, a sheep killed and spitted upon a long green branch, and the roasting process began. Tired of staying alone, and dreading the long evening without light, save from the fire in our hut, we walked down to their rendezvous. They did not seem displeased that we had taken this liberty, but indicated to us a seat upon a log, and later, put a sack filled with leaves behind our backs to break the force of the wind. Here we sat to watch the roasting, and to regale ourselves with the pleasing odor, for our appetites were keen upon that mountain-side. Our supper of black whole-wheat bread and roast mutton had a particular relish that night.

Both women seemed to feel tenderness for Stoyan. "He was a handsome man," Tsilka wrote, "so much so that we often said, 'even the dirt on his face is becoming him [sic].' He was tall and athletic, his movements were smooth and graceful. He had dark blue eyes, at times sad and pathetic, then again resolute and fierce."

Sometimes Katerina sounded like a woman in love.

THE STATE DEPARTMENT, meanwhile, was having no luck identifying the kidnappers. The same two names cropped up over and over again: Sarafov and Vacilov. Neither, however, turned out to be credible suspects.

Sarafov had not only fallen out of favor with the Prince and the Supreme Committee (SC), he had antagonized his former allies within the IO. The lieutenant had been expelled from Bulgaria. Where he'd gone, no one was sure. British intelligence reported him headed for London. But then he had been spotted in Odessa. Finally, he turned up in Paris, a city he knew well. Sarafov protested his innocence to a reporter from *Le Temps*, but his published remarks had more the character of a wistful admission than a denial. He would, no doubt, have preferred to be in the thick of the action. In fact, he had nothing whatsoever to do with the kidnapping.

As for Vacilov, Miss Mary Haskell had originally identified him as the man she'd seen running from her window in the moonlight. She may have been under the suggestive influence of her father and Mr. Baird who knew that young Vacilov belonged to the local revolutionary committee. After Miss Stone's disappearance, Vacilov had been heard boasting in Sofia cafés that a kidnapping would convince the tight-fisted American missionaries to contribute to the Macedonian cause. His loose talk got him arrested by Bulgarian police. He was released shortly after, ostensibly because no evidence had been offered against him—but, in fact, no one had been allowed to offer any. At any rate, young Vacilov had lost much of his bravado. Charles Dickinson called him in for a tongue lashing, which he endured meekly. He finally agreed to travel to the Macedonian border to gather intelligence, but he returned empty-handed. Vacilov was a small-time player.

There had, in fact, been a third suspect whose name appeared periodically in American reports. His name was Doncho Zlatkov. Identified as a former "postman" from Dupnitsa, Doncho had taken to brigandage early in his career. One revolutionary historian would describe him as an old *haramii*, chieftain of a band, who was employed occasionally as a mercenary by the SC. Immediately before Miss Stone was kidnapped, Doncho and his men had left Dupnitsa. But this band was smaller than the one that had abducted the women.

Although he would figure prominently in the mythology of the case, he was also innocent of the kidnapping. In fact, Doncho and his band of approximately twelve had been recruited by the princely government to track down Miss Stone's kidnappers and liberate the captives. Bulgaria didn't bother informing Washington that this rescue effort was in the offing.

The State Department, meanwhile, had exhausted its own sources of intelligence. After Sir Alfred Biliotti's man dropped out of sight, the American delegation in Serres was helpless. Now, instead of maintaining a cover of secrecy, it began to advertise its presence in Macedonia by feeding stories to newspapers in Sofia. Peet and Gargiulo had rejected Dickinson's strategy of hard bargaining and were prepared to release all the money collected to free Miss Stone. But a week passed, then two. No letters, no telegrams, no midnight callers. They were authorized to release more than $60,000 in gold, and now no one stepped forward to claim it.

HAD CIRCUMSTANCES been more favorable, President Theodore Roosevelt might have escalated directly to a display of American seapower. Roosevelt had staked his career on rebuilding the navy. In the forty years since the Civil War, the fleet had gone into decline. Even the new steel-hulled battleships built to be powered by steam were refitted with sails. Coal was too expensive and coaling stations too far-flung for comfort.

As assistant secretary of the navy, Roosevelt had breathed new life into the invalid. Quietly, under the very nose of the pacifist McKinley, Roosevelt began making plans for war. In February 1898, the destruction of the *U.S.S. Maine* in Cuba, possibly the result of an accidental explosion in a powder magazine, gave him his opening. Commodore George Dewey sank the Spanish fleet in the Philippines, a victory that stunned the world. The United States of America had to be reckoned with militarily, especially as fate catapulted Roosevelt into the presidency.

High on the President's agenda was building a new fleet, a "Great White Fleet" of steel-hulled, steam-belching giants that would keep Europe out of the Western Hemisphere and lend muscle to treaty making.

But the complications of gunboat diplomacy would become all too apparent. Anchoring a warship was one thing; landing troops on foreign soil was another. It could be expensive, bloody, and embarrassing. When it came time to move cavalry into Cuba, the navy found that its ships didn't have room for the horses. Riders had to charge on foot. Fortunately, Spanish resistance was disorganized.

Subduing the Philippines turned ugly, and U.S. troops were drawn deeper into the jungle. Americans were captured and tortured. They retaliated with a vengeance, emerging victorious but hardly glorious. During the Boxer Rising of 1900, the navy was able to deposit marines on the Chinese mainland to make its celebrated rescue of Western diplomats in Peking. It did, however, arrive four months too late to save Miss Stone's fellow Bible Women from a beheading in Paotingfu. And when the embassy crisis had passed, there was the sticky question of how, when, and at what speed to withdraw troops, so as not to appear to be in retreat.

The Americans were novices at global gamesmanship. As of the fall of 1901, Theodore Roosevelt's White Fleet was not yet a reality. The U.S. Navy was still a mongrel of steam and canvas.

The Miss Stone affair presented an unusual set of problems that were outlined with remarkable economy by the *Troy* [New York] *Daily Times:*

> Certainly our army could not make a march across Turkish dominions, and equally certain our fleet could not pass the Bosporus to get at eastern Bulgaria. There are too many international complications involved in either of these projects. Bulgaria, like Switzerland or Bolivia, is completely protected by its geographical position. One

might as well quarrel with the Grand Lama of Thibet or with the Man in the Moon. The Bulgarian Government could stand up and make faces at Uncle Sam as long as he pleases without running into any real danger. Meanwhile Uncle Sam would not have even the mild satisfaction of sending the Bulgarian envoy back home under diplomatic censure. There is no Bulgarian envoy to send.

There were rivers from the Aegean coast into the interior, but unlike China's Yangtze, they were too swift to be navigable. Besides, they led nowhere but to a wild, unfamiliar wilderness with no friendly forts for refuge. On their home turf, the *comitadji* would always have the advantage. They knew the terrain and could hide in one of a thousand caves, ravines, or swamps.

In a report to the State Department, Dr. Henry House tried to convey the bewildering vastness of the border region:

> From the plains as one looks at them [the mountains] present the regularity of ranges but I have often been struck with their appearance from the mountain tops. It is one enormous sweep of country, hill rising above hill and mountain top above mountain top, stretching out as far as the eye can reach. It was only a year or two ago as I was passing over the mountain heights of Perin that I was amazed at the extensive regions of plateau, wood, and peaks and defiles that I then tho't what an excellent place for revolutionists to hide away from their business. I remarked then it would seem about impossible for Gov't troops to track them out to their fastnesses.

The U.S. State Department did not seem to own a current map of Macedonia.

The American officials handling the Stone case were in possession of only one irrefutable fact: the kidnappers spoke Bulgarian. As of December 1901, the State Department used the terms *Bulgarian* and *Macedonian* interchangeably, still unaware that Bulgarian supremacists and Macedonian autonomists were at war with one another.

IN THE YEAR 1901, not even the Great Powers—England, Germany, France, Austria-Hungary—that had drawn and redrawn the boundaries of the Balkans to suit their political convenience could have made an intelligent distinction between a Bulgarian and a Macedonian. Both descended from a fierce Asiatic tribe that migrated west in the seventh century. Some of these tribesmen, the Bulgari, married local Slavs and later they were all converted to Christianity. The kingdom they founded in 681 near the present coastal city of Varna swelled into an empire under Tsar Simeon, 893-927. Its power ebbed and surged until the early thirteenth century when Tsar Ivan Asen II extended Bulgarian control over much of the Balkan peninsula.

The Bulgarians were among those defeated during the Ottoman sweep across the Balkans. And for the next five centuries, they lived under Islamic rule, sinking deeper into a morass of nameless and oppressed peasantry.

Although the Turks allowed freedom of worship to their conquered peoples, there was no ambiguity about who was master. Christians were regarded as unclean, and Christianity itself a "corrupt invention of the Evil One." No Christian could hope to prevail against a Turk in an Ottoman court. Peasants paid heavy taxes. The most painful of these was "boy tribute."

Every three years, an officer appeared in villages throughout the Balkans and rounded up the healthiest ten-year-old males, who were then led off to an Anatolian work farm. The Ottomans had recognized early on that Christians made not only good soldiers but able administrators. The boys were educated, trained to peak physical condition, and converted to Islam. That many of these conversions were insincere didn't trouble the Ottomans. They assumed that a child who went through the motions of Islamic ritual would soon experience the change in his heart.

Although they were officially slaves, many of these boys went on to brilliant careers in the military and public service. From the Ottoman perspective, these promising youths had been rescued from a life of certain misery in a Balkan mud bog. The mothers who watched their sons marched off to Anatolia no doubt felt differently, particularly as they realized that those boys would be trained to fight their own people. What was shattering to families devastated the culture as well. Until it was abolished by the reforms of the seventeenth century, boy tribute leached from the conquered Christian states of the Balkans their most vital young men.

It was not until the mid-1700s that the Bulgarians rediscovered their own culture. This was due to the work of a radical Orthodox monk, Father Paissi of Hilendar. Paissi resisted not only Turkish domination of the Balkans but Greek domination of the church. While reading old manuscripts, he discovered passages that suggested former Bulgarian glory. From these, he wrote, in rudimentary Slavonic, the *History of the Bulgarian People.*

Paissi fired the imagination and passions of young Bulgarian men who were desperate for hope. His work became the bible for young revolutionists. By the early nineteenth century, these boys were being educated in greater numbers. Ottoman officials, particularly those in the provinces, believed that no good could come of this. As the Vali of Salonica explained the problem to a Western visitor:

> It is the fault of the Bulgarian schools. In these nests of
> vice the sons of the peasants are maintained for a number

of years in idleness and luxury. Indeed, they actually sleep on beds. And then they go back to their villages. There are no beds in their fathers' cottages, and these young gentlemen are too fine to sleep on the floor, they try the life for a little, and then they go off and join the revolutionary bands.

The Vali had articulated the problem perfectly. The young were given modern education, only to return to lives of medieval hopelessness. Sultan Abdul Hamid's regime was hard on scholars. According to one turn-of-the-century memoirist, Leon Sciaky, the Turks "hunted down and destroyed anyone suspected of progressive thought."

Bulgarian boys watched as other Balkan states—Greece, Bosnia, Serbia, Montenegro—won their independence from the Turks, yet when they tried to mount their own revolution in 1876, they were crushed. Liberated by the Russians in 1878, they were allowed to enjoy that freedom only briefly before the Treaty of Berlin cut them in half with the stroke of a pen. A "Bulgarian" then was a Bulgar who by an accident of fortune happened to be living north of an arbitrary line of demarcation. A "Macedonian" would be one of his luckless cousins to the south.

FOR A TIME, at least, Bulgarians on both sides of the border considered themselves a single aggrieved people, a single revolutionary movement. After another failed uprising in 1878, many young Macedonian men fled north to the principality. There, they regrouped as the Supreme Committee.

The SC understood the importance of courting public opinion. Boris Sarafov wined and dined visiting foreign journalists and took them to Sofia's only theater, which specialized in farce at the expense of the Turks. His purpose was to show the Macedonian revolutionist as a man of the world, capable of holding his own in the salons, boudoirs, and summit rooms of Europe.

The committee's money-raising apparatus was fine-tuned and far-reaching. In addition to Sarafov's cultivation of European heiresses, the SC wrote appeals to Macedonian expatriates in England and the United States. Within the principality, collectors from the SC made the rounds of well-heeled Bulgarians. If a merchant didn't make donations voluntarily, he would certainly be visited in the night by an enforcer. Macedonian revolutionists entered the Bulgarian army, and many became high-ranking officers. They saw to it that military rifles and supplies made their way south to their rebel brothers. And they trained for the inevitable rising.

THE BULGARIANS who remained in Macedonia set up their own revolutionary headquarters in Salonica. The cradle of this internal movement was the Gymnasium, or high school. Modern and well equipped, this institution seems to have operated in full view of the Turks as it turned out some of Macedonia's most prominent revolutionaries.

Among its first graduates was Gotse Delchev, who would eventually be hailed as a martyr. He enrolled at the state military academy in Sofia but was soon expelled for radicalism. He returned to Macedonia to work as a teacher by day, an agitator by night. Over the next ten years, he recruited many other young teachers—some employed, others who had lost their positions because of revolutionary beliefs. These young men considered themselves Bulgarian, yet chose to pursue autonomy because they thought a free Macedonia would be more acceptable to the Great Powers of Europe than a "Greater Bulgaria" already rejected by the Treaty of Berlin.

In its early years, Delchev's movement spun its wheels aimlessly. He and his men suffered from no illusions that they could get their hands on enough dynamite to dislodge the Turks. All they could hope to do was to commit some small act of violence that would provoke a reprisal. If that reprisal were bloody enough, it would get the attention of Christian powers of Europe, which would then step in to mediate. The tactic had been used with some success by the Bulgarians whose murder of Muslim neighbors provoked the reprisal that sparked William Gladstone's outrage leading to European intervention. That bloodbath, however, did not result in a free Bulgaria, only partial autonomy for the principality and continued enslavement for the Macedonians. The revolutionists' hope was that the Great Powers would now see their way clear to intervene and this time give them complete freedom from the Turks.

In late 1898, Delchev and several comrades drew up a practical plan. They divided Macedonia into seven precincts, which would be patrolled by the organization's military wing, the *cheti*, or roving bands of armed men. They were the Bulgarian *comitadji*. Each town had its revolutionary committee that answered to a regional committee, which in turn was beholden to one of the seven district committees, all of which reported to Delchev and the central committee in Salonica.

What they could not construct, however, was a blueprint for winning over the Macedonians.

It was said that Gotse Delchev truly loved the poor and that they returned his love. But he was unusual in his ability to touch their hearts. The majority of his followers, mostly the young, educated elite, were disgusted with the peasants because they were slow to rouse to revolution. The fact that these people were occupied eking out a living did not seem to them a compelling excuse for their lack of political consciousness. The peasants, for their part, often cheered on the *comitadji* who robbed Turkish *beys* and murdered their overseers, particularly if they could share in the booty. But the ranks of these Robin Hoods were shot through with ne'er-do-wells who lived off contributions collected from the people. When the *cheti* needed provisions, they strong-armed the peasants into supplying them. If the IO's secret police suspected a villager of treason, he was executed.

The Supreme Committee assassinated editors; the IO executed peasants. Inevitably, they turned on one another.

Although they shared the same desire for liberty, the IO and the Supreme Committee envisioned different outcomes. The SC, well-armed, well-trained, and flush with the patronage of Prince Ferdinand, naturally saw themselves as the liberators of Macedonia. They looked down on their more primitive comrades of the IO as a fifth column of schoolteachers unqualified to plan or launch a popular rising.

Delchev and his comrades were left feeling like poor relations. They were poorly armed. Most carried old Czech-made Krimki, which the Bulgarian army considered obsolete. During the spring of 1900, Sarafov had managed to purchase under the table over a thousand sleek, modern Mannlichers. Only two hundred, however, found their way to Macedonia. This infuriated the leaders of the IO, who believed that the Supreme Committee was intentionally humiliating them.

Hostility between the two groups reached a flashpoint in early 1901 when, at Delchev's command, the IO broke entirely with the Supreme Committee. Shortly after, the Turks swooped down on IO leaders in Salonica, arresting them and shipping them off to prisons in Asia Minor.

With Sarafov's fall from power a few months later, the Sofia chairmanship passed to General Tonchev. He inherited not only all of the fund-raising machinery of the movement, but control over the official revolutionary newspaper and command of the police and military. The general sent troops over the border to rout what was left of the Macedonian rebels. And so, in the late summer of 1901, the ragtag survivors within the IO found themselves fighting on two fronts: against the Turks and the Supreme Committee.

OUT OF THIS confusion and betrayal emerged Yané Sandansky. A balding man in his early thirties, Sandansky was *voivoda*, or chieftain, of a band in the Serres region. In 1901 he was not a high-ranking member of the Internal Organization. Amid the speculation about Boris Sarafov as mastermind of the Stone kidnapping, Sandansky went unnoticed. His name occasionally appeared on lists of suspects passed from the missionaries to the State Department. The reporter William Curtis mentioned him only in passing as a "notorious desperado," misidentifying him as "Juan Zandanski." But none of the investigators seem to have taken him seriously.

Little is known about Sandansky's early childhood. He was christened Ivan. His nickname, Yané, stuck with him for life. Considering the fame he would later attain as a *voivoda*, he was, according to his biographer, Mercia MacDermott, a relatively mild youth who read omnivorously and raised doves. His father had belonged to a *cheta* during the Russo-Turk War. The Sandansky family was among those who found themselves on the wrong side of the border when the Great Powers split Bulgaria. As a teen, he joined a youth group organized by socialist teachers in Dupnitsa. When the teachers were run out of town by authorities, Yané took over leadership of the organization. He formed his own *cheta* of eight men who patrolled the Raslog District. He was, for a time, warden of a Bulgarian penitentiary. He never married. Not much more is known about his private life. Even in his memoirs, he limited himself to his exploits as rebel chieftain.

In time, Sandansky would drift further to the left to form a full-fledged "Sandansky wing" of the IO, but in the summer of

1901, he was still developing his ideas based on the works of Karl Kautsky, an adherent of the philosophy of Marx and a leader of the German Social Democracy movement.

At least one other member of his band shared Sandansky's political sympathies. That was his lieutenant, Krüstio Asenov, a tall, robust man with a blond beard and deep, soulful eyes. The nephew of a famous freedom fighter named Xadji Dimitur, Krüsty had tried his hand at teaching before becoming a revolutionist. He too was a disciple of Kautsky.

Sandansky's second lieutenant, Khristo Chernopeev, was stamped from a different mold. One Western journalist would describe him as "a small man with a face which, when in repose was that of a peasant; straight, brown, wiry hair, cut short, sticking up obstinately; round features, dark gray eyes under heavy eyebrows, and a small sandy mustache . . . when he smiled—in that smile was all that was super-peasant."

Chernopeev had only three years of grade school education, but he'd spent ten in the Bulgarian infantry, rising to the rank of *podporuchik,* or lieutenant. His interest in politics was piqued not by Kautsky but Boris Sarafov. Three years earlier, he'd left the army to help the general train boys from the Supreme Committee in military tactics. He'd become leader of his own *cheta* of sixteen, which was destroyed by a skirmish with the Turks in February 1901. A month later, Chernopeev switched his allegiance from the Supreme Committee to the IO, organizing resistance against the SC on the border. Sometime within the next five months, he'd hooked up with Sandansky.

Chernopeev was crude, undereducated, and bad tempered, but Sandansky, whose band was made up largely of teachers and boys, needed his military expertise. During the late summer of 1901, Sandansky and some fourteen followers were on the run from Tonchev. They were so poorly armed, however, that whenever they encountered a patrol from the SC, they had to run rather than fight. They needed guns, and that required cash.

The IO's leaders were imaginative, though not particularly effective, fund-raisers. One of the first schemes, suggested by Delchev, involved having a postal worker in Kyustendil, on the Bulgarian side, steal $80,000 from his office cash box. The thief fled across the border to Macedonia, where he passed the bag of money to a courier named Vassile. Pursued by Turkish patrols, Vassile buried the bag in a sandy river bottom. A sudden deluge apparently dislodged the money, carrying it downstream. It was never found. (Delchev was so distraught over the loss of the cash, he would wake from nightmares calling out "Vassile. Vassile. The gold!")

The IO then tried its hand at kidnapping—the first proposed victim being a Suleiman *bey*, a Turk who played backgammon every night in a Macedonian café with one of Sandansky's confederates, Sava Mikhailov. The Turk quarreled with the café owner, however, and on the night he was to be kidnapped, he failed to show up. Sandansky and Chernopeev considered a surprise attack on Suleiman *bey* in his *harem*, but before they had a chance to put this plan into action, the intended victim suffered a heart attack. Chernopeev was reportedly so angry that as he and Sandansky rode out of town, he tossed several of the bombs that had been made to divert attention from the kidnapping. They didn't go off.

In the summer of 1901, Sandansky and his band plotted to kidnap Prince Boris, the six-year-old son of Ferdinand, while he was taking riding lessons at a mountain resort. Delchev was squeamish. Little Boris was already the object of public sympathy; his mother, Princess Maria-Luisa of Parma, had died a year earlier. Although the revolutionists were prepared to resort to assassination and other impersonal cruelties to further the interests of their cause, kidnapping a motherless child was beyond the pale.

Talk then turned to taking an American missionary. The idea seems to have come from Sava Mikhailov, the backgam-

mon partner of Suleiman *bey*. He was a teacher and chairman
of the IO in Dzhumaia. He'd been educated at the Boys' Institute in Samokov. Whether he bore the Congregationalists any
ill will is not clear. But the revolutionaries felt generally put
out with the missionaries. The Americans might mutter privately against the Unspeakable Turk, but they wouldn't put
their convictions into action. Nor would they back the movement with money. Sandansky and his comrades shared the
unshakeable conviction that the board was rich. A kidnapping
for ransom would force them to come up with cash. The act
could be blamed on Turks, who would be forced to pay an
indemnity. The beauty of the plan was that the Americans
would suffer no loss in the end, and the Sultan would be supplying them with the cash to buy arms.

The original candidate had been Dr. Henry House, who was
due to visit the Bansko area during the late summer. He'd can-
celled that trip. Chernopeev would profess to have been
relieved. "Dr. House has always been a friend of the peasants,"
he later told an American journalist. "When we heard that he
had decided not to come our way, I, for one, only half regretted
it. A few days later we heard that Miss Stone was in Bansko. I
didn't mind Miss Stone so much. She often preached against us,
telling the poor peasants that God would right their troubles and
not the 'brigands.' All harmless stuff—nobody took it seriously,
but it made the business less difficult for us to gulp down."

The chairman of the Sofia committee denounced the proposed kidnapping as an "impure work." The district committee
of Bansko objected on grounds that the town might become the
target of Turkish reprisals. When Sandansky assured the *Banskali* that Miss Stone would not be taken until she was outside
the town gates, the local committee relented. Delchev and the
top leadership, however, held firm in their opposition to the plan.

Sandansky decided to act without permission. Disguised as
villagers, he and Chernopeev shadowed Miss Stone after her

arrival in Bansko that August. On at least one occasion, they were prepared to kidnap her as she made one of her long walks around the town, but they were deterred by the proximity of a Turkish garrison. According to Sandansky's memoirs, local Bulgarian Protestants cooperated with them, passing along information about her whereabouts, including the time of her departure.

IT WAS CLOSE to five in the afternoon on September 3 when the brigands' advance man arrived with news that Miss Stone's caravan was on its way. Sandansky's men, several dressed in ragged Turkish uniforms, had been crouching for hours behind rocks and trees near the Hanging Rock. They'd received reinforcements from a nearby town and numbered about thirty. Villagers, however, hadn't been able to bring them food, and they were starving. The boys were frightened and the older men nervous, with good reason. Not one of them had ever pulled off a successful kidnapping.

As Madame Usheva rounded the rock, Sandansky and his men surged forward, forcing their victims off their mounts, into the stream, and up a mountainside.

When they reached the clearing, the *chetnitsi* forgot their disguise and tore into the travelers' hampers of food. Only after eating the sausage and other pork did they realize that they'd blown their cover.

When Madame Usheva fainted, the kidnappers were in a near panic, as they would now have to choose a substitute.

"There were a lot of young girls in the party," Chernopeev recalled, "but we were afraid of the gossips. 'There's Mrs. Tsilka,' said the guide. 'She's married.' We liked her looks; she wasn't too young, and she looked matronly. But if we had known what was coming—the baby, you know—we'd have taken our chances with an unmarried woman. Or we'd have done without a chaperone. We paid heavily for our conventions."

The *cheta* split up, one contingent heading north with the prisoners, the other traveling in the opposite direction as decoys. Before the Turks could be alerted, Sandansky and Chernopeev had spirited their captives over the border into Bulgaria.

Sandansky had hoped to find sanctuary on the Bulgarian side. Perhaps he was counting on the sympathy and protection of Macedonian officers in the Bulgarian army. But he'd miscalculated. Within two days after Miss Stone's capture, the frontier bristled with Bulgarian regulars who were searching village to village, house to house. Sandansky and the band, who were being hidden by villagers in the town of Frolosh, soon crossed back over the mountains into Macedonia to take their chances with the Turks. They stayed near the border, first in Leshko where Asenov once taught, moving on to Selishte, where Miss Stone wrote her first ransom note.

The women were frightened, Chernopeev recalled. When Miss Stone complained that her elderly mother would die of grief, he replied, "Weep or don't weep, we don't care. The dance we have begun we will carry through to the end."

Chernopeev had taken upon himself the role of the Bad Man. He was good at arranging "dramatic scenes," as he called them. But as he was soon to learn, the business of inflicting terror entailed unforeseen risks. And looking into the face of a stern Christian spinster seems to have produced in Chernopeev and his cohorts a terror that they had never experienced in battle.

Stone's defiant nature revealed itself shortly after her capture. As she was being led away into the forest, she insisted on going back to retrieve her umbrella. Her captors were too flustered to stop her. When Chernopeev warned the women that they would be shot if they tried to run, Miss Stone replied, "You have taken the responsibility of stealing us from our God-given freedom, and [you] must therefore find a way to restore us; we shall not make it easier for you by attempting to escape."

"Bluff never pays," he would later explain. "We tried to keep it up. But what can you do with an angry, elderly and very respectable woman glaring at you? Once, she made a sudden move with her umbrella—she always carried that umbrella and her Bible and the old bonnet—well, it may have been imagination on my part, that move with the umbrella, but I stumbled backward through the doorway of the hut, to save my dignity."

Sandansky seemed even less equipped to handle Miss Stone. Although he was the Chief, Sandansky had, in the private estimation of Chernopeev, "the instincts of a French dancing master."

"I've seen the perspiration stand out on his bald head, with winter frost about us," Chernopeev told the American journalist. "I've seen him go off by himself among the trees and clench those big hands of his and grind his teeth. Well, he got his reward. He was handed down to history as the Good Man."

Asenov was the only man who proved Miss Stone's match. Stoyan—"The Bear" as she liked to call him—was her sentimental favorite. Although the two of them quarreled incessantly over the wording of the ransom notes—Miss Stone refused to write false statements—she was bent on saving his soul.

"She got after Krüsty Asenov with her Bible," according to Chernopeev. "She wanted him to read a marked chapter. He said, 'I'll read your chapter if you will read a pamphlet I have. You look into my creed, and I'll look into yours.'"

Chernopeev recalled how Krüsty took the Bible and gave her a pamphlet by Kautsky in exchange. The next day when he asked her if she was ready to exchange views, she stumbled. She'd understood nothing. Asenov then recited some biblical verses from memory. "You see," he said, "it's easier for me to learn of your creed than it is for you to learn mine."

Miss Stone did not let up. When she noticed one of the younger boys, Meeter, puffing on a cigarette, she launched into a temperance sermon. Some of America's finest young men who volunteered for service in Cuba, she told him, were rejected because tobacco had weakened their hearts.

"Not long after," recalled Miss Stone, "I was delighted to see Meeter trying to live without his smoking."

EIGHTEEN DAYS—the deadline set out in the first ransom letter—had stretched into two long months. It had become clear to Sandansky that this was not going to be the quick, low-risk operation that he'd envisioned. The *cheta* had failed in laying the blame on the Turks. It had failed to extract quick cash from the missionaries. And yet the rebels had succeeded beyond their wildest imaginings. The American public, stirred, had taken their demands seriously. American and European newspapers were reporting that Miss Stone's fellow citizens had raised the entire amount! It was unclear, however, who had control over this money.

From the beginning, Asenov had acted as the band's chief go-between—"Noah's dove," one of his biographers put it. After Miss Stone's first ransom letter went astray, he was the one who shoved the second through Mary Haskell's window. He was the "dark-haired young man" who visited her father and Mr. Baird, and was the one who carried back encouraging news that the missionaries were ready to deal. He was the one who was intercepted in Dupnitsa by Nikola Malashevski with the letter from Kasurova and a report that the American government was now in possession of the ransom fund.

Missionaries were unworldly and pliant. Diplomats were cynical and eager to impress their superiors and were likely to play a more roundabout game. There would be threats, posturing, and still more delays.

Krüsty Asenov, worried that the American, Dickinson, might regard him as an illiterate peasant, shed his schoolboy disguise and, on the morning of his first meeting with Dickinson, showed up dressed in a fine European suit, which, along with his impressive bearing and literary Bulgarian speech, left a very favorable impression on the consul general. Dickinson infuriated him by insisting that the newspaper accounts were wrong. Americans had not raised anything like $110,000.

Asenov and Chernopeev fumed that they were being played for fools and walked out of the talks.

As Dickinson withdrew to Constantinople to play his waiting game, Sandansky and his captives recrossed the border into Bulgaria to sit out the winter. Peet and Gargiulo, meanwhile, were still in Serres, waiting in vain for someone to contact them.

IT WAS NOW late December. Snow and ice made a military rescue impossible, at least by American marines, Turks, or Bulgarian regulars. But Doncho, the old Bulgarian bandit, had under his command a band of seasoned mountaineers. Their sturdy ponies could negotiate ravines and peaks that more conventional forces wouldn't even attempt. And by now, he was on the move, under orders from General Tonchev to track down Sandansky, take the women alive if possible, and wipe out the *cheta.*

Having received intelligence that they were the targets of a manhunt, Sandansky and his band studied the woods for suspicious movements. Both Stone and Tsilka sensed the heightened anxiety. Katerina wrote,

> The chief began to show signs of uneasiness. It seems that
> the place they had chosen to hide us was not as safe as
> they thought. They had noticed one or two hunters who
> could very well have been spies. Provisions had been hard
> to obtain without risk of detection. That day we saw the
> men gather and engage in earnest discussion, then all of

them but two grabbed their rifles and disappeared toward the path by which we had come. Within less than two hours the men returned together with as many new guerrillas whom we had not seen before. The chief came and told us to get ready to leave at once.

The descent was even worse than the climbing. The path was slippery and the horses found with difficulty their foothold. The party halted at the foot of the mountain under the shelter of a group of trees. The men, wrapped in their cloaks, lay on the ground and began to snore. We were told to remain on our horses. After some rest the men were up again and we resumed our journey. We were very tired and the chief knew it, but he told us that the place was not safe and we had to go further.

After midnight, the party stopped at a hut. It had no windows or chimney, only a door. Five of the men—Sandansky, Chaoosh, Antony, a man called Alamas, and the Doctor— stayed behind to guard the women; the others disappeared into the mountains. Asenov and Chernopeev had gone ahead to investigate the recent murder of an IO district leader, Alexander Iliev, who had been temporarily stationed in the town of Maleshevo to guard a supply line from Sofia. Asenov and Chernopeev had intercepted a courier who was carrying a letter from Doncho to the Supreme Committee. It told how he had invited Iliev in for a parley and a drink, promising to obey the rules of *cheta* hospitality. Later, as Iliev lay sleeping, Doncho smashed his skull with an axe.

Asenov and Chernopeev were enraged over the murder of their friend and comrade. They'd ridden off to take revenge when they received the news that Doncho and his men had doubled back and were somewhere in the area of the cabin where the women were being held.

Tsilka noticed her captors were anxious. She recalled:

They often looked through the cracks of the door. Then the chief gave some orders. Chaoosh was to guard the door, the others were stationed at different points around the hut. We saw that some danger was threatening us but we were afraid to ask any questions.

We were left alone in the hut; I was lying down while Miss Stone was standing near the door. We heard quick footsteps and whispering. Then one of the men rushed in . . . and was out again. Suddenly, we heard several shots and somebody yelling. I sprang up and rushed to a corner. It was now so dark that I could not see Miss Stone, only heard her breathing. Then the chief came in and caught us both by the arms and pushed us into a small closet where a man was standing, holding a gun partly projected through a small window. "Get those women out of here," he cried. "There is no room for three of us." But the chief told him to keep quiet and look outside.

It seems that we had been attacked and the first assault of the attack had been [repulsed]. By and by the shooting became less frequent and by the morning ceased altogether. All night long the five men had stood keeping the attackers off the hut.

Miss Stone, one of the kidnappers would insist, dropped to her knees begging Sandansky to kill her rather than let her fall into the hands of an unfamiliar enemy.

By dawn it was quiet. Sandansky led the women under the eaves of the hut to the horses. But as Tsilka was being helped into the saddle, another shot rang out of the woods. The women were hustled back inside and hidden in the cellar.

"By now," Tsilka recalled, "the shots above had become

more frequent. We heard a shot very near to the trap door of our cellar and a groan. Then the board was lifted and a man came down to us. It was The Doctor. He told the chief that he had killed one of our men because he found out that the man was a spy. He looked very pale and troubled because he had killed not in battle but in cold blood and considered this as a murder."

The "spy" was a boy from the town of Troskovo. He had approached the cabin carrying a white flag and bringing news that Doncho had retreated. The *chetnitsi* suspected they were being lured into a trap and shot him. Doncho and his band in fact had taken off.

Sandansky worried that the gunfire might have alerted the Turks, and he contrived a plan for the little party to walk out over a steep hill in single file at a distance of twenty steps from one another. Mrs. Tsilka, due at any time to go into labor, struggled to keep up, but she couldn't make it. Finally, it was necessary to put both her and Miss Stone on horseback. Tsilka recalled:

The chief was walking rapidly in front looking in every direction, from time to time waving his hand to make us hurry. For more than two hours we drove our horses stumbling over fallen tree trunks; once we had to wade across a river. Then we came upon a villager who was immediately surrounded by our men who menaced him with their guns. But he said that he knew about us and that the rest of our band were all "over there," and pointed to a hut almost invisible from where we stood.

Soon, the men streamed out from the hut and ran to us surrounding us, shouting welcome and congratulating us joyfully. It was nearly noontime. We dismounted and were led into the hut [where there were] two shepherd cloaks spread for us by the fire. The men were all very kind and attentive to us and showing their sympathy in every possible way.

"It may seem strange," said Miss Stone musingly, "but this is one of the happiest days of my life."

AGAIN, THE LINE between captor and captive blurred. The men drank to celebrate. Even Miss Stone gave in to the moment and withheld her disapproval. The giddiness soon passed, however, as Sandansky and company took stock of their situation. Doncho had nearly made off with their captives. He'd probably intended to collect the ransom. As things stood, any freelancer could claim to be holding the women and dupe the Americans out of their money.

Sandansky, Asenov, and Chernopeev decided to do the one thing they'd vowed they wouldn't: reach out to Dickinson.

CHAPTER NINE

The Baby

⟨∞⟩

The ransom of Miss Stone and her companion has been delayed by circumstances for which neither the Turks nor the "brigands" are responsible. A third captive—a very little, but no doubt, a very embarrassing one—has been added to the number.

The London *Daily Graphic,*
January 31, 1902

S ECRETARY HAY WAS FRUSTRATED by Peet's lack of progress. He cabled John Leishman, still on furlough in Paris, and ordered him back to his post. The diplomat left his family on Christmas Day, taking the Orient Express back to Constantinople. He found Spencer Eddy, looking exhausted. The Stone affair had taken its toll on him, and he was given a leave of absence.

Leishman prepared to devote himself to the Peet mission when he received a disturbing note from Charles Dickinson. The consul general was exultant: his waiting strategy had paid off; the kidnappers had blinked.

Leishman had come to regard Dickinson as expendable.

Now, it appeared, this irritating man was trying to insinuate himself back into the matter.

The diplomat's reply was polite but blunt. Although he had no objection to Dickinson's man trying to get a letter to Miss Stone, it would never do to have more than one set of negotiators in the field. He warned Dickinson to stay out of Bulgaria.

But the consul general had no intention of being dismissed. Since mid-December, he'd been corresponding on the sly with Dr. Henry House, who was pursuing a connection of his own. House had received two letters from a Bulgarian pastor of Samokov, a suspected sympathizer with the Macedonian cause. This minister, Marko Popov, wrote to House on December 7 and again on December 13 that he should go to Bansko if he wanted to find the kidnappers. The American missionary passed this information along to Peet and Gargiulo, but they were so preoccupied with Sir Alfred Biliotti's messenger that they apparently ignored it. House wrote Popov asking him to tell Miss Stone's captors that the Americans needed a more "distinct word." Then he sent Popov's original letter along to Dickinson with a note saying that he was prepared to go to Bansko if his services were required.

Two weeks later, "distinct word" arrived via the consul general's old intermediary, Boyadzhiev. The bookseller reported to Dickinson that the band might be ready to settle for less than the original amount. How much did the Americans have to offer? After conferring with Dickinson, Boyadzhiev wrote a letter to the *cheta* setting the ransom at 14,500 liras—about half of the original demand—with time and place of delivery to be agreed on. He also dispatched a letter to House, now in Serres with the Peet delegation, that a tentative bargain had been struck and he should leave at once for Bansko.

House delayed sharing this news with Peet and Gargiulo. After watching them bungle the Biliotti connection, he didn't want to jeopardize this new opportunity. When he finally let them know, on the eve of his proposed departure to Bansko, they were angry. They suspected that he was working as Dickinson's agent.

Gargiulo cabled Constantinople with the news that Miss Stone was alive, but he didn't bother telling Minister Leishman that the break had come through Dickinson's man, not his own.

Leishman wrote to Dickinson, "This would indicate [Peet and Gargiulo] are making progress . . . and encourages me to believe that we can safely leave the matter in the hands of the Committee."

Leishman's smugness faded over the next several days when, thanks to scattered particulars in Gargiulo's cables, he learned that the architect of this new initiative was in fact Dickinson. When he confronted the consul general, Dickinson responded coolly that he would have informed the legation before dispatching House to Bansko, but there hadn't been time.

Leishman then fired off a letter to Dickinson containing a list of allegations, including one that the consul general had offered the kidnappers an extra 400 liras as an incentive to deal through his emissary rather than Peet's. Dickinson replied that he knew of a certain letter Leishman had written to Miss Stone in which he'd tried to outbid Dickinson and House.

AS THE DIPLOMATS traded accusations, Katerina Tsilka was fast approaching her due date. Even before the attack by Doncho and his band, she'd begun having labor pains. For several days afterward, her discomfort increased.

"Mrs. Tsilka one night was compelled to climb," recalled Miss Stone, "and, overcome by her weakness and pain cried, 'Leave me here to die. I cannot go any further.' Thereafter she was supported far more tenderly than they had ever dreamed they could support a captive."

After ten hours or so of traveling, the women were taken to yet another tiny hut, this one almost entirely occupied by two large wine casks.

"Just under the one opposite the doorway, between it and the glowing open fire built upon the earth floor," Miss Stone would recall, "were spread the straw and leaves for our bed. Upon this we sank down exhausted and were soon in a deep sleep. It seemed to me not long after when I was roused by Mrs. Tsilka moving about, quite contrary to her usual custom after the fatigues of such a night's journey. She said that she was so restless and in so much pain that it was impossible to go to sleep. Brigands were urging travel the following night but it became clear due to developments during the day that Mrs. Tsilka could not travel."

"I had on two thick pairs of stockings and heavy boots," Tsilka recalled, "but still my feet were cold."

She removed her engagement and wedding rings, entrusting them to Miss Stone to give to her husband. She also left a message for her mother and asked Stone to tell her family how often she'd thought of them during the past four months of captivity.

Miss Stone was agitated. They had no bed, no linens, and no antiseptics. She was a maiden lady with no experience in these matters and was obviously going to be of limited help in the birth. The kidnappers were also nervous, the specter of the highwayman's curse still looming over them. They brought an elderly woman from a nearby village in the expectation that she could manage the mysterious process of birthing.

She was a "good little woman," according to Katerina. "The spaces between her heavy wrinkles were embedded with dirt, accumulated there for months, perhaps years. The gray hair hung loosely over her forehead and eyebrows. Her head was covered with a kerchief which had been white once upon a time. She also wore a black garment so patched that there was very little left of the original. Half of a sleeve and the collar were entirely gone. Her feet were bare and chapped from the cold and exposure. She looked at us with great surprise and reverence."

The *baba* appeared so backward that Tsilka guessed she had never met anyone outside her own family. While she may have had some experience at midwifery, her best advice was to sprinkle sacred water on the mother and have her to blow into a tin box.

Tsilka asked her to take a place by the fire, and she would call her if she were needed. As twilight approached, the old woman was "nursing her knees and shaking her head as a sign of approaching calamity."

Katerina would have to deliver her own baby. She recalled, "I was standing now with both hands tightly clutched at the rings of the wine cask. My strength was gone, and yet there was no one to help me."

By ten in the evening, it was over. On January 4, in the vicinity of Troskovo, Macedonia, Mrs. Tsilka gave birth to a daughter. She named the infant Ellen, after her mother and, of course, Miss Stone. Tsilka gave baby "Elenchie" to the *baba* to wrap, while Miss Stone made her a hot drink of boiled barley. The two older women now chattered with excitement.

The strain of labor, coupled with what was most likely postpartum depression, sent Tsilka into a fit of weeping. She was sure that the men were standing outside talking about how to take away her baby and kill it.

The youngest walked in and asked timidly, "Is it a boy?"

"A blessed girl," Miss Stone replied. The young man frowned.

"Well, if it were a boy," he said, "we would make a brigand of him, but a girl does not make a good brigand, although there are stories told of girls who became *voivodi*." He thought a little more about it, then added, "I don't know, after all, we may make her the daughter of the *cheta*."

The boy poured himself some wine from the cask, inadvertently spattering some of it into Tsilka's face as she lay reclined, her head under the spigot. Then he said, "I shall take this wine to the *cheta*. We must drink the health of the little brigand."

Two or three hours later, the Chief himself appeared in the cramped doorway. He walked over to the fire where he stood as if deep in thought.

The newborn's cries seemed to startle him. Everyone else kept still. Finally, Miss Stone broke the tension by picking up the baby and handing her to him.

"At first he appeared confused and embarrassed," Tsilka recalled, "but as he watched the little helpless morsel in his strong arms a smile passed over his face . . . he bent his head closer to baby's face. He was no more a brigand to me, but a brother, a father, a protector to my baby. He now made up his mind to have a good time, so he sat down by the fire and began to warm baby's feet. My heart jumped with joy."

The Chief seemed concerned that the baby might catch cold. He handed the infant back to Miss Stone, asking her to draw up a list of necessities. He returned shortly with barley, prunes, sugar, and tea.

Tsilka drifted off to sleep, then awoke suddenly and was unable to find her baby. Then she saw the Chief as he sat near the fire with his back turned to her, his head nodding as he dozed. Elenchie was sleeping in his arms. Tsilka's eyes traveled down his body to the revolver at his side, coming to rest on the dagger that helped kill the Pomak. She thanked God that there was gentleness in the man.

He awoke the next morning cheerful and full of pet names for the infant—"little brigand, the daughter of the *cheta*." His favorite was "Kismetchie," or "Good Luck." He seemed as pleased with her as if she were his own child.

Near the end of the next day, the Chief asked if his men

could see the baby. The women made preparations for a crude reception. The scene had the bizarre enchantment of a visit from the Magi. As each man entered, he shook hands with the new mother. Finally, there were two rows of armed men hunched into the tiny cabin. As they drank, they made eloquent speeches to the infant as she was passed from one to the next.

According to Tsilka's recollection, "Miss Stone was the queen of the occasion. She talked to them, she laughed with them, she made them feel perfectly at home. The mother was radiant; she forgot that she lay in straw, she only thought that her baby was safe. One said that they must give baby presents. He himself offered to make her a pair of sandals. Another one said he would make her a whistle, and the chief offered to make her a brigand's outfit."

The buffoon, Chaoosh, asked to hold the baby.

"Grasping her in [his arms]," Miss Stone recalled, "he seated himself at once before the fire, Turkish fashion, and rocked her back and forth. Then he proceeded in his quick imperative way to give me a lecture on the proper care of a baby. Of course, I had uncovered the little face to let him see her. 'You must not do so,' he said, 'you will cause her death of cold. You have not grown up with babies as I have,' he added, as he gave her back."

One of the brigands noted that no *cheta* had ever had a child born to it. To immortalize the event, he suggested that "the baby's name, Ellena, shall be written on our guns."

After giving the baby a kiss, each of the men said "goodnight" and stepped outside into the darkness.

Tsilka was in so much pain that she was unable to turn on her side. It hurt her to cough, and she was scarcely able to sit, let alone ride. Yet only a day after the baby's birth, Turkish patrols had been spotted near Troskovo, and the band was in danger. The men had also been drinking, and they were growing belligerent. They grumbled that women shouldn't be giving the orders. Gospozha would have to travel, sick or not.

They built a large wooden box that looked like a coffin. Then, placing a rug and half of a filthy quilt on the bottom, they lowered Tsilka into it. Unfortunately, it was too heavy to lift, so they made a lighter one, which they hung on one side of a horse against a counterweight of stones. As it was hoisted, the box slid loose and crashed into a stand of trees. Tsilka was unharmed but left feeling, in Miss Stone's words, "miserable and tortured."

The baby, meanwhile, was wrapped in a gauze shirt with a cloth napkin tied around her legs. She was swaddled in a layer of cotton and several more layers of wool. Her arms were tied to her sides to prevent them from working loose and exposing her tiny fingers to frostbite. One of the band had been chosen to carry the bundle, but he wouldn't give up his rifle, so Miss Stone took the child, cradling her under one arm in a sling while using her own free hand to hold the pommel.

They all worried about how to keep the infant quiet. She'd taken her first meal from a strip of thin cotton cloth dipped in barley water. Miss Stone recalled, "The baby took hold of it with great eagerness, testifying to her appreciation of it by very audible smacking. Mrs. Tsilka joked that the baby got her smack from the brigands who fell 'audibly' upon their food 'like pigs eating at troughs.'"

The women had sewn lumps of sugar into the baby's blanket to pacify her, but the band hadn't been traveling long when the sugar ran out.

"I heard the pathetic cry of my darling," Tsilka recalled:

From where I got strength I do not know, but I pushed at the ropes tied around the box, and raised myself in a sitting position. It was blowing and snowing, and the men rushed to me and ordered me to lie down and cover myself. I was defiant. "My baby please. . . . I can nurse it here. O Chief, please, please give me my baby."

My wish at last was granted. I seized the little ball (it looked like a ball) and pressed her to my heart. She nursed and sobbed. Only three days in the world and so much trouble! While I was nursing her, two or three brigands took their *kepes* off their backs, hung them on their guns, and made something like a tent around us.

THEY CONTINUED this way for about a week, traveling nights, spending the days in cottages or huts. Mrs. Tsilka tried to bathe the baby if the apartments were not too chilly and if she could persuade the men to find warm water and a tub. Diapers, which the brigands had managed to procure, were in short supply. These were difficult to wash and even more difficult to dry. They couldn't be hung in the sunlight for fear of attracting attention. They had to be strung up, therefore, before smoky wood fires that left them gray and gritty. The huts were so poorly ventilated that the captives' eyes were raw and rimmed red from the soot. They caught lice. The itching was unbearable.

Miss Stone quarreled constantly with Sandansky: the baby needed water for a bath, Gospozha needed food, they all needed rest. He would end an argument by stamping out and slamming the door. Elenchie suffered from a stomach ailment, which her mother treated with a dose of castor oil. She took it like a trouper, making little smacking noises. Then she caught a cold, and it was clear to everyone around her that if she were to be dragged out and around on wintry nights, she would die from exposure.

Sandansky considered leaving mother and child with villagers. On its face, this plan would have solved many problems. Stone was the more valuable captive. She was an American citizen. Money from the subscription drive had been raised in her name. Moreover, the need for a chaperone was now a charade. Miss Stone would insist that she'd pleaded with the band to leave Tsilka and her baby someplace where her mother could come to her, or at least where she could have "the ministries of women and some comforts of a home."

Mrs. Tsilka remembered it differently. Later, she wrote that when the suggestion to leave her and the baby with village women first came up, Miss Stone objected, saying, "I don't part from Gospozha." (Tsilka offered this as an example of personal loyalty, but in fact, Stone may have been reluctant to lose the protection of traveling with mother and child.)

Sandansky put off a decision to separate the women. He was expecting at any moment to hear from the Americans. Since Doncho's attack, Miss Stone had been aware that her captors had reopened negotiations for their release. She'd overheard the men fretting over the possibility that some imposter would claim the ransom.

A messenger arrived in the night carrying a letter from Boyadzhiev. It was a memorandum of agreement stating that the Americans were willing to pay 14,500 liras, a little over half the amount originally demanded. They required proof, however, that the captives were alive. The women were to answer in their own handwriting a couple of personal questions, the answers to which only Dr. House would know.

Stone seized a pen and wrote in her irregular, open scrawl, "Last night in my dreams I was talking with Mrs. House and I asked her whether she remembered that less a few days eight months have passed from the time I sent off your family to France."

Tsilka had been asked to provide two names: the first, of a close friend she'd had in East Orange, New Jersey, and the second, the name of her superior at a New York hospital where she'd once worked. She answered, "Miss Belle Judd" and "Miss Anna Maxwell."

Miss Stone added a postscript, "Saturday evening Jan. 4ᵗʰ, 1902 . . . Ellena G. Tsilka was born. Everything was and is well with the child and the mother, through God's wonderful mercy."

Sandansky, Asenov, and Sava Mikhailov left camp that same night, agreement in hand, for Bansko.

Dr. House, meanwhile, had managed to convince Peet and Gargiulo that he should go alone to meet with the brigands. Finally, they agreed, but only after he promised that once he'd made contact, he would send for them immediately.

The legation's code was apparently breakable. At least, the contents of government cables seemed to be finding their way into the hands of those with money to pay for them. So the three men devised their own clumsy cipher, which as House later revealed, was based upon a tiny English dictionary sold at a bookstore in Constantinople. It would allow them to correspond confidentially with the legation.

It was a three-day ride by horse to Bansko. House slipped past Turkish troops and into the home of Ivan Gratchanov, an "old and trusted friend." He waited for word.

During that first week in January, there was a spell of mild weather. Dr. House sat in the open air and wrote letters. Three days, then seven, then nine passed with no news from the *cheta*.

Peet and Gargiulo, who had moved from Serres to Dzhumaia to be closer to Bansko, were frustrated by the long silence. They wired their advance man for news, but he had nothing to report. Privately, House suspected that the band's messenger had been killed.

After dining in town on the evening of January 16, he received a visit from a "confidential helper," Konstantin Petkanchin, who brought good news. The brigands' man had accosted him in the street and told him that the negotiator from the band was still alive. The meeting would take place the following night at Gratchanov's house.

The Gratchanovs' place was on the northern edge of town. Its back yard faced a stretch of land that was unguarded by the Turks. On the evening of January 17, House tied up a fierce dog on the Gratchanovs' property. Again, he waited.

A little before midnight, he heard a rustling near the barn. In the darkness, he could see movement. When he went down to the garden to let his visitor in, he was surprised to find not one man but three, dressed in a sort of uniform of coffee-brown homespun material with white cloths wrapped around their ankles. They wore shaggy black cloaks and carried modern rifles. Ammunition belts were draped across their chests.

The three made a quick search of House's room. One took his place as guard at the door. Another threw his cape on the floor and sat on it. The third man, whom House now took to be the leader, was tall, with a straight beard and light complexion—most likely Asenov. (Unlike Haskell, Baird, and Dickinson, Dr. House had never met any of the kidnappers in person.)

"You doubtless have your letter of authenticity," House asked him. The tall man reached into his knapsack and pulled out a sheath of papers. On the first was a letter from Boyadzhiev signed with a code-name, "D. Todorov." He certified that captives should be freed on payment of 14,500 Turkish liras with the place and time of delivery to be determined by the bearer.

The tall man also produced a sheet on which a brief paragraph had been handwritten in both English and Bulgarian:

We give the present authorization to its bearer, a member of the band in whose hands we are held captives . . . with the right to receive the ransom demanded for us, but with the added powers to treat the question of our ransom to its

final conclusion. [Signed by Ellen Stone and Katerina
Stephanova Tsilka]

This was to assure House that he was dealing with the bona
fide captors. On the back of the memorandum of agreement, he
found the women's handwritten responses. House nodded his
approval.

The sum of the ransom was agreed on all around. The
14,500 liras would be paid in gold Napoleons so that they
couldn't be marked and could be spent anywhere in Europe or
Turkey. The other terms, however, remained to be negotiated.

House produced a piece of paper that had outlined methods
by which such a large amount of gold could be transported and
delivered. They were under five headings, written in Bulgarian,
all having been discussed with the committee and predicated
on the notion that the exchange be simultaneous.

"These I was permitted to read to them," he recalled, "but
they brushed them all away with a word, 'impossible.'" The
money, they demanded, must be paid "in coin, full weight,
unmarked, at a place in the mountains which I know, and at
least ten days before the deliverance of the captives. I could not
move them an inch from these last terms."

The brigands were obviously hoping to put as much distance as possible between themselves and the Turks. House
saw the danger in this and told the men he would need to con-
sult with his colleagues. At this, they became furious. He'd
misled them, they said, into thinking he had the sole power to
negotiate.

The revolutionaries launched into a litany of humiliations
that they had suffered at the hands of the Turks, the Greeks,
the Serbs, and now the Americans. They would not be toyed
with any longer. As they alternately insulted him and tried to
win him over to their holy cause, House held his tongue.

Hostage negotiation, he would observe, was "a rather delicate business."

After about two hours, the missionary managed to calm them by promising that he would deliver their ultimatum, along with his own endorsement, to his colleagues, Mr. Peet and Mr. Gargiulo. But he must have some assurance that the women wouldn't be killed.

"There is a rope for us in Constantinople and in Sofia," one of the men replied. "Our word of honor is all we have."

HOUSE WAS IN the saddle at dawn, and he reached Dzhumaia within the day. Peet and Gargiulo were dismayed when they heard the terms. A ten-day delay? Sofia and Constantinople were already rife with rumors that the kidnappers intended to kill their captives to keep themselves from being identified. Wouldn't this ransom-first arrangement give them incentive to do just that?

Gargiulo wired the news to Leishman. The diplomat was relieved to hear there had been progress. Payment in advance was not what he'd hoped to hear, but neither was it unexpected. In early January, he'd sounded out the State Department on the subject. Assistant Secretary of State David Hill had written back, "The precedents of brigandage make simultaneous payment and release of captives a uniform rule."

This had not, however, been the British experience. Sir Alfred Biliotti passed on to the U.S. Legation in Constantinople details concerning a certain Colonel Synge, a British officer kidnapped twenty-three years earlier by Greek bandits. His abductors demanded a twenty-four-hour delay before releasing him. Sir Alfred's own experience with Turkish brigands in Anatolia had taught him that these men had a certain code of honor, which allowed a certain reliance on their promises.

"It will be most difficult if not impossible," the British consul opined, "to come to terms as to the manner of payment of the ransom and rescuing the prisoners without running the risk of putting faith in the word of the captors."

Leishman authorized Gargiulo to accept the offer, but to try and soften the terms.

Miss Stone, meanwhile, had been awakened during the early morning hours of January 17 by men who thrust into her hand a note from Dr. House. He acknowledged having received her letter. Now, he told her, he was on a mission to persuade the rest of the ransoming committee to believe, as he did, that the money must be paid in advance.

"We were terribly perplexed," Stone recalled. "And the brigands were angry beyond all bounds."

One of the men held a tin kerosene lamp close to her hand as she wrote an indignant appeal. She declared that her captors had lowered their ransom demand because she and Mrs. Tsilka were women and because of that had endured special suffering in their captivity: It is *our friends*," she insisted, who "have prolonged our sufferings to five months, and are continuing to prolong them."

Mrs. Tsilka appears at that point to have grabbed the pen from Stone and scribbled furiously:

> *Who are these people who dare to be the cause of the lengthening out of our sufferings? Cannot they sympathize with my little daughter, who is in constant distress? Our eyes are swollen with smoke, which is constantly like a cloud in the room, and I can scarcely talk because of it. It is not a room, but a hole! Imagine my sufferings as I see my little one suffer.*

The hostages' plea must have reached the committee on or about January 18, in time for Gargiulo to pass along details from it in his first dispatches to Leishman. The captives, he wrote, had offered to assume all personal risks to themselves, if their "friends" would only release the money that had been collected in their behalf. In theory, this meant that the government and the missionary board would be absolved of blame if the ransom was paid and the women were later murdered.

Leishman passed along this dubious assurance to the State Department.

John Hay did not tend to view the Stone affair sentimentally. Earlier in January, he'd mused to Leishman in a confidential memorandum that departmental thinking had produced only three solutions: pay the full amount and try to collect an indemnity from Turkey, attempt a rescue by force, or send warships to Varna in the interests of coercing Bulgaria to coerce the brigands into releasing the hostages. "The department," he continued, "would be pleased to have your opinion on a fourth course which appears to be open, namely, to terminate the negotiations, leaving the brigands the alternative of indefinitely retaining the captives without hope of ransom."

When the Secretary wrote this, on January 2, the climate seemed favorable for plan four. The national dailies had pulled back on their fund drives as word reached them that publicity only served the interests of the kidnappers. (Mr. Curtis had apparently lost interest in the case and continued his travels.) The Stone story had retreated from banner headlines into boxed updates. Under these conditions, it might have been possible for the State Department to toss the ball back into the brigands' court. But circumstances were due to change. Grigor Tsilka, who until now had borne his grief in silence, was talking to the press.

CHAPTER TEN

The Gold

In so small a place as Serres it is absolutely impossible for foreigners to conceal themselves; their every movement is known and reported in the Konak and the Bazaar. Directly a stranger arrives in the place he becomes a centre of interest. . . . In this country, where there are no theatres, no race meetings, and no football, every man is a politician. Commerce, at least in the interior, is practically non-existent; the day's business may be disposed of before breakfast. Whenever men congregate they discuss, not syndicates, or mining trusts, or municipal undertakings, but the everlasting (Eastern) Question.

William Maud, The London *Daily Graphic*,
January 22, 1902

GRIGOR TSILKA was a private man. None of his missionary colleagues could say they knew him well. Of his childhood, there's no record except that he was born an Orthodox Christian in the village of Vithkucq. He was native Albanian, ethnically distinct from Slavs and religiously distinct from the overwhelmingly Muslim population of Western European Turkey. When Grigor was five, his father, Marko, moved the family to Monastir, then capital of the Ottoman *vilayet*. It was the center of the "Renaissance," a movement that aimed, among other things, to make Albanian the language of Albania. The Turks considered this seditious and forbade it.

Young Grigor became a Protestant. The circumstances of his conversion are unknown. By the late 1890s, he was on record as studying at the Boys' Institute in Bulgaria. He was a handsome, engaging youth who the Reverend Edward Haskell observed "has a quicker sense of humor than the average Slav." Gifted linguistically, young Tsilka eventually mastered Bulgarian, Greek, Turkish, Vlach, and English, which he spoke with an American accent.

The missionaries had hoped that Grigor would become a native minister to the as-yet-untilled field of Albania. But he declined the pitiful salary offered to him by the American Board and sailed for New York. That was 1897. By that time, Katerina had been in America about four years.

Grigor met Katerina in the Adirondacks where she was visiting a sick relative. He, to the best of his descendants' recollection, was working as a carpenter. He'd apparently abandoned his plans of becoming a minister, but Katerina persuaded him to reconsider. He graduated from Union Theological Seminary in the spring of 1900. Shortly after, he and Katerina married. They had much in common: both were Protestants, and both had grown up under Ottoman rule. Their union was as much political as it was passionate.

Katerina had her own reasons for hating the Turks. One Sunday in 1879—she was a child of about six—a mob of *bashibazouks* had stormed through Bansko killing everyone in their way. She and her family, including a three-week-old baby brother, fled to the mountains.

"Although the silence was almost complete," she recalled,

"we saw many people running, as we did, for their safety. I felt sleepy and tired from the very beginning, stumbled and fell down, but was immediately up again and running uphill as in a nightmare. Thus we ran many hours, until finally we stopped at a place where immediately I fell asleep to wake up only the next morning and see the sun pouring through the trees on a miserable crowd of silent men (and women) staring at nothing, and children whimpering for the hurts received from stumbling and falling during their flight."

The *bashi-bazouks* had sacked Bansko, killing those who couldn't escape. "Father lost all his moveable property," Katerina recalled. "But that was easily forgotten since none of the family had lost his life."

Grigor and Katerina returned to the Balkans in the spring of 1900 and after the happy interlude in Monastir, they settled in Kortcha.

Grigor did not apparently share Katerina's despair at being posted to "the deeps of the sea." Kortcha was near the town where he'd been born, and he had friends there who were celebrated local figures. The Kyrias family—notably Gerasim and his two younger sisters, feminists by the names of Sevasti and Paraskevi—had founded a girls' school where they taught classes in Albanian, in defiance of the Turkish ban. Although the school received money from the American Board, it remained under the control of the Kyriases, who were unabashed nationalists.

Gerasim was perhaps the best known of the clan. He'd been kidnapped in 1884 by bandits and released six months later after fellow Christians in Britain, America, and the Balkan peninsula passed collection plates, raising over $3,000 in ransom. The experience broke his health, though, and he died a few years later of consumption. His sisters carried on his work with their younger brother, George.

Grigor Tsilka's name was linked to George Kyrias in missionary correspondence as early as 1892. After graduating from

Miss Ellen Stone, a Congregationalist missionary, spent over twenty years in the Balkans before she was kidnapped on September 3, 1901, by Macedonian insurgents. Descended from Miles Standish, she was as tough as any of her captors.

Katerina Tsilka, the Bulgarian nurse and teacher who was also taken by the rebels as a "chaperone" for Stone. She was bright and passionate. Her yearning for education led her into the Protestant fold, but her sympathies lay with the revolutionaries.

3

Miss Stone's Bible class. Five were with her when she was captured.

4

Sava Mikhailov, Yané Sandansky, and Krüstio Asenov: the kidnappers.

The ambush at Hanging Rock.

Confined for months in various dark, cramped spaces, Stone underlined the Bible until her ink ran out. Tsilka, who was pregnant at the time they were kidnapped, gave birth, without assistance, to a baby girl.

7

Interpreter Alexander Gargiulo was the State Department's *ex-officio* member on the negotiating mission. He controlled the purse strings but was proud and easily offended.

8

Charles Dickinson, U.S. Consul-General to Constantinople, was a former newspaper publisher from upstate New York. A shrewd man of business, he used hard-nosed tactics that alienated the Bulgarians and Russians.

9

William W. Peet, treasurer of the Bible House in Constantinople, was tapped by kidnappers to receive Miss Stone's ransom letter. As a negotiator, he sided with Gargiulo against Dr. Henry House, the missionary in Salonica.

10

Alvah Augustus Adee, the second assistant secretary of state in charge of the Stone affair, was an eccentric man with encyclopedic knowledge of foreign affairs. He dismissed Dickinson's rescue-through-bribery plan as "opéra bouffe."

Dr. Henry House, head of the Salonica mission, was the first American to learn of the kidnapping. Of the three negotiators, he was the only one to speak Bulgarian. His steady nerves and common sense gave him an advantage in the negotiations.

President Theodore Roosevelt, who inherited the Stone crisis, believed in a strong navy and the sanctity of womanhood. One option open to him: Send in the fleet. But send it where?

Members of the American delegation dine with local Turkish gentry. Left to right, center. Gargiulo, Peet, and William Maud, the London *Daily Graphic*'s "artist-correspondent."

14

Mrs. Tsilka and infant Elenchie. The child was kept paci-
fied by lumps of sugar sewn into her blankets.

15

The ransom money left Constantinople by train in the company of Croatian
bodyguards and a U.S. marshal. Deep in the Macedonian wilderness, it was met
by Turkish dragoons who drove their horses to the brink of exhaustion so that
their cargo would not be waylaid by bandits.

Grigor and Elenchie. The kidnappers carved her name on their gunstocks and called her the "Lucky Child."

A fire at a local inn distracted Turkish soldiers and raised the question: Was it set intentionally to provide cover for the payment of the ransom?

A rare photograph of the captives' homecoming shows Mr. Tsilka carrying his baby daughter. To his rear, Miss Stone and Katerina (hatless).

Miss Stone on the gangway of the *Deutschland*, April 10, 1902. Her triumphal return to America was marred by controversy. Editorials accused her of merchandising her suffering. Her missionary colleagues cringed when she sang her captors' praises.

Katerina and Elenchie on the cover of their touring brochure, spring 1903. Madame Tsilka was "pretty, with . . . just enough of a foreign accent to add charm." And she was a gifted storyteller.

the Boys' Institute, Grigor applied for a colporteur's license that would have allowed him to carry religious books throughout Albania and Bulgaria; the Turks denied it. His association with the Kyriases had caused him to be marked, fairly or unfairly, as a subversive character.

THE TSILKA FAMILY—Katerina, Grigor, and baby Victor—had all their necessary identification and traveling papers in order when, during the summer of 1901, they began their journey to Bansko. During that six-week visit, they introduced their baby to his grandparents. Joy quickly turned to distress over the child's illness. After his death, both parents were surely consumed by grief. But they were not inactive. That, at least, was the opinion of Minister Leishman in Constantinople.

John Leishman had come to believe that Grigor, if not Katerina, had a hand in the kidnapping of Miss Stone. As he later explained to Hay, "The Turkish officials are under the impression that the husband of Mrs. Tsilka who accompanied Miss Stone was implicated in the conspiracy and some go so far as to include Mrs. Tsilka and even Miss Stone herself. As far as Miss Stone is concerned I would consider it absurd and impossible and highly improbable in the case of Mrs. Tsilka but it is quite within the range of possibilities that [Grigor] Tsilka knew more or less about what was going on but whether he was a party before or only after the act is still a matter of conjecture."

At first glance, Leishman's suspicions concerning Grigor Tsilka seem implausible. Albanian nationalism, after all, sprang up separately from the Macedonian resistance, and these two movements were sometimes at odds with one another. When Katerina brought her husband home to meet her people, she was introducing him as a foreigner. He was her *Albanian* husband—not Bulgarian, not Macedonian, but an outsider.

And yet, as Katerina herself pointed out, Albania and Macedonia shared a common lot. They were the last of the Balkan states to win their freedom from the Turks. Whatever their linguistic or ethnic differences, Grigor Tsilka, the Stephanov family, and the Protestants of Bansko were all Christians. And they were all united in their hatred of the Turks.

During his six- or seven-week stay in Bansko, Grigor lived in daily contact with the Protestants and the revolutionary committee, virtually all of them aware of the plot to kidnap Miss Stone. They would have needed to go to unusual lengths to exclude him from the secret.

Grigor and Katerina almost certainly did not participate in the planning of the kidnapping. The brigands' own memoirs make it plain that the idea was wholly that of Sandansky's *cheta* and that Bansko's local revolutionary council had tried to scotch the plan. It is doubtful that the Tsilkas could have done anything to stop it, short of alerting Miss Stone. In doing that, they would have branded themselves traitors, marking themselves and Katerina's family for death.

On the morning of September 3, Grigor and Katerina had set out on the road at least two hours in advance of the rest of the party, possibly to alert Sandansky and his men to the caravan's approach. If that indeed was the case, Grigor and Katerina were probably under the impression that the kidnapping would be of short duration—days, weeks at most—and that the presence of old Mrs. Usheva would ensure that Miss Stone would be treated kindly.

The Tsilkas could not have foreseen the possibility that Katerina would be seized as a substitute. They could never have intended that to happen, not with Katerina so far along in her pregnancy.

As she was being led away, Miss Stone later recalled, she looked back and saw Grigor sitting on his horse, chin in his hand looking dejected. She could not have guessed the full extent of his worries.

During the days immediately following Katerina's kidnapping, Grigor was the object of sympathy. Missionaries passed among themselves stories about how the poor man, wild with grief, had gone back to search the mountains for his wife. Then, of course, he had to deliver the terrible news to her parents. During the weeks ahead, however, they would come to view him more skeptically.

Tsilka's story changed with each telling. Originally, he had identified his captors as Turks. As that myth was dispelled by testimony from others in the party, Grigor's own account evolved. Early in October, Dr. House wrote to Consul-General Dickinson in Constantinople that Tsilka was now saying that the "Turks" threw back their cloaks revealing uniforms of the Macedonian Committee. By the time Grigor was finally deposed by Dickinson in mid-November, he would declare that the kidnappers' cloaks had partly obscured the uniform of the Macedonian Committee, but that he'd spotted and recognized it instantly. Moreover, he said that he had recognized early on that the brigands were not Turks and assured Miss Stone, in English, "Do not be afraid, they are Bulgarians."

The missionaries were also troubled by things that Grigor had left out. In early October, John Baird, who had been one of his most enthusiastic sponsors, went to Bansko on a fact-finding mission. He reported back to Dickinson that Grigor had apparently withheld information from the Turkish police. He'd failed to report the presence of the students and the Protestant club's servant in Miss Stone's party and was silent on the subject of the Pomak.

None of the party who straggled into Bansko the morning after the kidnapping mentioned to the Ottoman police inspectors who interviewed them that the kidnappers had killed a Muslim. They withheld this news, Henry House explained to the State Department, because they felt it might inflame the local revolutionary committee. There was also the question of the Turks. Islamic rite required that a body be washed and wrapped in a clean cloth. Abandoning it was a moral offense. Privately, House scolded the students for the omission.

Grigor later gave his old mentor, Lewis Bond, a highly sanitized version of the episode, which the missionary passed along to a friend in America:

> A little in advance of this party of Protestants was a man on horseback, presumably bound for Djumaya. This man was severely wounded, and our friends were halted by a party of brigands numbering from thirty to fifty, according to the varying estimates. . . . All were obliged to dismount and go into the woods two or three miles off the road. The wounded man, who seemed to be a Turk, walked with great difficulty, and when they came to a halt he was put out of his misery.

Grigor later circulated a story that after they were released by their captors, he and his companions began the march back to Bansko bearing the body of the murdered man. This is difficult to imagine: the students as well as the muleteers had fled by that time, which would have left Grigor, the only remaining male, to carry the dead man. This version is not corroborated by any other account.

The missionaries had hoped Grigor would stay in Bansko so that if suspects were found, he could identify them. But in late November, when rumors of Katerina and Miss Stone's death began circulating, he traveled to Samokov and then Sofia to pursue his own connections. Until then, Grigor had avoided reporters. But on November 16, the day of his deposition before Consul-General Dickinson, he gave an interview to Reuters.

He told the wire service reporter that he had just received a letter from his wife. She and Miss Stone were well and the brigands were in no hurry for the money. The letter had apparently reached him by way of the influential Madame Kasurova. Grigor was developing sources of information that were as good as, if not better than, those of the U.S. government.

Grigor and one of the young teachers who had been traveling with Miss Stone the morning she was taken—she was later identified as his niece—arrived in Serres on January 12. It was the same date that the bookseller Boyadzhiev's agreement arrived in the kidnappers' camp for Miss Stone's signature. They found the city humming with rumors of gold.

FOR SEVERAL WEEKS, the Americans and their dragoman had advertised their presence in the Bulgarian newspapers to encourage the brigands to make overtures. At the same time, they hoped that they would remain invisible to the European and American press. Now, however, they were being dogged at every step by a correspondent from the London *Daily Graphic.*

The *Graphic* was a tabloid. It enjoyed the distinction of being the first big city daily to run illustrations—some photographs and many more lavishly detailed engravings. One of its leading correspondents, William T. Maud, was celebrated for his nerve and enterprise. He'd covered Lord Kitchener's campaign in Khartoum. During the Boer War, he'd been wounded while under siege with the British army at Ladysmith. There he'd served as an honorary aide-de-camp to Major General Archibald Hunter. Maud was also familiar with Eastern Europe and handy with a sketch pad. The designation "artist-correspondent" worked to his advantage at border crossings. The Turks bristled at the mention of "correspondent" but would let a harmless artist pass. (Maud brought his personal secretary, a certain Mr. Herman Charri, who had been a servant of General Charles Gordon at Khartoum. He must have been an unobtrusive man, as he is mentioned only once in Maud's dispatches.)

Public interest in the Stone case was slackening when Mr.

Maud was offered the assignment. He accepted on forty-eight hours' notice and on December 22 boarded an Orient Express to Constantinople, arriving to find that Peet and Gargiulo had left two days earlier for Salonica. Overtaking them there, he presented letters of introduction. He was, he explained, a *British,* not an American, correspondent, presumably a practitioner of a higher order. But Peet and Gargiulo had seen how the press had sabotaged Charles Dickinson's mission in Sofia. They informed Maud that his presence would be "fatal to success."

Faced with the prospect of returning home empty-handed, Maud decided to remain and shadow the American mission. And so as Peet and Gargiulo boarded the train for Serres, Maud trailed a few discreet steps behind.

After Peet and Gargiulo checked into the Hôtel Salonique, Maud continued on to La Gloire de la Turquie, an establishment whose only distinctions, he noted dourly, were its name and its proximity to the British vice consulate.

Fortunately for his readers, Maud had an artist's eye for detail. He wrote:

A glance at the visitors' book showed that no one had stayed here for fifteen days: Seres [*sic*] is not a fashionable resort. My bedroom is small, but it looks upon the street, and is lighted and aired by five windows and two doors. It boasts of no stove or fireplace, but heat is generated by a *manigal*—a large copper dish, filled with ashes and red-hot charcoal. The suffocating fumes that rise from this crucible are supposed to be ameliorated by a lemon which smoulders in the ashes. Meals are served in the visitors bedrooms, being brought thither from a restaurant some distance away. A divan runs the whole length of the room, and is so placed that anyone who sits upon it receives the concentrated draught of the five windows. The street is narrow—so narrow, in fact, that I could almost shake hands with the lady in the opposite house, who follows my movements with apparent interest.

For the next two weeks, Maud and the missionaries played cat and mouse. On their frequent walks around the city, they would bump into one another and tip their hats. Finally, boredom overcame suspicion, and they began exchanging social visits. Maud fawned over Gargiulo.

"What he does not know of the Eastern Question and Oriental methods of approaching," he assured his readers, "is not worth knowing."

He was also careful to cultivate the Turks, who were as "simple as little children and always gentlemen." The artist-correspondent drew the portrait of Ibrahim Pasha astride his magnificent steed, a cross between an Arabian and a Hungarian. Maud praised the general's appreciation for detail in designing his barracks so that a stream in which the soldiers bathed would run away from the town.

Flattery, no doubt, helped facilitate the passage of his dispatches through Turkish censors in Pera. Neither Gargiulo nor Ibrahim Pasha, however, would take Maud into their confidence. It was not until the unexpected arrival of Grigor Tsilka that the reporter's luck changed.

The Americans were holding Grigor at arm's length. House wanted him kept away from Bansko, if only because his presence might attract Turkish spies. Gargiulo distrusted him, afraid apparently that he might be an agent of the kidnappers or, worse, of Consul-General Charles Dickinson. Grigor, in turn, had little faith in the Americans. The first round of talks had faltered in part because of Dickinson's high-handedness. Gargiulo, the U.S. government's current representative, was arrogant in his own right. His open feud with Ibrahim Pasha threatened to jeopardize the new mission. While he could have had no way of knowing that the U.S. State Department was mulling over Secretary Hay's plan four (don't pay the ransom; sit tight and hope for the best), Grigor Tsilka may have suspected that the Americans had such a contingency up their sleeve. One way to keep them honest was to keep the public's attention trained on the hostages.

Grigor's earlier interview with Reuters had turned out well. He'd been irked by rumors that he'd stood idly by while his wife was carried off. Now he managed to get it into the record that he'd offered himself in his wife's place, and "for answer he received a thrust with the butt-end of a rifle." The London *Daily Graphic* had run the story and, its interest piqued, had assigned the tenacious Mr. Maud, whose dispatches had once again aroused the interest of Europe.

Grigor and his niece now agreed to give an interview to Maud. The girl, identified variously as Donka and Athena, described to the British correspondent how, when they were first set upon by the brigands, she saw their blackened faces and had "laughed heartily" because she thought they'd done it for fun. Maud then turned his attention to the man he called "Mr. Ligord." (This was apparently from a misunderstanding of the name "Grigor.") The dead Pomak had been found and the survivors of Miss Stone's party had yet to make a public comment on the matter. Grigor now opined that the murder had been committed to intimidate them. It had worked because they were all very frightened.

Maud sent back to his paper sketches of both: the niece as a delicate girl in a high lace collar, her posture artificially erect; "Mr. Ligord" as a serious young man in a neatly trimmed beard and starched cravat. His eyes, close-set and piercing, suggested that he was a member of the intelligentsia. His brow was furrowed with concern, inviting the public to join him in the vigil for his missing wife.

Maud was pleased with his coup, but he stalked larger

quarry. If he kept a close watch on the commission, they would lead him to the gold, and the gold would lead him to Miss Stone.

Since arriving in Serres in late December, Maud had doled out generous amounts of *baksheesh* to stablehands who could tell him who arrived in the city and who was planning to leave. The bribes appeared to pay off when, on the day of his interview with Tsilka, a horse keeper came to him with a tip: he'd overheard the Americans making plans to leave early the following morning for Nevrokop, a hot springs area about five hours' ride to the northeast.

Maud, however, suspected that the informer had been sent to mislead him. And sure enough, the Americans had hired two four-horse carriages and would be leaving early the next morning—not for Nevrokop but Dzhumaia. The correspondent packed his own bags and at six o'clock the following morning showed himself at the Hôtel Salonique, where Peet and Gargiulo's carriage was still at the door. No doubt startled to see him, the pair insisted that they were headed for Nevrokop; then they rode away in the company of twenty-five calvarymen to the northwest.

At Maud's urging, the British vice consul sent a messenger to the civil governor asking him to provide Maud with an escort. The request was denied. Undaunted, the correspondent set out on his own, with only a dragoman, Mr. Charri, and their muleteers. The little party followed telegraph poles to Demir Hissar, where Peet and Gargiulo were to spend the first night. Their entourage passed directly under the missionaries' windows on their way into town. Maud and his company found their own humble accommodations. The correspondent ate a meager dinner of sardines and potted meat, and turned in early.

Maud's persistence must have impressed the Turks. The following morning he found a ten-man military escort waiting. Two cavalcades pulled out on the road to Dzhumaia—Peet's first, Maud's behind. They waved to one another. Throughout the day's ride, one caravan would pull ahead, then fall behind, and the other would pull ahead.

"A strong north wind was blowing down the gorge from the snow-fields," Maud wrote.

> It was bitterly cold and it cut like a knife. . . . The soldiers put up the hoods of their overcoats and tied long woolen scarves over their heads. The horses laid their ears back, and they staggered when it caught them on the broadside. The sheltered bends in the road gave one time to recover, and here, crouched over little fires, their faces and hands purple with cold, were the navvies who were building the road to Djuma-I-bala [Dzhumaia]. This important high road winds along the left bank of the Struma River, and the roar of its dark waters mingled with the crash of floating ice.

WHEN THE CAVALCADES STOPPED for the night, Maud and the American delegation were invited to dine at the home of a local *bey*.

"Climbing with difficulty a broad staircase," the correspondent wrote, "we crossed a verandah and entered a spacious apartment, where a huge log-fire blazed in a marble chimneypiece. The leaping flames lit up the room, which was roofed with a carved wood ceiling. After allowing an interval for the thawing of his guests, the old Bey ordered in dinner which was served on a low round table, at which we squatted on the floor. The dinner commenced with excellent soup, followed by meats, vegetables, sweets and savouries, and then back to vegetables, sweets and meats. The arrival of pilaf marked the end of the feast. I noticed when we first sat down that the son of the Bey produced several sets of brand-new knives, forks, and spoons, wrapped up in tissue paper, but nobody used them, for if you dine *a la Turque* you eat with your fingers. At the end a servant entered with a polished brass dish, warm water, and soap, a distinctly necessary adjunct to the dinner."

By nightfall of the following day, the cavalcades pulled into "a little frontier town tucked into a fold of the mountain the white minarets of the mosques rising above tiers of tiled houses, behind them dark pine forests, and above all, the Balkans, painted blood red by the sunset."

Dzhumaia.

It was Thursday, January 16. Dr. House was in Bansko, still waiting for his first meeting with the band. He had communicated with Peet and Gargiulo strictly in cipher. The missionaries were keeping mum, their mission enshrouded, in Maud's words, by "a mystery quite oriental."

House met Peet and Gargiulo in Dzhumaia and after much soul searching agreed to meet the kidnappers' conditions: ransom before release. They cabled Leishman to send the gold.

EARLY IN JANUARY, Leishman had instructed the Imperial Ottoman Bank in Constantinople to keep $66,000 in gold Napoleons in two sacks of convenient size. The time lock had been purposely left off the vault so that there could be no delay.

A king's ransom now had to be moved across 350 miles of Balkan wilderness. The dangers were obvious. Sixty-six thousand dollars would surely excite the greed of bandits, not to mention the interest of Turkish soldiers whose pay was long in arrears. Up to this point, the gold was a closely guarded secret. The Peet commission suspected—rightly as it turned out—that the news of the transfer would leak the moment the gold left the bank. The courier, therefore, could either try to slink out of town and hope to escape undetected, or he could exit with a show of strength. Gargiulo wired Leishman advising him to provide the "strongest and most picturesque kavasses in Constantinople."

Shortly before 8:00 P.M. on Monday, January 20, two large bank satchels of gold were loaded onto a special car of the Oriental Railway in the company of a U.S. marshal, W. Smith-Lyte. He was accompanied by two consular bodyguards and a Mr. Lemmi, who was the legation's second-ranking dragoman and apparently Gargiulo's brother-in-law. The bank sent two Croatian bodyguards, one assigned to each bag of gold. The Ottoman government assigned six of its own soldiers to the detail. Marshal Smith-Lyte's orders were to take the ransom money to Demir Hissar, the closest railway station to Bansko. There he was to be met by a detachment of a half-dozen or so Turkish dragoons.

The Ottoman and American governments, as it turned out, had radically different expectations about what was to happen to that gold once it reached the end of the line. The Turks assumed they would be able to track the missionaries to a meeting place with the bandits. Then they would follow and arrest the anarchists, or at least identify them and hunt them down at a later date. (The Turkish foreign minister and the grand vizier deliberated privately about getting an Ottoman representative onto the negotiating committee.)

If the missionaries crossed over the border, that would prove what the Ottoman government had insisted all along: that the kidnappers were in Bulgaria. In that case, Bulgaria, not Turkey, would be liable for the indemnity if "the girl," as the Turks sometimes referred to Miss Stone, were to be killed.

The Americans, meanwhile, had their own agenda. They'd promised the brigands to hand over the gold at a time and place unknown by the Turks. The Ottomans had been kept in the dark about House's meeting with the kidnappers. General Ibrahim Pasha was not even aware that a deal had been struck until, a couple of days before the money was due at Demir Hissar, the general, an avid reader, was thumbing through a copy of a revolutionary newsletter published in Sofia and came across a mention of the brigands having visited the American, Dr. House, in Bansko.

Furious, he telegraphed the brigadier general in command at Raslog demanding to know how he'd let the missionary meet with anarchists right under his nose. The flustered officer quickly wired Nevrokop for more men to reinforce a blockade around Bansko.

In Constantinople, Leishman kept pressure on the Ottoman foreign minister, who brought a petition on the American's behalf to the grand vizier, who in turn presented it to the Sultan.

For all of a night and a day, the special railway car rattled along, Croat bodyguards sleeping on top of the gold. In the early evening of January 21, it arrived at Demir Hissar, a place described by William Peet as a "lonely nook among the hills at a long distance from human habitation."

There was no military escort waiting there, only the local civil governor, who assured them that soldiers would arrive by the next morning. The train left without Smith-Lyte and company, who spent the night in the stationhouse in a state of high alert.

The following morning, the governor showed up early. Still there were no soldiers. The ransom party waited. Not until about seven o'clock that evening did a detachment of twenty dragoons appear at the station. Their commander, a suave young officer who spoke perfect French, informed Marshal Smith-Lyte that they would set off the following morning. Meanwhile, an entire day had been lost.

Gargiulo fumed. He wired Leishman to pressure the Ottoman Foreign Ministry to order Ibrahim Pasha to stand down. That meant withdrawing troops from Bansko and the border region and promising that whenever Gargiulo dismissed the military escort, it would fall back, leaving him to work in private.

The situation placed Leishman in an awkward position. He

was an ambitious man who looked forward to the day when the U.S. Legation in Constantinople would be upgraded to full embassy status and he, if Providence smiled, would be appointed to the post of ambassador. For this to happen, he would need to remain on good terms with the Porte. The Turks had already been duped once when they were not told in advance about House's first meeting with the brigands in Bansko. Now the U.S. Minister was complicit in a plan to pay the ransom secretly under the very nose of Turkish officials.

Leishman also realized that it would be a significant blow to his aspirations if Ellen Stone were to be killed on his watch. He wrote to the Ottoman minister of the interior asking him to appeal through the grand vizier for an *Irade*, an imperial decree from the Sultan, to the effect that American demands would be met. (Abdul Hamid II did not so much give an order as grant permission with a nod or a gesture.)

On January 22, a proclamation came down from the palace that "the ransom money might be given on the Ottoman side if the number of bandits (at the negotiation site) be limited and no responsibility would be referred to the Ottoman state." Leishman agreed.

The gold by now was jostling its way north to Dzhumaia. Early in the trip, the brougham that the Turks had brought to carry the satchels hit a patch of stones, which ripped the floor out. The bags of Napoleons tumbled to the ground. The young Turkish calvary officer forced the horses almost beyond the limits of endurance so that the party would not find itself, come nightfall, stranded in a ravine.

As it neared Dzhumaia, the procession became increasingly conspicuous. More soldiers joined in along the way, swelling the party to one hundred. Midafternoon on January 24, Gargiulo and Peet, bundled in fur wraps, drove to the outskirts of town to greet the cavalcade. The anticipation of gold had caused great excitement, according to Maud. Many merchants closed their shops to watch the parade make its way to the barracks.

"Fifteen thousand pounds," the correspondent observed, "does not come into Djuma [*sic*] every day in the week."

Peet and Gargiulo spent the rest of the afternoon counting and repacking the Napoleons in burlap. Early the following morning, their military escort received the order to move. Instead of taking the caravan directly to Bansko, however, the Turks diverted it to the nearby town of Raslog, home of the district governor.

Gargiulo was apoplectic. He telegraphed Leishman, who complained to the Ottoman foreign minister that his orders to local civil and military authorities were being "countermanded, modified or disobeyed."

With no particular sense of urgency, the Turks finally escorted the gold to Bansko.

THE PROTESTANT parsonage in Bansko had been vacant since Pastor Hristov fled the preceding spring. The negotiators now took up residence there. The interior of the house was laid out with a wide-open living space running down the middle and two rooms on either side. Peet and Gargiulo shared one room where the gold was now kept in valises. Colonel Osman *bey*, a personal aide to Ibrahim Pasha, stationed himself in the room opposite. There were soldiers posted at the door of the house and several more guarding the gate to the street. The town was encircled by 250 troops.

Adding to the commissioners' difficulty was the fact that two more British journalists—one from Reuters, another from the London *Daily Telegraph*—had joined the party in Dzhumaia. Osman *bey* had invited them to come by and inspect the valises. Peet and Gargiulo, it seemed, could not make a move without being detected by either Turks or the foreign correspondents.

The kidnappers were holding tight to a demand that the ransom money be brought to them in the countryside. If Turkish troops ambushed them, they could escape into the hills. Dr. House, however, had another plan. He was still living at the Gratchanov house. It lay within the Turkish cordon, but on the outskirts of town. If the gold could be moved there, the kidnappers might be able to make it across the unguarded clearing in the back yard.

Again, House dispatched Petkanchin with a message to the brigands trying to persuade them to come into town for the money.

They agreed to try on Wednesday, January 29.

THE PROBLEM that now faced House, Peet, and Gargiulo was how to spirit the money out of the parsonage, past the Turks, to Gratchanov's house—and then replace the missing gold with something of identical weight.

Dr. House instructed Petkanchin to buy up all the lead in town and store it in the Gratchanovs' oven. He wrote:

> We fortunately were in a village one of whose industries was the making of cheap guilded [sic] leaden ornaments for village women and so we succeeded in getting the necessary weight; Then came the delicate work of extracting the bags of gold from the valises in which they were carried, and carrying them secretly over to my room and hiding them under my bedstead. We had also to carry over to Mr. Peet's room the lead and pack it neatly and safely in the Valises. This was dangerous & difficult because of the two squads of soldiers on guard. However, we succeed

[*sic*]. There were three English reporter [*sic*] watching all our movements and after it had been accomplished they came around to look at the valises which held the money. After examining and lifting them, one of them remarked that he could swear that they had not been touched.

According to one theory, there was a secret tunnel under the parsonage. Another holds that Gargiulo invoked his prerogative to have his Turkish escort fall back. But how much distance could Osman *bey* and his men have put between themselves and the commissioners in a village teeming with troops?

One revolutionary historian, Anton Strashimirov, would claim that Asenov, disguised as the village idiot, brought the lead into the parsonage cellar, where he exchanged it for the gold. One of Strashimirov's confederates, Ivan Kharizanov, insisted that the men took frequent walks to visit one another, ferrying a small amount of gold or lead in their overcoats with each trip. According to this account, the brigands set a fire to cover the exchange. There was, in fact, a large fire that week at a local inn that housed the British journalists' military escort. In the aftermath, a special panel, which included the correspondents themselves, declared the disaster an accident. The fire, as it turns out, occurred a day or two before the commission and the brigands actually met.

Regardless of how it occurred, the switch was executed so skillfully that no one could tell the bags had been disturbed— not even William Maud and his colleagues who had availed themselves of Colonel Osman *bey*'s invitation to inspect the valises.

EARLIER THAT WEEK, the weather had turned colder.

"Everything," House recalled, "seemed against us." Wednesday came. The brigands didn't show. The next day also passed without a sign. The kidnappers had apparently seen the town swarming with troops and suspected bad faith. A disappointed Gargiulo cabled Leishman, "Fear too late to renew negotiations here."

Leishman sent a reply urging patience because "the object is worth a hard stubborn fight." He encouraged the men to stay for another week if necessary.

The meeting took place on January 31 or February 1. That evening the British journalists were to dine with Turkish officers.

"Everything was ready," House wrote. "The savage dog of whom the bandits had complained of his barking before was this time shut up in the family oven. The getting away with 210 lbs of gold was no child's play and the bandits understood it so in the darkness we saw a goodly number of shadowy forms in our yard but only the original three with perhaps one more appeared in my room. Each bag was handed out [from] under my bedstead by me & passed to one of the others to be passed to the third into the hands of the chief & to be counted each time. Then we shook hands with our bandit-guests now enriched with $63,000."

The agony of failure, which, as House put it, had for so long hung over the mission like a thunder cloud, had passed away. The Turks and the correspondents had been outfoxed, and House, for one, was weak with relief, noting all the while that a treacherous passage lay ahead.

"We would now," he recalled darkly, "commence our season of waiting."

CHAPTER ELEVEN

The Chase

๛

Dear Mr. Dickinson,

Miss Stone ought to give an illustrated lecture with colored lantern slides. She should collect photographs and if possible photographic negatives (they make better slides) of Bulgarian scenes of interest and of the people. Women in native costume, brigands, things to illustrate her captivity etc—This is most important. The best place to have the slides made from these is at Newtons 3 Fleet Street London. He is expensive but worth his price.

Cleveland Moffett of *McClure's Magazine*,
Grand Hôtel de Bulgarie à Sofia,
November 15, 1901

THE KIDNAPPERS had promised to release the women within ten days—sooner if possible—in the vicinity of Serres. They'd even hinted that they might drop the captives off close enough to a telegraph station that Miss Stone could wire for help. But the ten days passed, and there was no sign of the hostages.

John Leishman began to sweat. Throughout the tortuous negotiations in Bansko, he'd urged the negotiators to be patient and take as much time as they needed. But now, the ransom had been paid, and it was all too apparent to his superiors in Washington that the kidnappers had not kept their end of the bargain.

Minister Leishman tried to place this development in the best possible light. "Although the period originally mentioned has now been exceeded," he wrote to the secretary of state, "do not attach particular importance to it, as the time for delivery of captives was made rather elastic."

That explanation would stretch only so far. The worst-case scenario was that the kidnappers had killed their victims. With the ransom in hand, the band had to move fast to get free of the Turks. The women might slow them down. More important, dead hostages could never identify them.

House, Peet, and Gargiulo clung to the belief that the kidnappers were still acting in good faith but couldn't deliver because they were on the run. On the night of February 8, General Ibrahim Pasha dispatched three new patrols to search for the anarchists. Gargiulo complained to the civil governor. The governor shrugged. The matter was in the hands of the military commander, whose actions he couldn't control.

In fact, Ibrahim Pasha seemed answerable to no one—not to the local governor in Serres, not to the foreign minister, not even to the Sultan. Why wasn't he punished for this supposed insubordination? There are two possibilities. The first is that the Ottoman military was in such disarray and the authority of the Sultan so eroded that every regional commander could act as a law unto himself. From Ibrahim Pasha's perspective, the Sultan's *Irade* had made the Ottoman military appear weak and submissive. This was an invitation to Bulgarian *comitadji* to pour over the border and infiltrate the district. It might also incite the Bulgarians to invade and reclaim Macedonia and then march on to Constantinople. Given these possibilities, Ibrahim Pasha could have considered defiance of the Porte entirely honorable.

The second possibility is that the Ottoman military in Macedonia was acting on two entirely separate sets of orders: one, a series of formal documents intended to placate the Americans; the other, a secret and contradictory body of directives authorizing Ibrahim Pasha to do whatever he must to ensure Turkish safety and honor.

By February 1902, the Turks would no longer have seen the need for pretense. After all, the ransom negotiations had failed. On the American side, however, the deception continued.

Peet and his fellows had undertaken an elaborate charade to convince the Turks that the negotiations had fallen through. The valises carrying the "gold" had been escorted back to the train by the Croat bodyguards, who then transported it home to Constantinople. The lead pellets were deposited ceremoniously in a vault at the Imperial Ottoman Bank. The Turks were none the wiser.

As the result of this, however, Minister Leishman was not only responsible for the lives of the captives; he was answerable for American misrepresentations to the Porte. He was in a testy mood, therefore, when he received another message from Gargiulo asking him to demand that the Turks not merely stand down but that they withdraw entirely from the border region.

Once again, Leishman went hat in hand to the Ottoman foreign minister. Tewfik Pasha issued yet another order to Ibrahim Pasha to restrain his troops. The Ottoman general, as usual, ignored it.

THE KIDNAPPERS were three days overdue, when, on February 16, Leishman's nerve failed him. "If captives are not returned by twentieth," he wired Gargiulo, "I shall assume that an act of bad faith has been committed, notify Government to this effect and immediately take the most drastic measures."

Leishman didn't specify what drastic measures he intended. The alternatives were already on the table: warships to Constantinople to intimidate the Sultan, warships to Varna to pressure the Bulgarians, or he could simply relay to the Turks the State Department's blessing to hunt and kill, which would mean that Washington and Constantinople had given up on recovering the women alive.

Leishman's sudden rashness caught the negotiators off balance. Gargiulo was tempted to go along, but House, alarmed by the U.S. Minister's new attitude, persuaded the dragoman to write the legation and plead for restraint.

The situation had become so delicate that the commissioners, cut off as they were in the provinces, felt they couldn't explain themselves in encrypted cables. Peet made plans to leave by steamer for Constantinople in order to talk to Leishman face to face. His purpose was to keep the U.S. Minister from doing anything impulsive. His mission was to calm and placate. And yet the man he took along as his companion on that trip was one of the least soothing figures in American public life, Samuel S. McClure.

S. S. MCCLURE was not as well known as Hearst or Pulitzer, but he was a media baron of the first order. Born to a poor and joyless Scottish family in Ulster, Ireland, he emigrated at the age of eight to America with his widowed mother. A voracious reader, he was also restless and driven. His thin face, judging from portraits taken in boyhood and through his later years, was illuminated by the fierce intensity of his gaze. McClure seldom failed to get anything he went after.

McClure distinguished himself not as a writer but as an

editor and innovator. He expanded the concept of a news syndicate to include fiction by William Dean Howells, Sarah Orne Jewett, and other contemporary American writers who were often overlooked in favor of their British contemporaries. What fascinated him was discovering how things worked. When, in 1859, he founded *McClure's Magazine,* his intellectual curiosity drove him to seek out first-rate journalists who could take difficult social and scientific issues, study them down to the bone, and then render them comprehensible to a lay reader. *McClure's* had published Lincoln Steffens on city and state government, Ray Stannard Baker on corrupt labor practices, and Ida Tarbell on Napoleon and Abraham Lincoln. He nurtured the original "muckrackers," precursors of American investigative journalism.

From the golden age of magazines, covering about forty years from the late 1800s into the early twentieth century, McClure rode high. His monthly was a truly national publication and for that, all the more influential. He had published articles on big game hunting by Theodore Roosevelt, then commissioner of the U.S. Civil Service. By September 1901, of course, Roosevelt had succeeded McKinley, and McClure was proud to claim the new President as an alumnus.

That same year, Sam McClure found himself facing possible ruin. Despite his editorial successes, he'd overextended in trying to acquire the Harper's magazine group. The resulting losses sent his health into decline. He undertook a series of rest cures, none of which seemed to have any lasting effect. He became increasingly manic, which wore out his staff. Miss Tarbell had to take a rest cure of her own. He'd long since made a nervous wreck of his wife, Hattie, who found herself taking the cure alongside him. In the fall of 1901, the McClures and their four children took up residence at a spa in Vevey, Switzerland, hoping to benefit from its milk and cream regimen.

After a day or two in bed, Sam was too bored to continue.

He moved his family to Lucerne, where he met with Ida Tarbell. Before leaving America, he had assigned her a long and difficult article on Standard Oil. She was overwhelmed and
needed encouragement.

It was during this same autumn of 1901 that McClure
became obsessed with Ellen Stone. Exactly how McClure's fascination with her developed is not clear. Her story was too
melodramatic for his taste. The simplest explanation is that his
competitive impulses were piqued. Several publishers and news
organizations were making bids through the missionary society
to buy the rights to the captive missionary's story. She was an
elusive prize. Moreover, she was a convenient focus for his
other anxieties. Sam McClure wanted to demonstrate to the
world that he still had his stuff.

McClure's first overture to Stone seems to have been made
through Charles Dickinson. In mid-November, the consul general wrote Miss Stone to tell her, among other things, that Mr.
Cleveland Moffett of *McClure's Magazine* had arrived in Sofia
the evening before and said he would contribute 1,000 liras
toward her ransom, provided she write an exclusive experience
for the magazine after her release. The offer, if not accepted at
once, would be withdrawn.

The kidnappers never passed the information along to
Stone.

When the State Department heard of this, Mr. Dickinson
received a stinging reprimand from Assistant Secretary of State
David Hill:

> *Department is informed that a New York Magazine has left*
> *a contract with you offering one thousand pounds for*
> *exclusive interview. Any such proceeding at this stage*
> *would be most prejudicial to chances of ransom and it*
> *would be excess of functions were you to favor one journal-*
> *ist in enterprises and deny favor to others.*

Dickinson and McClure, however, remained in contact. Later that month, McClure wrote from London that he would sweeten the deal by adding another 1,000 pounds if that would "turn the scale and lead to Miss Stone's immediate release." He offered the consul general a commission of 10 percent and sent him a draft for 20 pounds to cover any out-of-pocket expenses.

There is no record of a contract, either written or verbal, between the two men. Late in January, however, McClure wrote to his wife from Belgrade that he was going straight to Salonica. He arrived the following night and cabled her that she should write him there "in care of the American Consul General."

Adeline House had invited McClure to stay at the mission house. Sam reported to his wife that he was comfortable and content. "Right across the bay in front of my window is Mount Olympus," he wrote, awestruck. "Near here Alexander the Great was born." He was planning an expedition, he said, to meet House and the committee in the interior. For that purpose, he hired a dragoman named Grigor Tsilka, husband of the missing lady, Katerina Tsilka.

Grigor had mysteriously dropped out of William Maud's narrative around Serres. Now he resurfaced in Salonica as interpreter for McClure. How these two found each other—at the very moment when the gold and lead were being exchanged—is an unexplained coincidence. House perhaps wanted to keep Grigor as far away from the negotiations as possible and assigned him to watch over McClure, whose own reputation for disruption was legendary. The job no doubt paid well, and Grigor needed money.

McClure expected that Tsilka would take him far into the mountains to Bansko. He reveled in the fantasy of going *mano a mano* with the wilderness. His adventure, however, was cut short in Serres, where he was told that the hostage negotiations had failed.

McClure decided to stay in Serres to see what might develop. At this point, House, Peet, and Gargiulo had taken Grigor Tsilka into their confidence. McClure, meanwhile, was left in the dark, but, as he was an influential man, the committee took pains to humor him. They invited him to share their accommodations. They invited him to dine. McClure was flattered to be included in their small, select circle.

"All I write you must be kept absolutely quiet," he wrote his wife. "Absolute secrecy is vital. We are concealing matters from two governments and various reporters. Don't believe a line you read in the newspapers. They can't know. There are spies & counterspies & nobody believes anything anybody says."

Hattie McClure, no doubt relieved that her husband had found an outlet for his energy, wrote to him from Vevey: "My dearest Sam—I am very proud that you have really gone like a belted knight of old to rescue a fair one from the robber's den. Poor thing. I was afraid she would be abandoned but when you went forth to find her (the one who even as a child never came home without having accomplished his missions) I felt that her star was once more on the rise."

"I should prefer the belted knight business," he wrote back, "to living in this wretched town, in this hotel, which I cannot describe to you for you have no experiences that would enable you to understand my words. Imagine a water-closet sans everything with a pair of wooden slippers in the hall to stand on so you can enter & thus is separated from the kitchen by a flimsy partition that you can see through."

The wait dragged on. Sam McClure passed the time "rest-curing" and "walk-curing," growing all the while more paranoid and hostile, imagining that his competitors were gaining the upper hand. He hated the sight of William Maud, to whom he referred as "my enemy." Maud, he sniffed, was "very thick with the Turks." When he heard that a competing monthly,

The Century, had entered the bidding for Miss Stone's rights at $5,000, he vowed to Hattie that "whatever they offer, I'll beat them." When he could see no visible progress, he fumed, "A warship could settle the matter in an hour. Pity Miss Stone wasn't British."

By the middle of February, McClure decided that it was time to act. He cabled Theodore Roosevelt:

Have made thorough examination [of] Stone matter . . .
her release impossible as Turkish military officials persist
in massing troops vicinity [of attempted negotiations]
destroying value [of] Sultan's Irade. These tactics should
be met with a warship in Salonica . . . the governor of
which is responsible for region where negotiations take
place.
   S.S. McClure
   McClure's Magazine

The tycoon had been counting on the intimate relationship of editor to writer to gain the President's ear, but he had misjudged his influence. Roosevelt never replied.

McClure, meanwhile, had tired of life in the trenches. When Peet returned to Constantinople to reason with Leishman, the publisher accompanied him. His services, he wrote Hattie, were needed in the Ottoman capital.

UPON ARRIVING at the Palazzo Corpi on February 17, Peet found Leishman very anxious. Mr. Peet, he said, should go quickly to Sofia to strong-arm the Bulgarian government into guaranteeing the safe release of Miss Stone, something Charles Dickinson had tried four months earlier. For his pains, the consul general had been publicly humiliated and privately reprimanded.

Once again, Peet pleaded for restraint, observing that the brigands probably interpreted the increasing Turkish troop movements as a sign that the Americans had broken faith. If the kidnappers had "a grain of common sense," Leishman retorted, they would realize that their demands were "absurd" and beyond the control of the committee.

"It begins to look," he wrote to Gargiulo, who was still in Serres, "as if most damned treachery and possibly murder have been added to their list of crimes."

On Thursday, February 20, a messenger appeared in Bansko with assurances that the women were alive and would be delivered as soon as the band could put enough distance between itself and the Turks.

Mollified, Leishman agreed to hold off taking drastic steps to see what developed over the next few days.

Sam McClure, who had come to Constantinople ready to roll up his shirtsleeves and work, had been seized by a "curious bowell trouble" and was laid up in the luxurious confines of the Pera Palace. This new illness seems to have convinced him to give up the chase. On Saturday, February 22, he got a passport to Vienna. The following day, he dropped in on Minister Leishman to say good-bye.

Leishman had startling news. Don't leave for Austria just yet, he warned. Miss Stone might be delivered as early as Tuesday.

Cursing himself for having quit the field so soon, McClure caught the next train back to Salonica.

AT THE MOMENT the gold changed hands, Khristo Chernopeev was holding the hostages in a cabin near Sandansky's hometown of Vlahi, only about fifteen miles as the crow flies from Bansko. The women were tense and, they would write, more frightened now than at any other time since the baby's birth. They did not like or trust Chernopeev, whom they later claimed to know only as the "Bad Man." Of the entire band, he was least tolerant of the baby. When Stoyan and the Chief had set off for Bansko to negotiate with Dr. House, they were once again worried for their lives.

On the evening of February 1 or 2, the brigands crowded uninvited into the hut, apparently waiting for news. Two couriers arrived and tossed a satchel to Chernopeev. He and a few others withdrew to an inner apartment. When he came out, he handed a letter to Miss Stone. She read it silently:

My dear Fellow-Worker:
   Our hearts are deeply touched by your words and those of Mrs. Tsilka in your last letter. . . . We cannot tell you how we shall rejoice to see the hour when we shall greet you. We have now given the money, (14,500 Turkish)—and we have taken your receipt for the same, and as we rely upon the "word of honor" of the bearer of your letter, we expect to see you soon. We will go from here to Serres, and there await you with great joy. . . .

It was signed by House, Peet, and Gargiulo.

Katerina Tsilka couldn't wait for Stone to speak. "Is the money paid?" she asked one of her captors.

"Yes," he replied.

"The happiness we felt," she recalled, "was too great to be expressed in words."

MANY MORE DAYS passed, however, and the women, despite their heightened expectations, seemed no closer to freedom. A thick fog had enveloped the mountains. It was too dangerous to leave the cabin, which was, in Stone's recollection, "perched high on the rocks, from which the descent was so steep that we must make it by foot."

When the weather cleared, the caravan continued its nightly travel. "The journeys were as hard as ever," recalled Stone. "The nights just as cold."

The brigands gave no reason for the delay. Sandansky, in fact, had wired Chernopeev that he should set the women free. Instead of taking them south to Serres in accordance with the plan, however, Chernopeev led them north. He was probably suspicious that the Americans might tip off the Turks to the time and drop-off point. Once they let the women go, moreover, they could no longer be used as shields. For whatever reason, Chernopeev dragged the two women and the newborn over the foggy slopes for three more weeks.

One night, a brigand stepped into the hut and warned the women they should prepare themselves for a long journey. They must, he said, reach a distant destination before dawn. Katerina Tsilka recalled this journey:

> We got on our horses and began to descend on a steep path driven as fast as the horses could go. By midnight we noticed, to our great surprise, that we were traveling on a good wide carriage road, from where we could see on both sides to some light which seemed to belong to two towns in the distance.
>
> We thought this was our destination, but suddenly the horses were jerked aside to the banks of what seemed a big river. [To throw the Turks off the trail, Chernopeev crossed the mountains west of Bansko and there prepared to ford the Struma River.] Here we were told to dismount and crawl as quietly as we could to a sort of depression where we stayed together with the men of the party. It was very dark and the men were straining their eyes across the river. Presently, we saw something moving on

the other bank. Now, it was in the water and growing larger as it approached. I was staring at it, clutching the baby in my arms. Then there was a splash and a man appeared, leading a string of horses tied one after the other.

The leader gave an order, the men helped us on to two new horses and dismounted themselves. The leader grabbed the baby from me and holding it with one arm, led the way toward the river. George tied the reins of my horse to his saddle and told me to hold as tightly as I could on my saddle so as not to lose my balance while crossing the river. By now, the leader's horse had plunged into the water and we were following. I felt the back of my horse shudder as its feet went into the cold water. The saddle was swaying from side to side and I grabbed the mane of the animal and held on it as tightly as I could. Soon my legs were in the water and the cold was unbearable. I was keeping my eyes shut because looking into the water made me dizzy, but I felt jerked to the right. [The horse] seemed to stumble, to spring, and finally its feet were on firm ground. Then I remembered my baby in the leader's arm and turned to look for them. I could only see men's and horses' heads on the surface of the water. Then I heard the leader's voice shouting near me, "Is everyone alright?" Then Miss Stone's faint voice, "Child, is the baby safe?" At the same moment the leader was pushing the little bundle into my lap.

On the far side of the river, the men had been cautious, but now they apparently considered themselves safe. The boy, George, confided to Tsilka that a scout had brought word that details of the delivery plan had been reported to Turkish authorities, hence the delay. And they'd been forced to cross the river at this isolated spot because the bridges were guarded.

The women were taken to a "ruined, lonely house," where they were allowed to warm themselves and dry their clothes before an open fire. They stayed there throughout the next day. When dusk fell, the hostages were told that this was the night they were finally to be released.

Outside the house, men waited. One group rode ahead, while the others fanned out around the women. Soon, however, Katerina noticed that the escort had vanished, leaving only two boys (probably George and Meeter) disguised as gypsies. One led her horse, the other Miss Stone's.

At four o'clock in the morning of February 23, the gypsy boys deposited the women with their saddlebags in a desolate field under a pear tree.

"It was so queer to be released in such a way, "Tsilka recalled, "we could hardly believe it."

AT DAYBREAK Mrs. Tsilka left her baby with Miss Stone and, gathering a handful of pebbles to throw at snarling dogs, headed toward a nearby village. Coming down the road toward her was an elderly Albanian Muslim. She called out to him. He looked surprised, but when she told him that she was with the "Teacher Stone," he followed her to the pear tree where he showed great concern for the baby. The old Muslim led them into his village to the home of a Christian family. The women of the household recognized them instantly, brought them inside, and set them before a fire.

"Baby was the first to get comfortable," her mother recalled. "She stretched her arms as they were freed from her swaddling clothes, then opened her big dark eyes, surprised by the light of the fire. The women watched her with wonder, smiling, exclaiming and making the sign of the cross."

Miss Stone and Mrs. Tsilka were taken on to the larger town of Strumitsa and there deposited with the local Protestant pastor. There, they enjoyed a long hot bath.

"Baby Elenchie," recalled Ellen Stone, "was for the first time arrayed in one of the little dresses and caps we had made for her during our captivity. Very sweet looked the little maiden, with her arms freed from those swaddling bands, against whose confinement she had sometimes rebelled bitterly. The tiny face looked most bewitching under its frame of thick clustering dark hair, confined under the little close cap, whose row of hem-stitching were all the ornamentation which we could devise for it. When we were once more among the family, all hands were outstretched to take our baby, and she graciously condescended to be passed about among her admirers."

"I do not know how Miss Stone felt," Katerina Tsilka recalled. "But after the first moments of relaxation everything to me became blank and indifferent. Here I sat on a couch with baby in my arms while our friends crowded about us asking questions. Miss Stone was practically submerged among her friends, listening to them with a smile. Then she looked at me and said, 'Child take that kerchief off from your head, it makes you look ugly.'"

THE NEWS REACHED Serres at a little past ten o'clock on February 23. Dr. House had just returned to the hotel after preaching at an Evangelical service that Sunday morning. He found a uniformed messenger waiting at the hotel with a telegram for Mr. Gargiulo.

"Give it to me," House said. "I will deliver it to him."

"No," the courier answered. "I will only deliver it into his hands."

House invited the man to wait, but he was annoyed. It had been nearly a week since Peet had left House and Gargiulo alone in Serres. The hostilities between them erupted periodically into arguments.

On the night of their final negotiations in Bansko as House spoke with the brigands in Bulgarian, Gargiulo had persisted in tugging at his sleeve asking for translation. House ignored him.

It was now House's turn to feel the sting of an insult. He was de facto negotiator, and the Turkish officer sitting in front of him held a message, which required, possibly, his immediate action. Fortunately, Gargiulo appeared not long after and opened the envelope. It contained word from the governor of Strumitsa to the Ottoman governor general of Serres that this very morning Miss Stone and Madame Tsilka had been found under a pear tree in a village about one hour's distance from town.

Gargiulo, this messenger would claim, had "kissed his hands and feet"—a common Turkish expression. For a moment, the quarreling stopped. "The tense strain," House wrote, "was relieved and peace at last filled our breasts. Our efforts had been crowned with success!"

That evening, Peet and Gargiulo set out for Salonica. A few steps behind them was the indefatigable William Maud.

MAUD HAD NEARLY burned his bridges with the Americans. The apparent failure of the ransom negotiations in Bansko left him disconsolate. He followed the progress of the "gold" back to the railway station and described it with all the gravity of a mourner following a funeral cortege.

"It was with bitter feelings," he reported to London, "that we saw them go, for with them went all hope. We have scrambled up precipitous mountains behind them; we have splashed through foaming torrents beside them. They were like old friends to us. We knew every knot and stitch in their canvas covers."

He'd taken the missionaries to task in print for their ineptitude as negotiators, suggesting they'd have done better to include him in their deliberations. Maud's colleagues from the *Daily Telegraph* and Reuters had given up and gone home. Maud stayed. It was obvious to him that Peet, House, and Gargiulo were still encamped at the Hôtel Salonique waiting for some impending development. And so he waited too.

Maud was at work writing in his little room at the Gloire de la Turquie that Sunday morning when a messenger of the provincial governor entered, out of breath. The women, he said, had been found. (This courier was the same man who'd brought the message to Gargiulo. Although the missionaries had sworn him to secrecy, Maud had bought his loyalty through bribes.) The Englishman packed his bags and paid hurried respects to various local notables before following House and Gargiulo to the station. There was only one train out of Serres that evening bound for Salonica. Maud, Gargiulo, and House once again found themselves awkwardly sharing the same space. News of Miss Stone's release spread rapidly, and a crowd of people gathered on the platform to see them off.

At Salonica, their small party grew to include Dr. House's fourteen-year-old son, Charlie. The reunion with Miss Stone was likely to be memorable and his father wanted him to witness it.

Mr. Tsilka was also to join the party. Grigor, however, had been under stepped-up surveillance since McClure left Salonica. Earlier in the month, the Ottoman inspectorate of Bulgaria in Sofia wrote Constantinople that Tsilka was walking around "like a gypsy" without a care in the world. Now the Ottoman minister of foreign affairs wrote the grand vizier that Tsilka's husband "who is under your supervision in Thessalonica, must be kept there without escaping, as he is our unique source of information."

Gargiulo and the Houses found Grigor waiting for them when they arrived at Salonica station a little before daybreak on February 24. Suddenly he was surrounded by Turkish police.

"At that last moment," Maud recorded, "they refused permission for him to go, even though Mr. Gargiulo promised to be answerable for him. Let the evidence against him be what it may, one could only feel a profound pity for the bitter disappointment of Ligord [*sic*] as he watched the train steam out of the station."

Maud was the only journalist to make it on to the train that morning. The American, McClure, was nowhere in sight. Finally, Maud had an unobstructed shot at Miss Stone. The prospect left him dazed.

"Throughout the journey," he wrote, "I tried to realize that we were going to see [her], but the idea even escaped me. It seemed certain that something would happen—as it had happened so often before—to thwart our wishes. Even the bundle of ladies rugs and capes which Mr. House had with him failed to carry conviction, and I doubted it was only one more ruse to throw me off the scent."

The train rattled through a massive gorge following the banks of the Varda—"the Axius of ancient times," wrote Maud, and a river that the poet Homer deemed "the fairest stream that flows in all the earth." At the station, there were fresh horses waiting to take them on the five-hour trek over the mountains to Strumitsa.

At the last checkpoint, the Turks made them coffee. "I began to feel," Maud rhapsodized, "that Miss Stone was near."

As the party rode down into the town, Maud harvested details for his sketches. As his eye skimmed the old wooden houses with their overhanging second stories, he caught a glimpse of two women looking out of a window. One of them held a baby in her arms. He recognized them at once.

The party stopped at the gate of the Protestant pastor's house. A frock-coated gentleman in a fez welcomed them in English and led them up a stairway to an empty parlor. Dr. House shortly disappeared into a side room for a hushed reunion with Miss Stone. House would explain that she was feeling nervous strain and wasn't up to the rigors of a reception.

House satisfied himself that the ladies were unharmed. (Miss Stone did, in fact, have a bruised knee from a fall she had taken while blindfolded.) Dr. House wanted to know what they had told the Turks. Although the committee had wired ahead warning the women to talk to no one, the local Ottoman police chief had gotten there ahead of the telegram. The women thought he intended to congratulate them on their release. Instead, he interrogated them for the remainder of the Sabbath.

The Ottoman records of this interview indicate that the women were evasive. They knew their kidnappers only by nicknames, they claimed. The men had never spoken to them except to ask them what they'd like to eat. Mrs. Tsilka insisted they had never been kept in towns and that she couldn't remember if they'd crossed any mountains or rivers.

Gargiulo and Maud waited in the parlor while House spoke with the women. Half an hour passed, and Maud, who was making notes on the furnishings, noticed that Gargiulo was angry. The dragoman fancied himself Miss Stone's liberator, and for that he'd expected an effusion of gratitude. Instead, he sat ignored.

Gargiulo ordered the pastor to fetch Dr. House. The command was sufficiently emphatic that the door soon opened. Miss Stone and Mrs. Tsilka followed Dr. House into the room. The atmosphere in the little parlor was strained.

"I had prepared myself for an affecting scene," recalled Maud. "Something perhaps that would recall the relief of Ladysmith." Instead, there were polite handshakes. Puzzled over this, he speculated to his readership that this was the American way of showing joy.

Maud found Madame Tsilka "painfully uncommunicative." He fared slightly better with Miss Stone. The following day, as the women and their escort left town in a triumphal procession, Maud pulled his pony alongside the spinster's and ventured a remark about the well-tended fields that stretched out around them.

"Yes," she replied. "But how will those poor people escape when the trouble begins?"

Maud, oddly, did not pursue the point, but he had grown bold enough to ask her if she had indeed been taken into Bulgaria. Gargiulo, who was riding close behind, brought the exchange to a halt declaring, "There must be no flirting with Miss Stone!"

DURING THE GREAT rejoicing in Strumitsa, Katerina had been reunited with her brother Ivan, a Protestant pastor in the nearby town of Radovish. He'd brought bad news: Grigor had been arrested in Salonica. This, no doubt, was one of the sensitive issues that Dr. House had discussed with the women behind closed doors. As an American citizen, Miss Stone was unlikely to be taken into custody upon her return to the capital. Katerina, as a Turkish citizen, had no similar protection.

The prospect of her husband in a Turkish prison weighed heavily on Katerina as she rode over the mountains that morning to the train. About halfway down, the little party reached the town of Chipelli, a cluster of mud huts just below the snow line. On a patch of grass nearby, some young Turks, naked to the waist, were wrestling "utterly heedless," Maud wrote, "of the biting wind that swept through the pass. Suddenly, from round a bend, a dark figure came running towards us at full speed. He rushed past me like a hunted man and I saw that it was Ligord. His wife was riding close behind us, and with a startled, happy cry, she bent for his embrace. There was a brief halt while they, together, unwound the wrappings that covered the face of their little daughter." Grigor then took the child in his arms and carried her the rest of the way to the station.

Tsilka had been released because the American, McClure, had intervened on his behalf. The Vali of Salonica had no doubt seen the mounting excitement in anticipation of the women's arrival. For him to interrupt this celebration by jailing the father of the brigand baby would leave a bad impression.

House and Gargiulo had hoped the women could travel incognito. At Strumitsa station, they were taken to a separate room to protect them from curious stares. When they boarded the train around sunset, they were draped in cloaks, hats, and veils, but a fellow passenger recognized them instantly and handed Miss Stone an English-language newspaper with her photograph on the front page. Miss Stone marveled at how universal the interest in her case had been.

It was evening when they arrived in Salonica. Waiting to greet them on the railway platform was a throng of Miss Stone's missionary colleagues, the American vice consul and his wife, as well as most of the English-speaking citizens of the city. The women were whisked off to the mission house where, in Stone's recollection, they felt safe "under the folds of the Stars and Stripes."

House, who had taken it upon himself to shield the women from the Turks, was frankly not sure how far the U.S. government could or would go to assist him. In the short run, his hope was to keep them visible. Over the next two weeks, many visitors streamed to the mission. Five ships of the British fleet dropped anchor in Salonica, and an unusually large number of officers and sailors came for tea.

The Blue Jackets all wanted to see and hold the baby. Scattered among them was a fresh crop of correspondents hoping to interview Miss Stone. Poor Maud found himself shoved to the sidelines. His cause was lost. S. S. McClure, it turned out, had already gotten to Miss Stone and secured her promise to write a series of articles to appear in his magazine. Besides the written pieces, she would be giving fifty-four lectures for which she would be paid the startling sum of $29,000. (Mrs. Tsilka had been retained for a smaller amount, but she couldn't publish or speak until Miss Stone's run was finished.)

Maud's *baksheesh* couldn't compete with a media lord's checkbook. McClure also enjoyed the advantage of having Grigor Tsilka in his employ, which may have explained why he was the first person allowed to board the train when it pulled into Salonica. There, finally, he sat face to face with Miss Stone.

Unlike Maud, who was dumbstruck in her presence, McClure tended to regard Miss Stone with new-found detachment. She was, he wrote his wife, just what he expected her to be—a cross between their children's nanny and Miss Ida Tarbell, herself a spinster.

McClure spent only a few minutes with the women.

"It was the hardest contract I ever made," he wrote to Hattie, who was still rest-curing at Vevey. "But I won against the world."

"The baby," he observed absently, "is just a baby."

CHAPTER TWELVE

Persona Non Grata

◖◗

The kidnapping of another American woman would bank-
rupt the Ottoman Empire.

Anonymous Turkish minister,
The London *Daily Graphic*, October 21, 1901

IF ONLY BRIEFLY, Elenchie Tsilka was the world's most
famous baby. She was baptized on March 23 by Dr. House at
his home in Salonica. After having been imprisoned for seven
weeks in a ball of flannel and sugar lumps, she was free to wave
her limbs to her heart's content. The House children doted on
her, especially six-year-old Gladys, who, sitting proper as an
English nanny, held the infant in the garden.

For Miss Stone, the scene was bittersweet. "It was a terrible
heartwrench," she wrote, "to leave 'our baby' and her mother
for we had so long been everything to each other."

Three days later, however, Miss Stone set off for Vienna in
the company of *McClure's* editor Ray Stannard Baker. She
would describe it as a quiet departure. In fact, she was trying to
give the Turks the slip.

Since Miss Stone's arrival in Salonica, the Ottoman government had been trying to take her deposition. She refused, argu-

ing that as an American citizen she could not be forced to tes-
tify. She and Mrs. Tsilka had already been interviewed by the
police chief of Strumitsa, and that, in her mind, excused her
from further duty.

News of Miss Stone's intransigence had made its way into
the dinner conversations of foreign diplomats in Salonica. She
had been evasive. She couldn't remember names or specific
conversations. She couldn't identify landmarks because she and
Mrs. Tsilka had been forced to travel at night and during the
day they were held in dark places. She'd never had a conversation with her captors. She didn't know their real names. She'd
never stayed in a village, or a town.

According to Sandansky's biographer, Mercia MacDermott,
Miss Stone knew perfectly well that her captors carried her
over the border into Bulgaria. "When her guard denied it and
assured her that they were still in Turkey," wrote MacDermott,
"she pulled out a compass and pointed out the directions of
Kyustendil and Dupnitsa, saying that she could tell from the
state of the forests—which were young and thick—that they
were in Bulgaria, not Turkey." Caught off-guard by her sophisti-
cation, Sandansky was said to have burst out laughing.

The Europeans felt that the American missionary lady was
lying to protect someone.

While unfamiliar with this Western practice of selling
rights, the Ottoman inspector in Sofia tried to explain it to the
grand vizier:

> It would be no surprise if she tries to acquire money and
> fame through this event. To ensure her future life and get
> money, she may be expected to make a contract with a
> newspaper or journal to publish her six months long life
> story among bandits. In addition to that, she would no
> doubt participate in various conferences and tell people

about this awful adventure. It would therefore be better if she would not be permitted to travel to the U.S. for a while.

Learning that Miss Stone had slipped away to Austria, the grand vizier sent an angry letter to Leishman. If the errant missionary did not come at once to Constantinople, he would send an envoy to Vienna to take her deposition. If she didn't cooperate, he would demand her arrest.

By the time she crossed the Austrian border, however, Miss Stone was beyond the reach of the Turks. Her fame had preceded her, and her progress from Vienna to New York, Ray Baker recalled, was a "continual skirmish with reporters."

Early in April, Baker and Stone sailed on the *Deutschland* from Liverpool. For the past month in Salonica, they'd been collaborating on Miss Stone's first article. They spent the Atlantic voyage hard at work on the second. When their ship docked in Jersey City at noon on April 10, the quay was crowded with well-wishers, curiosity seekers, stevedores, custom house officials, along with, Baker estimated, some twenty reporters and "photo grabbers." Miss Stone's brother, Charles, was allowed to board first. He reappeared leading his sister triumphantly down the gangway to the arms of her nieces and nephew.

THERE WAS NO ready escape for Katerina Tsilka. As a Turkish citizen, she was subject to Ottoman law. Local authorities ordered her to stay put. She was summoned repeatedly to appear at court. Dr. House finally prevailed on the Vali to hold these interrogations at the mission house. Cradling Elenchie in her arms, Katerina would arrive for questioning in the company of her husband, Dr. House, Dr. Haskell, and for a time, at least, Samuel McClure.

Every day the Ottoman prosecutor asked her the same questions. Every day she gave the same vague replies. Finally, she refused to say anything further and remained at the mission under virtual house arrest.

She wrote to U.S. Minister Leishman in Constantinople:

> Is there any possibility [of] shortening our case with the government here? Both my husband and myself have been thoroughly examined, and now I do not see what they are waiting for. My husband has been without work for the last seven months, and now we are spending all the means we (have) . . . it is very hard on us.

Leishman didn't favor her with a reply.

Realizing that no help would be coming from the Americans, Grigor finally bribed a court official with a gold Napoleon, and the Tsilkas slipped out of town.

Leishman's coldness, of course, was due to the fact that he was convinced that Grigor Tsilka had advance knowledge of the kidnapping. He'd arrived at this conclusion due largely to information supplied to him by Gargiulo. But even the American missionaries were coming around, with great reluctance and even greater sadness, to the U.S. Minister's point of view. On the whole, their Bulgarian brothers showed a greater allegiance to the revolutionary movement than to the Protestant faith.

John Baird wrote an angry letter to Dickinson describing how the former pastor of Bansko had warned him to stonewall American investigators about the "Kottmeya." Baird averred that Pastor Hristov had closer ties to these rascals than was proper and he swore that he would tell Minister Leishman anything that would help him bring the guilty to justice.

Baird was among those who wanted to see "some of the guilty swing." It was time, he believed, for Teddy Roosevelt to remove the velvet glove and bring down his iron fist—on someone. The humiliation visited upon the American public could certainly now be avenged by arrests, trials, and executions. But the government in Washington had fallen curiously silent. The only word that the State Department would let out for publication is that it had petitioned the Porte for an indemnity, but this was only a legal formality. An exhaustive inquiry would be made to determine responsibility.

AMONG THE THRONGS of people waiting for Miss Stone on the dock in Jersey City had been lecture agent Major James B. Pond. A tall, elderly man with a brusque manner, Major Pond had been the impresario for Henry Ward Beecher's famous tours of America and Europe. He had once paid the African explorer Henry M. Stanley $50,000 for a series of fifty lectures, picking up all the expenses of his speaker and a companion.

Pond had outbid McClure for Miss Stone's lecture rights, offering Miss Stone $29,000 for fifty-four appearances She would be speaking on the Chautauqua, a populist speakers' bureau that booked musicians and guest lecturers in lyceums and revival tents around the nation. Chautauqua was very popular at the turn of the century as it was the only contact many rural families would ever have with culture. In Miss Stone's case, Pond decided not to open with a splash—New York would have been the logical choice—but rather bring her out gently in front of the most sympathetic audience possible, her hometown congregation.

The First Congregationalist Church of Chelsea, Massachusetts, was packed on the evening of April 15. One local newspaper placed the crowd at nearly 1,000 ticket holders. The organ behind the speaker's platform was draped with a large American flag. When Miss Stone appeared in the doorway in the company of her brother, Charles, and a Mr. Durning, editor in chief of *The Congregationalist*, the crowd waved their handkerchiefs in enthusiastic welcome. Miss Stone, who appeared overcome by emotion, bowed again and again.

Despite her majestic appearance—she had chosen a handsome black gown with a cluster of American Beauty roses attached to the bodice—she seemed uncomfortable in her new role. As she began to relate tales of her captivity, her lack of experience as a public speaker showed. According to a reporter from the *Boston Evening Transcript*, who reviewed a performance she gave later in the week at the Tremont Temple, she had a habit of "suddenly dropping her voice, clipping her periods and rushing through groups of words which, unminded by a small group of listeners, often make a large audience sigh for the sustained tones [of] a trained lecturer."

Fortunately, she had taken Cleveland Moffett's advice and prepared a stereoscopic slide show that featured photographs of herself and Mrs. Tsilka in their brigand clothes. (The Turks had confiscated these, but Gargiulo had gotten them back saying the women had requested them as "mementos of their adventure.") The presentation included shots of Miss Stone's pet Salonica tabby, which went over very well with the crowd.

The surge of hometown sentiment notwithstanding, Miss Stone's celebrity was already drawing censure. The editors of *The Missionary Herald* tried to rationalize her $5,000 arrangement with McClure and nearly $30,000 contract with Major Pond, explaining that "literary men, travelers, explorers, and others, who have the ear of the public, have written magazine articles and books, and have given lectures up and down the land, receiving large remuneration." The paper cited one case in which a prominent writer was applauded for undertaking such a tour to satisfy his creditors. And Miss Stone should be praised equally for trying to repay those who had contributed to her ransom. A less sympathetic daily, however, suggested that she was "merchandising her suffering." And a particularly vicious item in the *Ramsey County* (Minnesota) *Courier* accused Miss Stone of "exhibiting herself in the same manner as the woman of the side show who bites the heads off of snakes."

Miss Stone's family had apparently foreseen these dangers. At least one of her brothers had tried to persuade her not to go through with the magazine deal. Just before she signed the contract, she appeared to waver, but McClure's forceful personality overrode her qualms.

To disarm her critics, Miss Stone issued a public statement saying that when it appeared that a recital of her captivity would be productive of financial results, she accepted in order to reimburse those who had "embarrassed themselves" by helping provide her freedom. She also announced a bequest of $500 to establish a school in Macedonia offering education to "poor boys so they would not have to resort to brigandage." (One of her colleagues observed cynically that most of the leaders of the Macedonian movement seemed to have been unemployed teachers.)

Miss Stone's public relations problem did not go away. American audiences quickly became impatient with her. They were waiting for tales of Barbary captivity, but she did not gratify them with titillating particulars. And, she refused to blame her kidnappers. In fact, as she told a crowd of admirers in Boston, those boys had worked hard for their booty. The villains, she insisted, were the Turks.

"Twenty-four years will have gone [by] since the Treaty of Berlin," she exhorted her audience at First Congregational, "and no nation, no government has raised its hand to say that the Sultan shall fulfill the promises he made in that treaty for the protection and development of the little Christian nations which are under his rule. Revolutionary committees represent the protest those people are making against the indifference of the world."

Miss Stone was using her lectern to promote the Macedonian cause; certain of her missionary colleagues were scandalized. As much as they despised the Turks—Dr. Haskell still referred to the Ottoman Empire as that "reactionary, tyrannical, heartless monstrosity"—they did possess a basic sense of fairness. The Turks were innocent of the kidnapping. Miss Stone's attack on them now struck the Reverend George Marsh for one as "regular sickening bosh."

Miss Stone made time in her busy schedule to attend a meeting of the American Board in Oberlin, Ohio. Here again she tried to plead the cause of the revolutionists. Dr. Barton and others called her aside and warned her to bide her tongue. After that, she tempered her remarks, even though it seemed to her "like treachery to be silent."

IN THE COLD gray light of retrospection, it is difficult to imagine that Miss Stone helped plan her own kidnapping. She could be passionate—an old friend had supposedly heard her declaim from a pulpit, "Oh Bulgaria, my adopted country!"—but she was not politically sophisticated. As Chernopeev would later reveal, Miss Stone was chosen in part because she'd tried to persuade the people to put their faith in God, not revolution. Even if she'd agreed to her abduction as a quick and quiet way to raise cash for a cause, she would have been restrained by the prospect that any word of her capture that reached her aged mother might easily kill her. A more likely explanation for the radicalization of Miss Stone is that she was co-opted by her captors.

Years later, old women in Bansko would wink and chuckle among themselves about how Miss Stone had fallen in love with Yané Sandansky. (If she did harbor romantic fantasies, they most likely centered upon the strapping Asenov, with his large, sensitive eyes and perfect literary Bulgarian.) But the seduction of Miss Stone by her captors ran deeper than any spinster's fantasy. She had been carried away by force, but the men who held her at gunpoint one minute were bringing her flowers the next. Even as she lived under a death sentence, her would-be executioners cooked her a Thanksgiving turkey. They could have killed the baby, but instead they'd doted on little "Kismetchie," carving her name on their guns. Even if they had not sworn Miss Stone to secrecy, she would have kept their secrets because their secrets became her own. By the time she was released, Miss Stone saw no conflicts between her loyalty to her native country and her loyalty to the brigand's holy cause. Was it not, after all, an American's responsibility to rescue fellow Christians?

IN MAY, the first of her five articles, "Six Months Among the Brigands," appeared. It was not the triumph McClure had foreseen. Despite Ray Stannard Baker's conscientious efforts, Miss Stone's account, though full of colorful anecdotes, was light on substance. She failed, for example, to mention that the kidnapping had a political motive. By early July, Major Pond concluded that Miss Stone's tour was a "failure." (Miss Stone saw the ordeal through to the finish. As late as March 1903 she was writing from the road in Salina, Kansas.) Having staked so much of his personal reputation on the celebrated missionary, McClure had been blind to her shortcomings.

"The Stone matter is surely wonderful," he'd written Hattie after reading a draft of the first article. "It is the best stuff the magazine ever had & will be a great success."

By midsummer, however, he had to acknowledge that Miss Stone's articles "weren't pulling." Katerina Tsilka, on the other hand, was gaining new and respectful notice. Her one and only article for *McClure's*, an account of Elenchie's birth, had been assigned almost as an afterthought. In a letter to his wife, McClure described it as lacking the literary quality of Miss Stone's work, even if it was "necessarily more thrilling."

Mrs. Tsilka was the more gifted storyteller.

AFTER THEIR ESCAPE from Salonica, the Tsilkas had gone to Monastir, where they hid quietly for a time at the home of Grigor's parents. Then, hiring a carriage under assumed names, they continued on to Kortcha. The Turks apparently lost the scent, for it seems that the Tsilkas passed a relatively peaceful year in Kortcha working at the girls' boarding school. Grigor was on the payroll of the American Board but earning almost nothing.

"Mr. Tsilka has not been satisfied with his salary," Lewis Bond wrote ruefully to headquarters in Boston. "I don't think we can ever satisfy the preachers who are educated in America."

In the spring of 1903, the Tsilkas left for the States.

Now that Miss Stone's tour had ended, Katerina was free to begin her own. Her prospects seemed poor. A year had passed, and none of the perpetrators had been caught, let alone tried and executed. The odor of national disgrace clung to the affair.

Katerina Tsilka, however, vanquished all obstacles with a bravura display of charm and determination. The photograph that accompanied her touring notes shows her as an elegant Western-style matron, her glossy black hair swept into a loose bun. Elenchie, now fifteen months old, is perched on her mother's knee in white ruffles. She had her mother's resolute jaw and her father's dark, intelligent eyes.

Katerina was under the exclusive management of the Slayton Lyceum Bureau, but soon a dozen other lecture agencies were bidding for her favors. In April, she arrived in Chicago, home base of the *Record-Herald* and its peripatetic reporter, William Curtis. Since his attacks on Charles Dickinson in the fall of 1901, Curtis had been occupied writing his book. In the fall of the previous year, he'd taken a few nasty swipes at Miss Stone. But the curmudgeonly correspondent was now captivated by Katerina Tsilka. The lady, he found, had become "quite a lioness."

"Her success has been very great as a lecturer both in the

East and in the West," he wrote in the spring of 1903. "She is pretty, with attractive manners, fluent speech and just enough of a foreign accent to add to the charm." She was not so serious and matter-of-fact as Miss Stone, he went on to explain. Whenever she brought out the baby, the audience "went wild."

Little Elenchie seemed to have no fear of the crowds who came to hear her mother speak. She scampered freely over the stage, searching the faces below her to find a child her own age. Once she hid behind the organ and wouldn't come out until someone called "peek-a-boo." Admirers entertained her by building block houses for her to destroy. One gave her an apple, which she bit and judged "very nice." She spoke English and became annoyed with her parents when they spoke Bulgarian.

Like Miss Stone, Katerina Tsilka had only kind words for her captors. Again and again, she insisted that the brigands were just good Christian boys persecuted by Turks. Despairing of justice, they'd fled to the mountains to fight for freedom.

It is fair to say that most of her American audiences were deaf to this political message. Even after all of the news accounts, lectures, and stereoptical slides, they were not sure of Macedonia's exact location or how it, in fact, differed from Bulgaria—wherever that was. The only place where Mrs. Tsilka's words hit home was the U.S. Department of State.

IT HAD BEEN a year since the hostages were delivered, and the State Department, which had promised a thorough investigation of the affair, had come up empty-handed. The leading suspect was still Boris Sarafov, but—as usual—there was no proof against him. (He had, in fact, patched up his quarrels with the IO and joined them in the mountains.) Although Yané Sandansky's name had been mentioned in a couple of reports, no one seemed to believe he had the stature to pull off a job like the Stone kidnapping.

Charles Dickinson was now of the opinion that pressuring Bulgaria to find the kidnappers was the wrong approach. Trying and failing to bring the suspects to justice would damage American prestige. Better, he suggested, to persuade the Turks, the Bulgarians, or both, to pay back the ransom by taxing villagers on either side of the border. This would reduce their incentive for giving aid and comfort to the insurgents. As Dickinson was officially persona non grata at the court of Ferdinand, he could not return to Sofia to propose this plan.

The one last face-saving gesture for the Americans would be to squeeze an indemnity out of the Sultan. The kidnapping had occurred on Turkish territory, and the ransom had been paid there. Under international law, the United States could make a case. Adee passed this idea to the American solicitor general for a legal opinion. Judge W. L. Penfield was dubious. "Throughout this entire affair," he wrote in reply, "the Ottoman Government appears to have acted well" as opposed to the "weakness and culpability of the Bulgarian government." A claim of indemnity, he warned, would only play into the hands of the Macedonian Committee.

Neither victim would identify or blame their kidnappers. Left hanging in the air was the suspicion—again, evidence entirely circumstantial—that the women had been conspirators. A public airing of the case might turn up facts that would embarrass both the U.S. government and the missionary society. So the government let the matter drop.

The identities of the kidnappers would not be revealed to the West for more than a quarter of a century. In the late 1920s, the dictated memoirs of IO leaders were published by Bulgarian historians. Until then, Americans knew Sandansky, Chernopeev, and Asenov only as the Good Man, the Bad Man, and Stoyan the Bear.

AND WHAT BECAME of the ransom money? The *Mis Stonki*, as it was called, had been whisked away from Bansko that winter night in 1902 by Sandansky, Asenov, and Sava Mikhailov. When they reached Dzhumaia, they were said to have spent three days counting and weighing the gold.

The newspaper *Struma*, published in the brigand stronghold of Kyustendil on the Bulgarian side, reported that during the last days of March 1902, IO delegates held a "secret congress" to debate how the money should be spent. This body supposedly decided to send armed bands into Macedonia. Historian Ivan Kharizanov, publishing in the 1940s, claimed that Krüstio Asenov bought new clothes for himself, Sandansky, and Chernopeev; then he took the money to Sofia to hand over to place in the safekeeping of Gotse Delchev.

The *Mis Stonki*, at least most of it, was frittered away on the IO's continuing feud with the Supreme Committee. What little was left went to buy guns for the revolution against the Turks, which was set for the late summer of 1903. But these arms made it to only one region, where on August 2, 1903, the Ilinden, or St. Elijah's Day, Rising began.

At twilight, Macedonian rebels stormed the mountain town of Krushevo, northwest of Monastir, where they murdered every Ottoman official. They raised red flags and declared a provisional government. The Republic of Krushevo lasted less than two weeks. A force of nearly 5,000 Turkish regulars and *bashi-bazouks* stormed the citadel, burning homes, murdering Christians, and carrying off young women. Bodies rotted in the streets. Dogs ate the corpses.

The splintered ranks of the IO withdrew to the swamps and hills. Their time-honored ploy of provoking the Turks, weathering the inevitable retaliation, and relying on the Great Powers to rush to their aid would fail. After Ilinden, the European Powers did send in teams of peacekeepers, but these fell far short of giving Macedonia its freedom. The best they could do was to force the Ottomans to make tepid reforms. Meanwhile, thousands of Macedonians fled north over the border to the principality.

The suffering of the refugees that winter was severe. In Sofia, Madame Bakhmetieva organized a fund for their relief. It was hoped that Bakhmetieva, with her ties to the elites of Washington and California, could tap into the vein of American generosity. The missionaries also did their best to raise money, but those efforts were in large part rebuffed. The Stone affair had made Americans wary of pleas from the Balkans. As Baird asked Barton, "Will such funds not find their way into the empty treasury of the revolutionists?"

By kidnapping an American, a citizen of a Christian ally, the IO had plucked the pigeon. Now it wouldn't fly.

DURING ILINDEN and its aftermath, Katerina Tsilka crisscrossed America, pleading the rebels' cause. There seems to be no record of the amount of money that Katerina raised on the Chautauqua circuit. When she arrived in Monastir late that November, however, she had collected enough from "friends" in America and England to buy a piece of property, presumably for an expanded girls' school.

Although some of the American missionaries wanted to see the Albanian mission thrive, others, like George Marsh, were by now alienated toward the Tsilkas and their radical friends. "I would be willing to try and extend work toward Albania," Marsh wrote in May 1906. "But at present it seems to me unwise. Mr. Tsilka urges it. [But] I am sorry to say that many of us have but small confidence in him. And I think that the basis of the pleas that the Americans should undertake mission work there is the wish and purpose to push revolutionary schemes under American protection."

Grigor made no secret of his politics. He and Katerina helped the Kyriases reopen the girls' school and operate it without a government permit. Sometime around March 1908, the Turks arrested him for revolutionist activities. Police had searched his office and found a photo of an Albanian soldier in full armor and what appeared to be a letter from a fellow revolutionary.

Tsilka's colleague Phineas Kennedy complained to local Turkish officials that they were interfering with American interests and would be hearing from Constantinople. But Minister Leishman showed no interest in helping the Tsilkas. He was apparently not even willing to allow the local Austrian consul who handled American affairs to act on Grigor's behalf.

Leishman had confided in U.S. Senator Henry Cabot Lodge that he had positive proof that Grigor Tsilka was a conspirator in the Stone kidnapping. Word of this reached Edward Haskell in Salonica. While harboring suspicions that Bulgarian Protestants had been deeply involved in the Stone affair, Haskell was concerned that Grigor's reputation was being tarnished without solid evidence. And so he wrote to Minister Leishman in Constantinople asking that he furnish this supposed proof that Tsilka was party to the capture.

There is no record of a reply.

All that Phineas Kennedy could do for Grigor was to persuade the Turks to allow him to go home for the birth of his child. Katerina was pregnant with their third. After the arrival of a healthy son, Skender, Grigor was returned to jail with no set trial date.

Grigor Tsilka was saved by a stroke of fate. In the summer of 1908, discontented Turkish officers staged a coup that would overthrow the 600-year-old Ottoman dynasty. Abdul Hamid II remained on his throne a short while longer but was finally deposed. His lord chamberlain was reading him the adventures of Sherlock Holmes when news of his ouster came. Upon hearing his sentence—exile to Salonica—the Sultan reportedly fainted.

Yané Sandansky and what remained of his following had joined forces with the Young Turks, making the dramatic gesture of riding into Salonica and handing over their rifles. In Albania as well, the Tsilkas, the Kyriases, and other militants felt in sympathy with and liberated by their former enemies.

Kennedy wrote euphorically to The Rooms, "It seems like a dream that Mr. Tsilka should now be a free man! All the prisoners here were released and he was the first. To-day an election is going on here in Kortcha to elect five men for the oversight of the local govt. and Mr. Tsilka is one of the promising candidates. Possibly God has been training him for such a time as this!"

Grigor seemed destined to play a major role in this new order. He and George Kyrias went as delegates to a congress in Monastir where they served on a committee to give Albanians a common language. The Tsilkas had a fourth baby, Stefan, and they could rightfully envision for their children a future of ever-expanding possibilities. Those hopes, however, were cut tragically short.

In 1912, Serbia, Greece, and Bulgaria entered an uneasy alliance to throw off Turkish rule once and for all. They succeeded, but in the scramble for territory that followed, Greeks and Serbs turned on Bulgaria. The Tsilkas were driven over the shifting borders. Grigor was imprisoned by Serbs for six months in northern Albania. It broke his health.

In 1914, he and Katerina made a visit to her family in Bansko when they heard the terrible news: Europe was at war and the borders to Albania closed. They had no choice but to remain the next four years in Sofia. In October 1918, as they were preparing to return home, Grigor fell ill with Spanish fever. In five days, he was dead.

Katerina, now a widow with four children, spent a good deal of time in Bansko. Not everyone found her Westernized ways to their liking. A young niece would recall her Aunt Katerina as a "very vain person" who arrived in Bansko with a servant and butler. Most *Banskali,* however, revered her as a patriot. On winter nights, she would entertain them by firelight with tales of her famous captivity.

Her kidnappers would also be lionized as patriots. Sandansky was the hero of folk songs. His photograph hung in many a Macedonian home. At Hanging Rock the *Banskali* mounted a plaque:

On the 3rd of September 1901, Jani Sandansky, Christu Asenov and Sava Michailov captured the American missionary, Miss Ellen Stone.

As Elenchie entered her teens, an aura of celebrity clung to her. She had graduated from the mission school at Samokov and had started college at an American school in Constantinople, when she fell in love with a young Communist named Georgi. In September 1923, he and his comrades joined a people's revolt, proclaiming Bansko a Soviet republic. It lasted only twenty-four hours. The Russians they hoped would come to their aid didn't. Georgi was taken by Bulgarian soldiers to a field and shot. Elenchie threw the ring he had given her into the Bosporus.

More grief followed. Kismetchie, the Lucky Child who was to have been the fulfillment of her mother's dreams—a confident, educated young woman of the West—contracted tuberculosis from a college roommate. At first, it seemed there might be hope. Elenchie, as it happened, had another admirer, George Carlton Minor, a clerk at the U.S. Legation in Tirana. After the failed coup in Bansko, he approached her mother asking for her daughter's hand in marriage. If Elenchie would become his wife, he promised, he could find a cure for her in Europe. They were married late in the year, and by December Elenchie had checked into a sanitorium in Karlsbad, Austria.

One of the last photographs of her was taken there. Her beautiful face was turned toward the camera smiling. She complained of the fatigue, but her eyes were burning bright with fever and, perhaps, hope. In a year, she was dead. Katerina, who had once written so lovingly about the birth of her baby daughter, fell silent on the subject.

SERBIA AND GREECE tried to dismantle Albania, but they failed. Briefly, after the Great War, Albania enjoyed independence. Fortunately, Grigor lived to see it. Macedonia would eventually be parceled into thirds: the Aegean sector including Salonica going to Greece, the Vardar lands to the west going to the Serbs, and the Pirin region going to Bulgaria.

Throughout most of the 1920s and 1930s, Katerina remained in Tirana, Albania, raising her children alone. She made her living as head nurse of the local hospital and later as director of a Red Cross orphanage. One of Katerina's four grandchildren, Eva, visited her *baba* there during the 1940s.

"She was at this time very old," Eva recalled, "but very educated, like a Protestant." Her grandmother allowed her to climb very high in the pine tree in her garden. Katerina had a little pianola where she played and sang hymns. Every night, she made the child take a cold bath to build her character.

Three of Katerina's children had been educated by American missionaries. So was her younger brother, Constantine. He went on to study at Yale and would later compile and publish the first English-Bulgarian dictionary.

Constantine had been doing post-graduate work in Berlin the year his sister was kidnapped. The one letter he wrote to Secretary John Hay complained not about his sister's captors but of the Turks' mistreatment of his elderly father. (There are no other mentions of Dimitur Stephanov's persecution.) After Katerina's release, Constantine traveled Europe and America as a publicist for the IO.

MISS STONE ALWAYS intended to return to her missionary work in the Balkans. But until the Turks were made to tremble in the face of American wrath—and cough up the $60,000 or so to reimburse the U.S. public—she would be persona non grata and unsafe in Turkish territory.

For nine years she waged a relentless letter-writing campaign to Theodore Roosevelt, John Hay, Hay's successor Elihu Root, as well as Senator Henry Cabot Lodge, a fellow Bostonian and close friend of the President. Late in 1907, Root wrote to Lodge reiterating the decision of the State Department to take no action. Lodge wrote Miss Stone regretfully that he felt nothing more could be done.

He proposed instead that the U.S. Congress honor Roosevelt's implied promise to the American Board back in 1901 to reimburse citizens who had contributed to the ransom fund. (What Miss Stone did with her own magazine and lecture earnings is unclear. Presumably she reimbursed her closest relatives who had been "financially embarrassed" on her behalf, but the claims of others remained unsatisfied.) A bill to provide that money passed the Senate four times, but never passed the House.

Every so often, the missionary society in Bulgaria issued a polite invitation for Miss Stone to return. But too many of her fellow workers had turned against her. Lewis Bond shared his misgivings about her with the society's corresponding secretary in Boston. "In regard to the question of Miss Stone's return to the Mission," he wrote, "I do not hesitate to give it as my opinion that as matters now stand in Macedonia it is inadvisable that she be stationed either at Salonica or Monastir—partly because of the belief of the Turkish officials that she was in collusion with the Bulgarian band which captured her & partly because of the way she has denounced the Turkish government in her public addresses in this country. I doubt if she would care to go back to Macedonia before a new form of government is established."

If the Bulgarian field had a crying need of reinforcements, he said, he had no objections to her posting in Samokov, although he feared her reputation might now be "too large" for that place. Philippopolis was another possibility, but he worried about her history of bad blood with George Marsh, the overbearing station chief.

The Reverend Marsh, in fact, did have strong objections to her return. In a letter marked "Private," he wrote to Dr. Barton in July 1903 that he considered it most unwise for the board to give Miss Stone any encouragement. Her life would be in danger unless she did exactly as the local revolutionary committees told her.

He then launched into a more freewheeling inventory of her flaws. She had been reckless to hold the Bible meeting in a region that was "on fire" with revolution. She had traveled without a guard, putting herself and the young women with her in grave danger. In the best of times, he said, she had been "ravenous for praise and adoration," which made life miserable for any native worker who happened to disagree with her.

During her years at Philippopolis, she developed an attachment to a Bulgarian girl. Miss Stone called her an "assistant," but in fact she took the young woman to live with her, "waiting upon her pet hand and foot." The girl, in return, plied her patroness with compliments.

Miss Stone was apparently eager for her protégé to marry Gerasim Kyrias, the Albanian pastor who was kidnapped by bandits in 1884. According to Marsh, Miss Stone was allegedly attracted by Kyrias's celebrity. The match fell through when the young woman decided she did not love Kyrias enough to move to Albania. Miss Stone had tried to persuade her young friend to move with her to Salonica, but the girl's parents apparently objected.

The nominal reason for Marsh's indignation was that Miss Stone had ruined the character of a promising young Protestant girl by pampering her. He suggested that Stone wanted to marry off her protégé to Kyrias and then live as a threesome.

Miss Stone suspected the source of these rumors, but she did not succeed in scotching them. Her only hope was to live them down. For the rest of her life, she remained scrupulously aloof from politics. When in January 1904, Katerina's brother, Constantine Stephanov, tried to organize meetings of New England Christians in order to raise money for refugees of the failed Ilinden Rising, Miss Stone refused his invitation to speak at the Park Street Church in Boston. As she explained to Dr. Barton, she'd turned down the invitation so as to distance herself from young Stephanov and a crony whom she described as "known revolutionists."

Still, a cloud of suspicion hung over her. When asked by a reporter from *The Congregationalist* in 1905 about her plans for the future, she replied, "I don't belong anywhere."

Her name remained on the mission rolls long after she'd retired to her home in Chelsea. She spent her later years attending temperance meetings and writing her memoirs. It was intended to be a thoughtful work, an illustrated history of the missions of Macedonia, with the last chapter devoted to her captivity. But in 1908, a fire destroyed Miss Stone's house in Chelsea. She was unharmed, but the manuscript burned. Whatever else she may have had to say about her life and times was carried away in ash.

Miss Stone died peacefully in the home of a niece on December 13, 1927. She was seventy-one.

AFTERWORD

Theodore Roosevelt continued to build his Great White Fleet. This armada would eventually boast sixteen modern battleships, all constructed of steel, run by steam, and largely independent of sails. Their white hulls and gilded bows made them gleam on the horizon like avenging angels. Later they would be painted gray, the better to avoid enemy fire.

In the summer of 1904, Roosevelt sent sixteen of those ships on a "goodwill cruise" of the Mediterranean. At each port of call—Lisbon, Trieste, Villefranche—their guns boomed a peaceful salute. They also rumbled an unmistakable message to the capitals of Europe: the United States of America was amassing a navy that would rival any save Britain's.

The United States had already flexed its muscle in the Caribbean. A single warship anchored at Colón was all it took to ensure the success of a Panamanian uprising, the upshot being America's control over the isthmus and, later, the Panama Canal. All it took was the threat of sending the fleet to Caracas to cause the Germans to withdraw from Venezuela. The Mediterranean, however, was the province of the European powers. And although America's warships had cruised those waters since the early 1800s, the United States had never made such a conspicuous display of its might.

After the Stone kidnapping, the Ottoman Sultan had punished the American missionaries by closing their schools and restricting their travel. John Leishman had requested Washington to send a gunboat, hoping that its presence in the Sea of Marmara would make his Imperial Majesty see reason. In late spring 1904, John Hay cabled Leishman that "during the next

six weeks an imposing naval force will move in the direction of
Turkey. You ought to be able to make some judicious use of
this fleet."

Even as this armada steamed toward the Dardanelles, the
State Department received news of a new crisis developing on
the coast of North Africa. On May 19, the U.S. consul general
in Tangier telegraphed Washington with the news that a "most
prominent American Citizen" had been kidnapped. The victim,
an aging industrialist named Ion Perdicaris, had been taken
along with his English-born stepson from their villa in the foreign quarter. Their captors were Berber tribesmen led by a warlord named Ahmed al-Aziz Mohammed el Raisuli.

Raisuli's quarrel did not seem to be with America but
rather with the Sultan of Morocco, a rival whom he wanted to
embarrass into meeting his demands: $70,000 in silver and a
couple of districts to rule. Since the life of an American was on
the line, these terms reached the desk of John Hay, who pro-
claimed them "preposterous."

Significantly, 1904 was an election year, and Roosevelt,
who'd come to the presidency by dint of a national tragedy,
wanted to win the office in his own right, preferably with an
overwhelming mandate. Earlier in the year, Roosevelt had
pledged his intent to intervene against brutality and lawless-
ness abroad. Now, foreigners had once again insulted the
national honor by kidnapping an American.

Unlike landlocked, impenetrable Bulgaria, Morocco lay on
the coast and was open to bombardment. Hay gave orders for
the North and South Atlantic and the European Squadrons to
change course for Morocco. By the time the Republicans gathered in Chicago during the first week of June for their national
convention, four American battleships, a fast cruiser, three protected cruisers, a protected carrier, and two gunboats sat in the
Bay of Tangier awaiting orders.

The nomination of Theodore Roosevelt was a foregone conclusion. The inevitability of it had practically lulled the conventioneers into a stupor. Then, on June 22, a clerk took the podium and read a bulletin just received from the Scripps-McRae news service. Secretary of State John Hay had issued an order to the U.S. consul in Tangier: *"We want Perdicaris alive, or Raisuli dead!"*

The assembly was electrified. The battle cry "Perdicaris alive or Raisuli dead" reverberated through newspaper headlines to the far corners of the nation. After the humiliation of the Miss Stone affair, Teddy was finally reading foreign rascals the riot act and sending warships to back up his threats.

What Americans did not hear above the din was the cautious conclusion of Secretary Hay's memo in which he emphasized that the United States wanted to avoid complications with Morocco or other powers, and he would not authorize a landing of marines. There was another detail to which the American public was not privy. The State Department had received word shortly after the abduction that Perdicaris was not even an American. He'd renounced his citizenship during the Civil War to keep his family estates from being seized by the Confederacy.

"This is bad business," Hay muttered to a colleague. "We must keep it excessively confidential."

Hay succeeded. Not until the 1930s would a historian unearth the Secretary's correspondence and publish the truth. By then, the matter was moot. Theodore Roosevelt had been nominated by acclamation and elected by a landslide. As far as any American knew, it was Teddy's tough talk and those battleships in the Bay of Tangier that had caused the brigands to fold.

Later that summer of 1904, three fast cruisers from the White Fleet continued east, dropping anchor at Smyrna on the western coast of Turkey. Within days of their arrival, the grand vizier conveyed to Minister Leishman his Majesty's assurances that every courtesy would be extended to the American missionaries and their schools.

It was good to be lords of the seas.

NOTES ON SOURCES

The Miss Stone Affair draws upon documents from the archives of the American Board of Commissioners for Foreign Missions in the Houghton Library of Harvard University and upon missionary periodicals from the Andover-Harvard Theological Library, both in Cambridge, Massachusetts. It also relies upon U.S. consular dispatches, diplomatic correspondence, and miscellaneous materials from the National Archives, as well as upon the papers and correspondence of Theodore Roosevelt, John Hay, Alvah Augustus Adee, and Charles Monroe Dickinson from the Library of Congress. Reports of U.S. fleet movements of the period can be found at the Naval Historical Foundation in Washington, D.C. Other contemporary documents and accounts come from the Public Records Office (PRO) at Kew and the British Library Newspaper Library in London, England; the Ottoman Archives of the Prime Ministry in Istanbul, Turkey; the Central State Archives of the Republic of Bulgaria in Sofia; and the American Farm School Archives in Thessaloniki, Greece. Articles from *Le Journal de Salonique* are from the private collection of Mr. Yiannis Megas.

Materials concerning the Stone family come from the *Gregory Stone Genealogy* (1918) and related materials in the Boston Public Library. Other genealogies and period histories may be found in the New York Public Library. The correspondence of Samuel S. McClure comes from the Lilly Library at Indiana University in Bloomington with the gracious permission of Mrs. Jane Lyon. Correspondence and photos of the Stephanov family are from the private collection of Dr. Richard Cochran of Big Rapids, Michigan. Anecdotal material concerning the Stephanovs and the kidnapping derive, in part, from interviews with Mrs. Tsilka's descendants: her great-nephew, Dr. Cochran, as well as her granddaughter, Eva Cilka, and great-granddaughter, Boriana Kolchakova. Many thanks to Valter Cilka for making available the unpublished memoir of his grandmother, Katerina Stephanova Tsilka. Local lore and genealogy came by way of interview with Georgi Ushev, town historian of Bansko.

Fortunately, many of the parties to the Miss Stone Affair published their personal memoirs: Miss Stone and Mrs. Tsilka in *McClure's Magazine* and the kidnappers themselves in accounts dictated at a much later date to revolutionary historians. I have drawn upon these extensively.

All dates have been converted from the Julian calendar to the Gregorian calendar, thirteen days later. Transliteration of Bulgarian and Turkish names follows Library of Congress guidelines. *Tsilka* is sometimes given the Albanian spelling *Cilka*. The designation *Porte,* or the *Sublime Porte,* refers to the Ottoman government. *Bey* and *Pasha* are terms denoting Ottoman gentility and nobility. The terms *Turk* and *Ottoman* are used interchangeably. The more contemporary *Muslim* replaces *Mohammedan* and *Mussulman*. *Salonica* has been used as a default reference for the ancient—and modern—*Thessaloniki*.

BIBLIOGRAPHY

BOOKS

Baepler, Paul (ed.). *White Slaves, African Masters: An Anthology of American Barbary Captivity Narratives.* Chicago and London: University of Chicago Press, 1999.

Bartlett, J. Gardner. *Gregory Stone Genealogy: Ancestry and Descendants of Deacon Gregory Stone of Cambridge, Mass. 1320–1917.* Boston: Stone Family Association, 1918.

Barton, James L. *Missionary and His Critics.* New York: Fleming H. Revell Co., 1906.

Bemis, Samuel F. *American Secretaries of State and Their Diplomacy,* Vols. 1, 9. Edited by Samuel F. Bemis. New York: Knopf, 1927–1929.

Brailsford, Henry Noel. *Macedonia: Its Races and Their Future.* London: Methuen, 1906.

Brands, H. W. *TR: The Last Romantic.* New York: Basic Books, 1997.

Christowe, Stoyan. *Heroes and Assassins.* New York: Robert M. McBride & Company, 1935.

Curtis, William E. *The Turk and His Lost Provinces: Greece, Bulgaria, Servia, Bosnia.* Chicago: Revell, 1903.

Eliot, Sir Charles. *Turkey in Europe.* London: Edward Arnold, 1908.

Forsythe, Sidney A. *An American Missionary Community in China, 1895–1905.* Cambridge, Mass.: East Asian Research Center, 1971.

Gernsheim, Alison. *Victorian and Edwardian Fashion: A Photographic Survey.* New York: Dover, 1963.

Gladstone, W. E. *Bulgarian Horrors and the Question of the East.* London: John Murray, 1876.

Glenny, Misha. *The Balkans: Nationalism, War and the Great Powers, 1804–1999.* New York: Viking, 2000.

Goodwin, Jason. *Lords of the Horizons: A History of the Ottoman Empire.* New York: Henry Holt, 1998.

Government Printing Office. *Foreign Relations of the United States: Affairs in China.* Washington, D.C.: Government Printing Office, 1902.

————. *Foreign Relations of the United States.* Washington, D.C.: Government Printing Office, 1903.

Hall, William Webster. *Puritans in the Balkans: The American Board Mission in Bulgaria 1878–1918: A study in Purpose and Procedure.* Sofia: "Cultura" Printing House, 1938.

Haslip, Joan. *The Sultan: The Life of Abdul Hamid II.* New York: Holt, Rinehart and Winston, 1973.

Hupchick, Dennis P. *The Balkans: From Constantinople to Communism.* New York: Palgrave, 2002.

Hurst, Michael. *Key Treaties for the Great Powers, 1814–1914,* Selected and edited by Michael Hurst. New York: St. Martin's Press, 1972.

Jelavich, Barbara. *The Ottoman Empire, the Great Powers, and the Straits Question, 1870–1887.* Bloomington: Indiana University Press, 1973.

Kaplan, Robert D. *Balkan Ghosts.* New York: St. Martin's Press, 1993.

Kennan, George F. *The Other Balkan Wars: A 1913 Carnegie Endowment Inquiry in Retrospect.* Introduction and reflections by George F. Kennan. Washington, D.C.: Carnegie Endowment for International Peace, 1993.

Ketler, Isaac. *The Tragedy of Paotingfu.* N.p., 1902.

Kinross, Lord. *The Ottoman Centuries: The Rise and Fall of the Turkish Empire.* New York: Morrow, 1977.

Kyosev, D. (ed.). *Gotse Delchev: Pismi I Drugi Materiali* (Letters and other Materials). Sofia: Bülgarskata Akademiya na Naukite (Bulgarian Academy of Sciences), 1967.

Larsen, Peter. "Theodore Roosevelt and the Moroccan Crisis, 1904–1906." Ph.D dissertation, Princeton University, 1984.

Lewis, Bernard. *The Muslim Discovery of Europe.* New York: Norton, 1982.

Lyon, Peter. *Success Story: The Life and Times of S. S. McClure.* Deland, Fla.: Everett/Edwards, 1967.

MacDermott, Mercia. *For Freedom and Perfection: The Life of Yané Sandansky.* London: Journeyman, 1988.

Macdonald, John. *Czar Ferdinand and His People.* New York: Arno Press and *The New York Times,* 1971. (reprint)

Mahan, Alfred Thayer. *Mahan on Naval Warfare.* Edited by Allan Westcott. Mineola, N.Y.: Dover, 1999. (reprint)

Marder, Brenda L. *Stewards of the Land: The American Farm School and Modern Greece.* Boulder, Colo.: East European Quarterly, 1979.

Martinenko, A. K. *Russko-Bolgarski Otnosheniya.* Kiev, 1894–1902.

Massie, Robert K. *Peter the Great: His Life and World.* New York: Ballantine Books, 1980.

Mazower, Mark. *The Balkans: A Short History.* New York: Modern Library, 2000.

McClure, Samuel Sidney. *My Autobiography.* Lincoln: University of Nebraska Press, 1997.

Miletich, L. (ed.). *Materiali za Istoriyata na Makedonskoto Osvobod-itelno Dvidzhenie* (Materials Concerning the History of the Macedonian Liberation Movement). Sofia: P. Glushkov, 1927 and 1928.

Mojzes, Paul B. "A History of the Congregational and Methodist Churches in Bulgaria and Yugoslavia." Ph.D dissertation, Boston University, 1965.

Moore, Frederick. *The Balkan Trail.* London: Smith, Elder & Co., 1906.

Morris, Edmund. *The Rise of Theodore Roosevelt.* New York: Modern Library, 2001.

———. *Theodore Rex.* New York: Random House, 2001.

Nankivell, Joice M. *A Life for the Balkans: The Story of John Henry House of the American Farm School.* Told by his wife to J. M. Nankivell. New York: Fleming H. Revell Company, 1939.

Norwich, John Julius. *A Short History of Byzantium.* New York: Vintage Books, 1999.

Pandev, K., and Daskalova, M. *Aferata Miss Stone.* Sofia, 1983.

Peet, William Wheelock. *No Less Honor.* Chattanooga, Tenn.: private printing, 1939.

Poulton, Hugh. *Who Are the Macedonians?* Bloomington: Indiana University Press, 2000.

Reed, John. *The War in Eastern Europe.* New York: Scribner, 1916.

Reid, Harry. *Bansko 1974* (unpublished).

Roosevelt, Theodore. *An American Mind: Selected Writings.* Edited with an introduction by Mario R. DiNunzio. New York: Penguin Books, 1995.

Roscoe, Theodore, and Fred Freeman. *Picture History of the U.S. Navy: From Old Navy to New, 1776–1897.* New York: Bonanza Books, 1956.

Sciaky, Leon. *Farewell to Salonica.* New York: Current Books, 1946.

Sherman, Laura Beth. *Fires on the Mountain: The Macedonian Revolutionary Movement and the Kidnapping of Ellen Stone.* New York: Columbia University Press, 1980.

Siliyanov, Khristo. "Ilindenskoto Vüstanie" (The Ilinden Rebellion) from *Osbovoditelni Borbi na Makedoniya* (The Liberation Struggles of Macedonia). Vol I. Sofia: Durzhavna Pechatnitsa (State Printing House), 1933.

Sonnichsen, Alfred. *Confessions of a Melancholy Brigand.* New York: Duffield & Co., 1909.

Strashimirov, Anton. *Krüstio Asenov*. Sofia, 1906.

Straus, Oscar Solomon. *Under Four Administrations from Cleveland to Taft: Recollections of Oscar Straus*. Boston: Houghton Mifflin, 1922.

Sulzberger, C. L. *A Long Row of Candles: Memoirs and Diaries, 1934–1954*. New York: Macmillan, 1969.

Tomov, Lazar. *Spomeni na Revolyutsionnata Deinost v Serskiya Okrüg* (Recollections of Revolutionary Activities in the Serres Region). Sofia: Izdatelstvoto na Nationalniya Süvet na Otechestveniya Front (Publishing Group of the National Council of the OF), 1952.

Tsilka, Katerina. *An Event in Macedonia: Memories of Mrs. Katerina Cilka*. Transcription and annotations by her son, Dr. Stefan Cilka (unpublished).

Vohra, Ranbir. *The Chinese Revolution 1900–1950*. Edited by Ranbir Vohra. Boston: Houghton Mifflin, 1974.

Washburn, George. *Fifty Years in Constantinople and Recollections of Robert College*. Boston: Houghton Mifflin, 1911.

West, Rebecca. *Black Lamb and Grey Falcon: A Journey Through Yugoslavia*. New York: Penguin Books, 1994. (reprint)

Yavorov, Peyu. *Gotse Delchev*. Sofia: Bülgarski Pisatel (Bulgarian writer), 1989.

Zimmerman, Warren. *First Great Triumph: How Five Americans Made Their Country a World Power*. New York: Farrar, Straus and Giroux, 2002.

PERIODICALS

American Monthly Review of Reviews
　　"The Balkan Question" (December 1901).

Athenian
　　Marder, Brenda, "The Stone-Tsilka Kidnapping" (February 1975).

Balkan Studies. A biannual publication of the Institute for Balkan Studies.
　　Dimitra Giannuli, "'Errands of Mercy': American Women Missionaries and Philanthropists in the Near East, 1820–1930," Vol. 39, No. 2 (1998).

Bellefontaine Weekly Register (Ohio)
　　"Ellenche at Chautauqua," 7 July 1905.

Chautauqua
　　Telford, Emma Paddock, "Why Brigands Thrive in Turkey" (September 1902).

Chelsea Gazette (Massachusetts)

"How Much Do They Pay," 27 October 1900.

"Missionary Held; Miss Ellen Stone Captured by Macedonian Brigands," 14 September 1901.

"Details of the Capture," 28 September 1901.

"For Miss Stone; Central Church Raised $199.15," 19 October 1901.

"Miss Stone Free at Last," 1 March 1902.

Chicago Record-Herald

"Bandits Who Abducted Miss Stone Make a Cash Demand for Her Restoration," 9 September 1901.

"President McKinley Is Dead," 14 September 1901.

"Aid for Miss Stone," 5 October 1901.

"Cannot Pay Brigands," 7 October 1901.

"Hope for Miss Stone," 8 October 1901.

"Miss Stone May Live" and "News of Miss Stone," 9 October 1901.

"Imperils Miss Stone," 11 October 1901.

"Fear for Miss Stone Assists Her Captors," 12 October 1901.

"Lose Trace of Miss Stone," 16 October 1901.

"Ransom Is Pouring In," 18 October 1901.

"No Trace of Ellen M. Stone," 22 October 1901.

Curtis, William E., "Will Pay a Ransom," 26 October 1901.

"No News on Freedom," 26 October 1901.

Curtis, William E., "Imperils Miss Stone," 30 October 1901.

"Hope for Miss Stone," 31 October 1901.

Curtis, William E., "Miss Stone Is Well," 1 November 1901.

"Demand Full Ransom," 2 November 1901.

Curtis, William E., "No Trace of Brigands," 6 November 1901.

———, "Captives Both Well," 7 November 1901.

———, "Liberty Is Now Near," 9 November 1901.

———, "Catch Four Brigands," 11 November 1901.

———, "Miss Stone Beloved," 12 November 1901.

———, "Delays Stone Rescue," 13 November 1901.

"Makes Unwise Move," 14 November 1901.

Curtis, William E., "Beauty of Bulgaria," 18 November 1901.

"Insists Miss Stone Is Alive," 20 November 1901.

Curtis, William E., "Turks' Rule a Curse," 20 November 1901.

———, "All Clews Run Down," 22 November 1901.

"Miss Stone's Fate in Doubt," 29 November 1901.

"Miss Stone Is in Bulgaria," 5 December 1901.

"Miss Stone's Release Near," 7 December 1901.

"Tries to Convert Brigands," 13 December 1901.
"Threat from Turkey to Expel Americans," 23 December 1901.
"Yields to American Protest," 3 January 1902.
"Miss Stone's Release Lacks Confirmation," 4 January 1902.
"To Free Miss Stone," 27 January 1902.
"Miss Stone Is Soon to Be at Liberty," 28 January 1902.
"Hitch in Stone Negotiations," 29 January 1902.
"Reports Miss Stone Has Been Liberated," 30 January 1902.
"Miss Stone Is Freed," 19 February 1902.
"Release Is Doubted," 21 February 1902.
"Miss Stone Is Free," 24 February 1902.
Curtis, William E., "Romance of Balkans," 16 May 1903.

The Christian Herald and Signs of Our Times
"The Abducted Missionary," 16 October 1901.
"Ransomed with Gold," 16 October 1901.
"Held by Brigands for a Ransom," 16 October 1901.

Churchman
"The Abducted Missionary," 26 October 1901.
"Chronicle and Comment," 1 March 1902.

The Congregationalist and Christian World
"Tidings About Miss Stone," 28 September 1901.
"Tiding from Miss Stone," 5 October 1901.
Clarke, James F., "Brigandage in Bulgaria and Macedonia," 12
    October 1901.
Dyer, Frances J., "Miss Stone, Girl and Woman," 19 October 1901.
"Advancing Congregationalism," 26 October 1901.
Goodrich, C. L., "Miss Stone's Companion in Captivity," 2 Novem-
    ber 1901.
"Miss Stone Heard From," 16 November 1901.
"The Case of Miss Stone," 23 November 1901.
"Miss Stone's Death Reported, But Not Confirmed," 7 December
    1901.
"Miss Stone Alive," 14 December 1901.
"The Case of Miss Stone," 21 December 1901.
"Miss Ellen M. Stone's Captivity," 25 January 1902.
"The Case of Miss Stone," 6 March 1902.
"Miss Ellen M. Stone Released from Captivity," 1 March 1902.
"Miss Stone's Release," 20 March 1902.
"Miss Stone's Journey to London," 5 April 1902.
Childe, Abbie B., "A Welcome to Miss Stone," 12 April 1902.
House, John H., "The Captivity and Release of Miss Stone," 19
    April 1902.

"Miss Stone's Busy Days," 21 April 1902.

"Miss Stone as a Lecturer" and "Miss Stone's Official Statement," 26 April 1902.

Gordon, George A., "The Essential Principles of the Pilgrim Faith," 7 June 1902.

Daily Graphic (London)

"The Kidnapped Lady, Alleged Complicity of the Macedonian Committee," 4 October 1901.

"The Kidnapping of Miss Stone. Proposed Relief Expedition," 18 October 1901.

"A Letter from Mme. Tsilka," 16 November 1901.

Maud, W. T., "In Search of Miss Stone, Among the Balkan Brigands," 30 December 1901

———, "A Daily Graphic Mission," 17 January 1902.

———, "In Search of Miss Stone, Among the Balkan Brigands: The Abortive Negotiations," 18 January 1902.

———, "In Search of Miss Stone, Among the Balkan Brigands: From Salonika to Serres," 20 January 1902.

———, "In Search of Miss Stone, Among the Balkan Brigands: A Monastery in the Mountains," 21 January 1902.

———, "In Search of Miss Stone, Among the Balkan Brigands: Marking Time," 22 January 1902.

———, "In Search of Miss Stone, Among the Balkan Brigands: The Mystery Deepens," 23 January 1902.

———, "In Search of Miss Stone, Among the Balkan Brigands: A Study of Faces," 24 January 1902.

———, "In Search of Miss Stone, Among the Balkan Brigands: Mr. Ligord's Narrative," 25 January 1902.

"Newsbrief," 27 January 1902.

Maud, W. T., "In Search of Miss Stone, Among the Balkan Brigands: The Advance," 30 January 1902.

———, "In Search of Miss Stone, Among the Balkan Brigands: Another Captive Release Delayed," 31 January 1902.

———, "In Search of Miss Stone, Among the Balkan Brigands: A Night in Rila Monastery" and "In Search of Miss Stone, Among the Balkan Brigands: A Stable Fire," 5 February 1902.

"The Captive Ladies; Where Are the Brigands," 6 February 1902.

"The Failure of Negotiations," 8 February 1902.

Maud, W. T., "In Search of Miss Stone, Among the Balkan Brigands: Travelling with the Ransom," 11 February 1902.

———, "In Search of Miss Stone, Among the Balkan Brigands: Arrival of the Ransom," 12 February 1902.

———, "In Search of Miss Stone, Among the Balkan Brigands: The Failure and Its Causes," 13 February 1902.

———, "In Search of Miss Stone, Among the Balkan Brigands: The Ransom at Seres," 14 February 1902.

———, "In Search of Miss Stone, Among the Balkan Brigands: The Captive Ladies Not Yet Released," 18 February 1902.

———, "In Search of Miss Stone, Among the Balkan Brigands: The Captive Ladies Still Unreleased, Growing Anxiety," 20 February 1902.

———, "In Search of Miss Stone, Among the Balkan Brigands: The Captive Ladies Release Yesterday," 24 February 1902.

———, "In Search of Miss Stone, Among the Balkan Brigands: The Ransomed Ladies; How They Were Released; A Caution from Constantinople," 25 February 1902.

———, "In Search of Miss Stone, Among the Balkan Brigands: The Search Ended; The Interview with Miss Stone; A Touching Meeting," 26 February 1902.

———, "In Search of Miss Stone, Among the Balkan Brigands: The Ransomed Ladies; Returned to Salonica; Incidents of their Captivity," 27 February 1902.

"Among Brigands . . ." (March 1902).

Maud, W. T., "In Search of Miss Stone, Among the Balkan Brigands: The Indemnity Question; A Visit to the Vali," 1 March 1902.

"Miss Stone's Captivity; Kismetcha, the Lucky Child," 3 March 1902.

Maud, W. T., "In Search of Miss Stone, Among the Balkan Brigands: The End of the Search; Miss Stone's Return; Ransomers and Ransomed; Their First Meeting," 5 March 1902.

———, "In Search of Miss Stone, Among the Balkan Brigands: The End of the Search; Return of the Ransomed; Madam Tsilka's Statement; The Meeting with Her Husband; A Tale that Will Never Be Told," 7 March 1902.

———, "In Search of Miss Stone, Among the Balkan Brigands: The Rescue of Miss Stone," 8 March 1902.

"The Release of Miss Stone," 10 March 1902.

"The Indemnity Question," 12 March 1902.

Den (Sofia, Bulgaria)

Kharizanov, Ivan, "Aferata Mis Ston," Vol. 1, Nos. 26–37, 11 September to 23 September 1945.

Everybody's Magazine

Lyle, Eugene P., "An American Woman Captured by Brigands" (June 1902).

The Independent
"Miss Stone and the American Board," 17 October 1901.

Le Journal de Salonique
"Echos de la Ville" (Saadi Levy, ed.) (May 1901–1902).
"Lettre de Constantinople," 30 May 1901 and 3 June 1901.
"Travaux Publics," 6 June 1901.
"Jardins Publics," 29 August 1901.
"Etablissements Orosdi Back," 26 August 1901.
"Histoire dé [sic] Brigands," 9 September 1901.
"Dernières Nouvelles," 18 November 1901.

Leslie's Weekly
Ross, James H., "Strange Sequel of the Capture of Miss Stone," 10 April 1902.
Telford, Emma Paddock, "The Brigands of the Balkans," 19 October 1901.

Literary Digest
"The Case of Miss Stone," 19 October 1901.

McClure's Magazine
Stone, Ellen M., "Six Months Among the Brigands" (May 1902).
———, "Six Months Among the Brigands" (June 1902).
———, "Six Months Among the Brigands; The Mother and Her Baby" (July 1902).
———, "Six Months Among the Brigands: Born Among the Brigands" (August 1902).
———, "Six Months Among the Brigands" (September 1902).

The Missionary Herald
Smith, Judson, "Touring with Missionaries in China" (February 1899).
Barton, James L., "The Collegiate and Theological Institute at Samokov" (April 1901).
"The Work of Brigands" (October 1901).
"The Case of Miss Stone . . ." (November 1901).
"The Case of Miss Stone . . ." (December 1901).
"The Captivity of Miss Stone . . ." (January 1902).
"The Release of Miss Stone . . ." (April 1902).
"The Escape from the Brigands . . ." (May 1902).
"The Balkan Missions" (June 1902).
Morse, Charles F., "Why Send Missionaries to the Balkans?" (September 1902).
"European Turkey . . ." (November 1902).
"Macedonia" (June 1903).

"Mrs. E. B. Haskell of Salonica" (July 1903).
House, John H., "The Situation in Macedonia," (July 1903).
Norton, Thomas H., "Influence of an American College in Turkey" (October 1903).
"From Macedonia" (February 1904).
"The Russo-Japanese War and Missions" (April 1904).
"Revival in Bulgaria" (March 1905).

Missionary Review of the World
"The Case of Miss Stone" (December 1901).

New York Daily Tribune
"Miss Stone's Companion," 19 February 1902.

New York Journal
"Miss Stone Is in the House of Bekir Bey," 13 November 1901.

The New York Times
"Brigands Carry Off American Women," 6 September 1901.
"The Captured Missionary," "President Shot at Buffalo Fair," and "Washington Stunned by the Tragedy," 7 September 1901.
"Mr. Hay Leaves Washington," 23 September 1901.
"The Capture of Miss Stone," 25 September 1901.
"$110,000 Ransom for Kidnapped Missionary," 28 September 1901.
"The Case of Miss Stone," 29 September 1901.
"The Kidnapping of Miss Stone," 30 September 1901.
"Miss Stone's Capture," 1 October 1901.
"Appeal for Miss Stone, the Captive Missionary," 5 October 1901.
"Large Donations for Miss Stone's Ransom," 6 October 1901.
"Churches Give for Miss Stone's Ransom," 7 October 1901.
"Brigands Give Miss Stone a Month More" and "Ransom Money Coming In," 8 October 1901.
"Little Ransom Money Coming In" and "Bulgarian Troops Seek Miss Stone," 9 October 1901.
"Miss Stone Still Alive," 10 October 1901.
"Troops Surrounding Miss Stone's Captors," 11 October 1901.
"Public Meeting Held in Aid of Miss Stone," 14 October 1901.
"An Appeal for Funds to Ransom Miss Stone" and "Search for Bulgarian Abductors Abandoned," 15 October 1901.
"Miss Stone Is Hidden in a Cave" and "Stone Driver Arrested," 16 October 1901.
"No News of Miss Stone," 21 October 1901.
"Hope for Miss Stone," 25 October 1901.
"To Search for Miss Stone," 29 October 1901.

Outlook
"Brigands and Missionaries," 12 October 1901.

Peru Daily Chronicle (Indiana)
"Only Half Is Raised," 9 October 1901.

Troy Daily Times (New York)
"A Difficult Task," 18 November 1901.

World (New York)
"The Beautiful Bulgarian," 22 September 1901.
"Ransom to Be Paid for Miss E. M. Stone," 26 September 1901.
"Miss Stone Found in Brigand's Camp," 28 September 1901.
"Miss Stone Still in Den of Brigands," 29 September 1901.
"Fund to Pay Miss Stone's Ransom Is $60,000 Short," 7 October 1901.
"How Brigands Murder Captive Whose Ransom Is Withheld," 20 October 1901.
"Bulgaria Scorns Our Warning About Miss Stone," 3 December 1901.
"Peet Thinks That Miss Stone Is Alive," 4 December 1901.
"Miss Stone's Fate Still Uncertain," 5 December 1901.
"Hard to Get Truth About Miss Stone," 10 December 1901.
"Collector for Miss Stone Thought to Be Fraud," 13 December 1901.
"Brigands Have Not Freed Miss Stone," 4 January 1902.
"Brigands Sign Paper to Free Miss E. M. Stone," 10 January 1902.
"Ellen Stone May Be Free Now," 27 January 1902.
"Miss Stone's Release Is Hourly Expected," 28 January 1902.
"Miss Stone Reported Free," 30 January 1902.
"Miss Stone Free; Tsilka Arrested," 10 February 1902.
"Mrs. Stone and Mrs. Tsilka at Last Are Set Free," 24 February 1902.
"'Free, Thank God, and Well,' Says Miss Stone," 26 February 1902.
"Miss Stone's Story of Captivity in Demand," 28 February 1902.

ARCHIVAL SOURCES

Andover-Harvard Theological Library, Harvard University, Cambridge, Mass. *The Congregationalist and Christian World*, Folio Periodical 445 (at depository). *The Missionary Herald*, Microfilm Periodical 3125.

British Library Newspaper Library, London. *London Daily Graphic*, 4 June 1890–16 October 1926, Nos. 1–11482.

Central State Archives of the Republic of Bulgaria, Sofia. Central State Historical Archive, CSHA. Fund 176, op. 1, archive units 1645, 1647, 1762.

Houghton Library, Harvard University, Cambridge, Mass. Administrator of Manuscripts. Microfilm located at Government Documents and Microforms, Social Sciences Program of the Harvard College Library. Microfilm Unit 5: Reel 579, Vol. 18; Reel 580, Vol. 19; Reels 505–506 (miscellaneous news clippings); Reel 576, Vol. 15; Reel 577, Vol. 16; Reel 578, Vol. 17; and Reel 581, Vol. 20. Also, Microfilm Unit 1: Reel 96, Vols. 209, 210.

Library of Congress, Washington, D.C. Manuscript Reading Room: Adee Family Papers (Papers of Alvah Augustus Adee, 1842–1924), LC Number: mm 79010231; Papers of Charles Monroe Dickinson, LC Number: mm 78018432; Letters of John Hay, LC Number: 71093245; Papers of Theodore M. Roosevelt, LC Number: mm 73038299. Newspaper and Current Periodical Reading Room: *Chicago Record-Herald,* Chicago, 1901–1914. *New York Evening World,* New York, 1887–1931.

Lilly Library, Indiana University, Bloomington. McClure Mss. Phillips Mss.

National Archives and Records Administration, College Park, Md. Record Group 59 (diplomatic dispatches by country): M35 (Russia), Rolls 58, 59; M46 (Turkey), Rolls 68–70; M77 (consular dispatches, Turkey), Roll 168; and T682, (Bulgarian Series), 1–30 (1 August 1901–26 August 1904). Also see M179 (Miscellaneous Letters of the State Department), Rolls 1112, 1113, 1118.

Naval Historical Foundation, Washington, D.C. Annual reports of the Secretary of the Navy, VA 52 A2 1901c.4, VA 52 A2 1902c.4.

Ottoman Archives, Sultanahmed, Istanbul. Irades (imperial orders): *Irade-i Hususî* (special orders) L 1319 #26, 112; Za 1319 #14, 17, 35, 36, 42. Yildiz Collection: Ministerial and other proposals. Y.Mtv. Files 222/95, 133; 225/76, 111, 141; 226/72; 424/41; 425/45, 47, 56, 80; 426/64, 96, 148. Archive of the Bureau of Privileged Provinces, A.MTZ-04. Files 15/8, 16/1, 17/3.

Public Record Office at Kew (National Archive of England, Wales and the United Kingdom), London. Reference FO195/2111-2133.

ACKNOWLEDGMENTS

What was intended as the short study of an obscure episode in American history turned instead into a three-year odyssey requiring research in thirteen archives containing documents written or published in seven languages using four separate alphabets. Naturally, I had help.

I owe a great deal to the published works of two American scholars, Randall Woods and Laura Beth Sherman. Their accounts served as an introduction to this remarkable case and pointed me in the direction of the missionary archives at Harvard and State Department archives in Washington, D.C.

I thank Villy Ioannu, with whose assistance I obtained documents from the Public Records Office at Kew and whose work at the British Library Newspaper Library in London unearthed the extensive writings of William Maud. He was not the first journalist, nor the last, to fall under the spell of Miss Stone. I cannot express the full extent of my gratitude to Zornitsa Semkova-Dimitrova, whose research and translation of documents from the Bulgarian Central State Archives made accessible the accounts of IO historians. Additional thanks to her husband and fellow historian, Ivailo Evgeniev Dimitrov, who with their son, Deyan, made me feel so at home in Sofia. Thanks to Randall Warner, archivist of the American Farm School in Thessaloniki, Greece, who not only shared her own materials but introduced me to other local archivists and historians, including Basil C. Gounaris of the Museum of the Macedonian Struggle, and Mrs. Thomi Verrou-Karakosta of the Institute for Balkan Studies.

The Ottoman archives in Istanbul would have been inaccessible without the assistance of Gultekin Yildiz, who translated hitherto unpublished documents from the original Osmanlica. His tour of old Constantinople made the Imperial past come alive for me. There is no better way to see an ancient city than through the eyes of a young historian.

As for Richard Cochran, I still find it hard to believe my good fortune at finding a descendant of Katerina Tsilka who is also a genealogist and a professional librarian, specifically dean of library and chief information officer at Ferris State University, Big Rapids, Michigan. Richard and his wife, Jennifer, exhibited unflagging enthusiasm for this project and their generosity in sharing documents from their private collection turned my pursuit of Miss Stone into a delightful journey of discovery.

Many thanks to the Tsilka relations in Bulgaria—Eva and Boriana—and, on the Albanian side—Valter, Aferdita, Selma, Skender, Alban, and young Eva, born one hundred years to the week after her late great-great-aunt Elenchie. My gratitude to Mercia MacDermott, Dr. Gilbert Schrank, Dr. Barbara Higdon, and Dr. Richard Cochran for reading this book in its intermediate stages. We do not concur on every point, but then Miss Stone's story raises issues about which reasonable men, and women, may disagree. The errors are solely my own. Thanks to Paul Dippolito, Thea Tullman, Beverly Miller, Cathy Dorsey, and Emily Takoudes for their attention to detail. Thanks as well to David and Patti Buck, Louis Perske, Barry and Tasso Feldman, Angel Velitchkov, Eleni Michaelidou, Matthew MacRoberts, Dune Lawrence, William Mooney, Dr. Carol Finkel, Bernadette Perrault, Gloria Korsman, Leslie Morris, Saundra Taylor, Rebecca Cape, Dr. Paul Rood, Louis Holland, Victor and Sarah Kovner, Mary Ann Whitten, former U.S. Undersecretary of State Evelyn Lieberman, and Stoyan Tonchev, former Bulgarian consul general to New York City.

I owe an accruing debt to my American researcher, Mervyn Keizer, as well as to Anja Schmidt of Simon & Schuster. Deepest thanks and gratitude to the significant three: Esther Newberg, David Rosenthal, and, of course, Alice Mayhew. And to my dearest two, Steven and Andrew.

INDEX

PHOTO CREDITS

1–2: *McClure's Magazine*, May 1902.

3: *McClure's Magazine*, June 1902.

5: "The Capture." Illustration by Frank Brangwyn, *McClure's Magazine*, May 1902.

6: "In a Sheepfold." Illustration by Claude Shepperson, *McClure's Magazine*, 1902.

7–9, 11: *McClure's Magazine*, September 1902.

10: Reproduced from the Collections of the Library of Congress.

12: Courtesy of Corbis.

13: "Turkish Hospitality at Belitza." Illustration by F. De Haenen based upon a sketch by William Maud, London *Daily Graphic*, February 8, 1902.

14: *McClure's Magazine*, August 1902.

15: "The American Mission on the Road to Djuma-I-Bala." Illustration by John Charlton based upon a sketch by William Maud, London *Daily Graphic*, February 15, 1902.

16: "A Fire at the Bansko Khan." Illustration by F. Matania from a sketch by William Maud, London *Daily Graphic*, February 22, 1902.

17, 20: From the collection of Dr. Richard Cochran.

18: Photograph by William Maud, London *Daily Graphic*. Republished by *McClure's Magazine*, October 1902.

19: *The Christian Herald*, 1902.

ABOUT THE AUTHOR

TERESA CARPENTER is a former senior editor of *The Village Voice*, where her articles on crime and the law won a Pulitzer Prize. She is the author of three books, including the best-selling *Missing Beauty*. She lives in New York's Greenwich Village with her husband, *Newsweek* columnist Steven Levy, and their son.